Windows™ 3.1 SmartStart

Meta Chaya Hirschl
Purdue University

Ron Person

Karen Rose

que
College

Windows 3.1 SmartStart.

Copyright © 1993 by Que® Corporation.

All rights reserved. Printed in the United States of America. No part of this book may be used or reproduced in any form or by any means, or stored in a database or retrieval system, without prior written permission of the publisher except in the case of brief quotations embodied in critical articles and reviews. Making copies of any part of this book for any purpose other than your own personal use is a violation of United States copyright laws. For information, address Que Corporation, 11711 N. College Ave., Carmel, IN 46032.

Library of Congress Catalog No.: 93-83862

ISBN: 1-56529-203-0

This book is sold *as is*, without warranty of any kind, either express or implied, respecting the contents of this book, including but not limited to implied warranties for the book's quality, performance, merchantability, or fitness for any particular purpose. Neither Que Corporation nor its dealers or distributors shall be liable to the purchaser or any other person or entity with respect to any liability, loss, or damage caused or alleged to have been caused directly or indirectly by this book.

95 94 93   4 3 2

Interpretation of the printing code: the rightmost double-digit number is the year of the book's printing; the rightmost single-digit number, the number of the book's printing. For example, a printing code of 93-1 shows that the first printing of the book occurred in 1993.

Screen reproductions in this book were created using Collage Plus from Inner Media, Inc., Hollis, NH.

Windows 3.1 SmartStart is based on Microsoft Windows 3.1.

Publisher: David P. Ewing

Associate Publisher: Rick Ranucci

Product Development Manager: Thomas H. Bennett

Operations Manager: Sheila Cunningham

Book Designer: Scott Cook

Production Team: Jeff Baker, Claude Bell, Jodie Cantwell, Paula Carroll, Brad Chinn, Lisa Daugherty, Brook Farling, Carla Hall-Batton, Wendy Ott, Juli Pavey, Caroline Roop, Marcella Thompson, Michelle Worthington

About the Authors

Meta Chaya Hirschl has taught information systems literacy in the Krannert School of Management at Purdue University since 1989. The course includes hands-on experience with personal productivity software packages, including Windows, Word for Windows, Excel, and dBASE III Plus. She has helped well over a thousand undergraduates through the challenges of their first use of microcomputers. Meta also worked as a manager with Andersen Consulting of Arthur Andersen & Co., where she assisted with the development and installation of information systems for such clients as IBM, NYNEX, and Consolidated Edison of New York. Meta received an M.B.A. in management information systems from New York University, graduating with honors, and a B.S. from Purdue University. She currently resides in West Lafayette, Indiana, with her husband and two daughters.

Ron Person has written many books for Que Corporation, including *Using Excel for Windows*, Special Edition; *Using Windows 3.1*, Special Edition; and *Windows 3.1 QuickStart*. Ron is the principal consultant for Ron Person & Co. He has an M.S. from The Ohio State University and an M.B.A. from Hardin-Simmons University.

Karen Rose is a senior trainer for Ron Person & Co. She has written several books for Que Corporation. Karen teaches Word for Windows and desktop publishing for Ron Person & Co. and has taught for the University of California, Berkeley Extension, and Sonoma State University.

Title Manager
Carol Crowell

Senior Editor
Jeannine Freudenberger

Editors
Barb Colter
Phil Kitchel

Editorial Assistant
Elizabeth D. Brown

Formatter
Jill Stanley

Trademarks

All terms mentioned in this book that are known to be trademarks or service marks have been appropriately capitalized. Que cannot attest to the accuracy of this information. Use of a term in this book should not be regarded as affecting the validity of any trademark or service mark.

Microsoft, Microsoft Word for Windows, Microsoft Excel, Microsoft Windows, and Microsoft Word are registered trademarks of Microsoft Corporation. IBM is a registered trademark of International Busi ness Machines Corporation. WordPerfect is a registered trademark of WordPerfect Corporation. 1-2-3 and Lotus are registered trademarks of Lotus Development Corporation.

Composed in *Garamond* and *MCPdigital* by Que Corporation

Give Your Computer Students a SmartStart on the Latest Computer Applications

Que's SmartStart series from Prentice Hall Computer Publishing combines the experience of the Number 1 computer book publisher in the industry with the pedagogy you've come to expect in a textbook.

SmartStarts cover just the basics in a format filled with plenty of step-by-step instructions and screen shots.

Each SmartStart chapter ends with a "Testing Your Knowledge" section that includes true/false, multiple choice, and fill-in-the-blank questions; two or three short projects; and two long projects. The long projects are continued through the book to help students build on skills learned in preceding chapters.

Each SmartStart comes with an instructor's manual featuring additional test questions, troubleshooting tips, and additional exercises. This manual will be available both on disk and bound.

Look for the following additional SmartStarts:

Word for Windows SmartStart	1-56529-204-9
Excel 4 for Windows SmartStart	1-56529-202-2
MS-DOS SmartStart	1-56529-249-9
WordPerfect 5.1 SmartStart	1-56529-246-4
Lotus 1-2-3 SmartStart *(covers 2.4 and below)*	1-56529-245-6
dBASE IV SmartStart	1-56529-251-0

For more information call:

1-800-428-5331

or contact your local Prentice Hall College Representative

Contents at a Glance

Introduction 1

1 An Overview of Windows 5

2 Getting Started 23

3 Operating Windows 49

4 Editing, Copying, and Moving in Windows ... 73

5 Managing Files 87

6 Using Object Linking and Embedding 125

7 Using Desktop Accessories 143

8 Using Windows Paintbrush 169

A Summary of Windows Shortcuts 199

B Help, Support, and Resources 217

   Index 221

Table of Contents

Introduction 1
    How To Use This Book 2
    How This Book Is Organized 2
    Conventions Used in This Book 3

1   An Overview of Windows 5
    Objectives 5
    Objective 1: To Understand the Advantages of Windows 6
    Objective 2: To Run DOS Programs under Windows 13
    Objective 3: To Identify Helpful Windows Features 15
    Objective 4: To Recover from a Crash 18
    Chapter Summary 19
    Testing Your Knowledge 20

2   Getting Started 23
    Objectives 23
    Objective 1: To Start Windows 25
    Objective 2: To Start Programs 25
    Objective 3: To Understand the Windows Desktop 27
    Objective 4: To Understand the Parts of a Window 30
    Objective 5: To Use the Mouse and Keyboard 34
    Objective 6: To Close Documents, Programs, and Windows 40
    Chapter Summary 44
    Testing Your Knowledge 45

3   Operating Windows 49
    Objectives 49
    Objective 1: To Control Menus and Use Dialog Boxes 50
    Objective 2: To Control Window Positions and Sizes 57
    Objective 3: To Switch between Programs 61
    Objective 4: To Get Help 62
    Chapter Summary 70
    Testing Your Knowledge 70

4 Editing, Copying, and Moving in Windows 73

Objectives 74
Objective 1: To Edit Text 74
Objective 2: To Copy and Move Text in Windows Programs 78
Objective 3: To Copy and Paste in DOS Programs 79
Objective 4: To View and Save Cut or Copied Data 81
Chapter Summary 83
Testing Your Knowledge 84

5 Managing Files 87

Objectives 87
Objective 1: To Understand the File Manager 89
Objective 2: To Select and Open Files and Directories 93
Objective 3: To Control File Manager Windows and Displays 101
Objective 4: To Manage Files and Directories 107
Objective 5: To Manage Disks 116
Chapter Summary 119
Testing Your Knowledge 120

6 Using Object Linking and Embedding 125

Objectives 126
Objective 1: To Link Data between Programs 129
Objective 2: To Manage Links 133
Objective 3: To Embed Data in a Document 136
Chapter Summary 139
Testing Your Knowledge 139

7 Using Desktop Accessories 143

Objectives 143
Objective 1: To Start the Windows Accessory Programs 144
Objective 2: To Track Appointments with Calendar 145
Objective 3: To Make Calculations with Calculator 155
Objective 4: To Watch the Clock 160
Objective 5: To Develop Skills with Solitaire
   and Minesweeper 162
Chapter Summary 165
Testing Your Knowledge 165

8 Using Windows Paintbrush 169
Objectives 169
Starting Windows Paintbrush 171
Understanding How Paintbrush Works 172
Objective 1: To Use the Toolbox, Line-Width Box, and Palette ... 173
Objective 2: To Save a Drawing 181
Objective 3: To Use the Painting Tools 182
Objective 4: To Add Text 186
Objective 5: To Edit a Drawing 189
Objective 6: To Print a Drawing 193
Chapter Summary 194
Testing Your Knowledge 195

A Summary of Windows Shortcuts 199
General Windows Shortcuts 199
Program Manager Shortcuts 204
File Manager Shortcuts 205
Desktop Accessory Shortcuts 208

B Help, Support, and Resources 217
Telephone Support 217
Support Organizations 218
Computer Bulletin Board Forums 219
Consultants and Corporate Training 220

Index 221

Introduction

Welcome to *Windows 3.1 SmartStart*. Whether you are a novice with computers and quake at the thought of turning on a computer or you are familiar with DOS programs, this *SmartStart* provides one of the easiest and fastest ways to master the Windows revolution.

You will find that Windows 3.1 makes personal computers more accessible, even to first-time computer users, and moves you further up the productivity curve. Controlled studies, surveys, and the experiences of thousands of students have shown that Windows programs help new users learn more quickly and help experienced users become more productive. Aside from increasing your productivity, Windows and Windows programs are more *fun* to use than character-based DOS programs.

What you learn in *Windows 3.1 SmartStart* carries over to Windows programs, such as Microsoft Excel, Microsoft Word for Windows, and Aldus PageMaker, because all Windows programs work in a similar way. After you learn the basics, you're well on your way to understanding any new Windows program. This *SmartStart* not only gets you going quickly but also gives you a head start on learning any Windows programs.

To illustrate various key concepts of Windows 3.1, popular programs like Microsoft Excel and Microsoft Word for Windows are used in the exercises. If you don't have a specific program that is mentioned, you may use whatever similar program you have. For example, you could substitute Lotus for Windows for Microsoft Excel. The basic steps are the same, and you will still learn the concept of the exercise.

Windows 3.1 SmartStart

How To Use This Book

Windows 3.1 SmartStart is designed for use in an instructional setting. It has been prepared and reviewed by people who have experience teaching Windows 3.1. Each chapter has a list of objectives with easy-to-follow exercises that guide you through clear steps. The exercises and concise explanations get you into the program and through your work without much page turning, rereading, or index flipping.

Each chapter in this book follows the same format. First, an overview of the chapter is presented, followed by a list of objectives. Key terms for the chapter are defined in order to prepare you for the material. Then each objective is explained with the aid of clear, step-by-step exercises. Illustrations show how the screen (or a similar program's screen) should appear. Some exercises are followed by short notes that describe important tips or cautions in using basic features of the program. At the end of each chapter is a section called "Testing Your Knowledge." Here you have the opportunity to check that you have learned the key concepts through true/false, multiple choice, and fill-in-the-blank questions. In addition, you will find project suggestions, giving you the opportunity to apply your new skills.

If you're an experienced personal computer user but are not familiar with Windows, you will find *Windows 3.1 SmartStart* an excellent way to come up to speed quickly. When you need more detailed information, you can turn to the **Help** menu found in Windows programs and to Que's line of Windows books, including *Using Windows 3.1*, Special Edition; *Using Excel 4 for Windows*, Special Edition; and *Using Word for Windows 2*, Special Edition.

How This Book Is Organized

Windows 3.1 SmartStart shows you how to operate Windows and some of the free programs that come with it. The book contains chapters on sharing data between programs designed for Windows, including Microsoft Excel and Microsoft Word for Windows and on sharing data between DOS programs such as Lotus 1-2-3.

Chapter 1, "An Overview of Windows," illustrates how Windows can improve your work and helps you decide which features are most important to the way you work.

Chapter 2, "Getting Started," explains how to start Windows and describes its capabilities on different computer systems.

Introduction

Chapter 3, "Operating Windows," covers the important concepts used in all Windows programs. You learn how to control window sizes, operate menus, select from the choices in dialog boxes, and enter and edit data. What you learn in this chapter applies to all Windows programs.

Chapter 4, "Editing, Copying, and Moving in Windows," teaches you the basics of working with all Windows programs. You learn how to open, close, and save files, and how to copy and paste text, numbers, and graphics within documents and between programs.

Chapter 5, "Managing Files," explains how to use the File Manager to copy and erase files, create directories, and format disks—all the disk-maintenance problems that were tough and time-consuming under DOS but now are easy under Windows.

Chapter 6, "Using Object Linking and Embedding," explains how you can link files together and how you start one program from within another.

Chapter 7, "Using Desktop Accessories," reviews the personal productivity programs that come free with Windows, including the Clock, Calculator, and Calendar. These small pop-up programs are convenient to use while you use other Windows programs.

Chapter 8, "Using Windows Paintbrush," describes an enjoyable and colorful Windows program that introduces you to drawing in Windows. Paintbrush works the same way as, and with a toolbox similar to, many of the powerful drawing, design, and drafting programs designed for Windows.

Appendix A, "Summary of Windows Shortcuts," lists the most useful shortcuts in Windows 3.1 and a few of the free programs.

Appendix B, "Help, Support, and Resources," directs you to sources for getting help with Windows and Windows programs.

Conventions Used in This Book

The conventions used in this book have been established to help you learn to use Windows quickly and easily. As much as possible, the conventions correspond with those used in the Windows 3.1 program and documentation.

In this book, *selecting* means highlighting text, and *choosing* means executing a command from a menu or a dialog box.

Windows 3.1 SmartStart

The keys you press and text you type appear in **boldfaced blue** type in the numbered steps and in **boldfaced** type elsewhere. Key combinations are joined by a plus sign: **Shift**+**F5** in numbered steps and **Shift**+**F5** elsewhere.

DOS commands, file names, and directory names are written in all capital letters. Options, commands, menu names, and dialog box names are headline style.

On-screen prompts and messages are in a `special typeface`.

An Overview of Windows

Windows is leading a revolution in personal computers. The Windows revolution makes people more productive with less work; yet Windows is easier to learn and use than DOS. The key to this phenomenon is that we can bring our knowledge of the world to computing. We don't have to learn a completely new way of thinking just to understand a strange set of symbols, like `C:\>`, the DOS prompt. So, for example, when we see a picture of a notebook, we think of a tool to write things. With this graphical orientation, we are immediately more familiar and comfortable with the computer, and so we can use it more productively. Windows is fueling this revolution in the way we use computers. This chapter shows you how.

Objectives

1. To Understand the Advantages of Windows
2. To Run DOS Programs under Windows
3. To Identify Helpful Windows Features
4. To Recover from a Crash

An Overview of Windows

1

Key Terms in This Chapter	
Desktop	The screen background area on which windows and icons containing programs are displayed.
Document	The data on which a program works. A document may be the data in a spreadsheet program, a letter in a word processing program, or a chart in a drawing program.
DOS	The disk operating system that coordinates hardware and software actions. DOS is the foundation underneath Windows.
Environment	The collection of objects, commands, and rules composing the work space in which Windows and Windows programs work.
Graphical User Interface (GUI)	A visual environment that helps you control computer programs more easily and more consistently.
Icon	A pictorial representation of a command, program, or document.
Window	A rectangular on-screen area that encloses one specific program or one specific document.

Objective 1: To Understand the Advantages of Windows

Windows is an *environment* (system software) surrounding the *disk operating system* (DOS). The pyramid shown in figure 1.1 illustrates how Windows works with your disk operating system.

DOS enables computer programs to run on your computer. Before Windows, computer users were faced with remembering difficult DOS commands. Users also had to learn different programs, such as Lotus 1-2-3 and WordPerfect, which shared no common menu structure or operating techniques. Much practice was necessary to become proficient in DOS-based programs, and hard work was required to master the power hidden inside them.

To Understand the Advantages of Windows

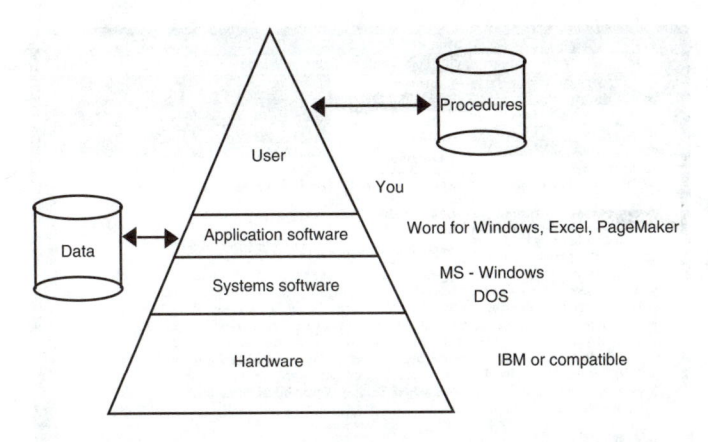

Fig. 1.1

How Windows works with DOS.

Windows eliminates these problems. It masks DOS, doing away with arcane DOS commands and improving the way DOS uses memory. Programs designed specifically for Windows—such as Microsoft Excel, Aldus PageMaker, and Microsoft Word for Windows—share common menus and operate the same way. Learning one program, therefore, helps you learn other Windows programs. And because pull-down menus and pop-up dialog boxes make all options available to beginners and experts, Windows programs are more accessible to all users—everyone moves up the productivity curve.

Learning Faster with Windows

People are visual beings. Most of what we learn comes through our sight. We remember best what we can place in a unique location, not what we tag with a text name.

Windows programs use what is known as a *Graphical User Interface*, or *GUI* (pronounced "gooey"). A GUI takes advantage of the visual way that people are accustomed to working and the way most people prefer to work.

Like the programs designed for Windows, a GUI uses *pull-down menus*. Many of the various Windows programs have the same menus, often in the same locations. For example, when you choose Format from the menu bar in a Word for Windows 2.0 window, the Format pull-down menu appears (see fig. 1.2). Almost all Windows programs use the same kind of menus, and many have menus with the same names.

An Overview of Windows

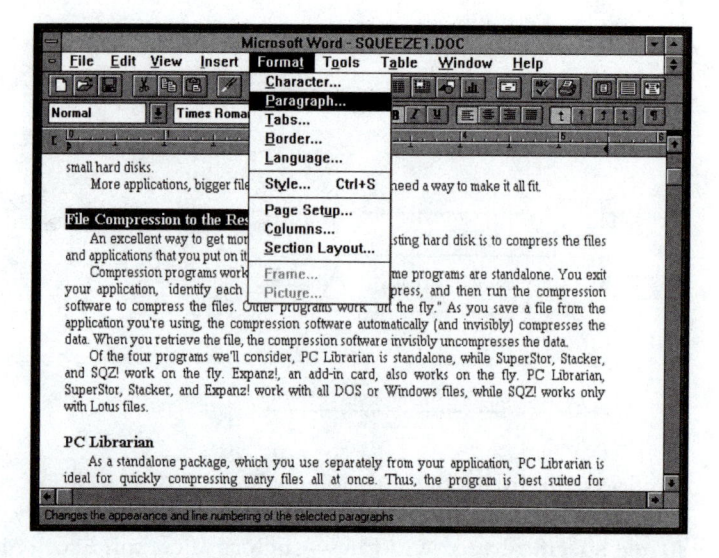

Fig. 1.2
A menu in Word for Windows.

Selecting a command in a pull-down menu from a Windows program produces a dialog box if the command requires additional information. All choices or options for the command are available in the dialog box. Figure 1.3 illustrates the use of a dialog box in Word for Windows.

Fig. 1.3
A dialog box in Word for Windows.

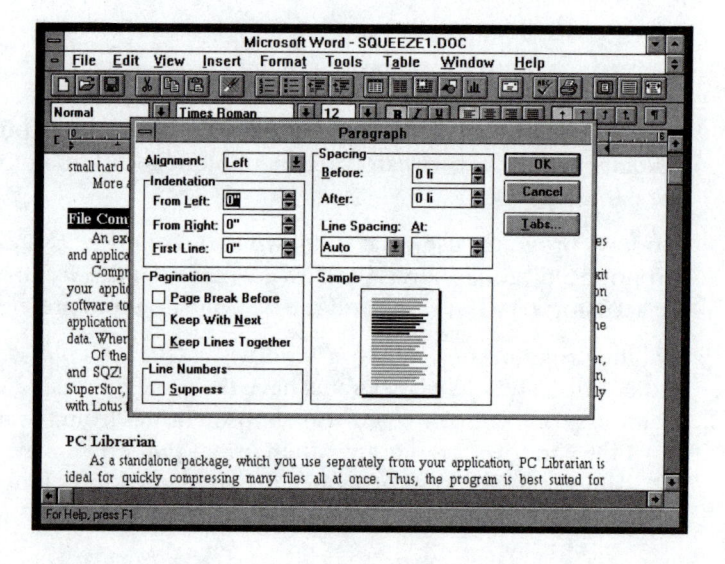

To Understand the Advantages of Windows

You don't need to move down through 10 or 12 layers of menus, as some DOS programs require. Because all your choices or options are immediately visible or are visible in a list that appears for that choice, a beginner and an expert have the same access to the program's features. Windows programs make their power accessible, not hidden beneath layers of menus.

Windows also uses *icons*, or small pictures, to represent items you can quickly identify. For example, every Windows application is represented in the Program Manager by an icon that gives the user an idea of its purpose (see fig. 1.4). The Program Manager makes it obvious which icon to select to start different programs.

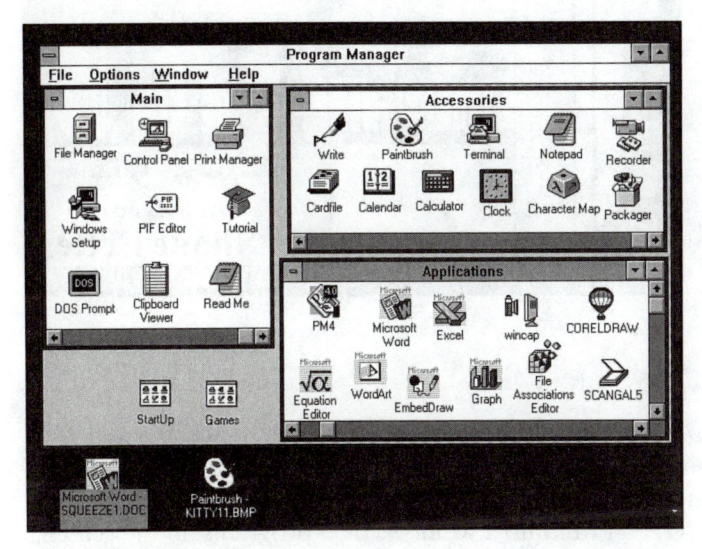

Fig. 1.4
Windows application icons.

With Windows and Windows programs, you can control programs the way you prefer. You can use a mouse-driven pointer while you are learning or drawing, use the keyboard during data entry, or use shortcut keys for speed. Many people first learn with the mouse and then use both the mouse and the keyboard as they become two-handed masters.

Sharing Operating Methods

Learning one Windows program helps you learn other Windows programs. Not only are the operating methods the same in different Windows programs, but many of the menus and commands are identical. Many menus and

An Overview of Windows

commands—such as File, Edit, Format, Window, and Help—are in the same locations and perform the same functions in different Windows programs (see fig. 1.5).

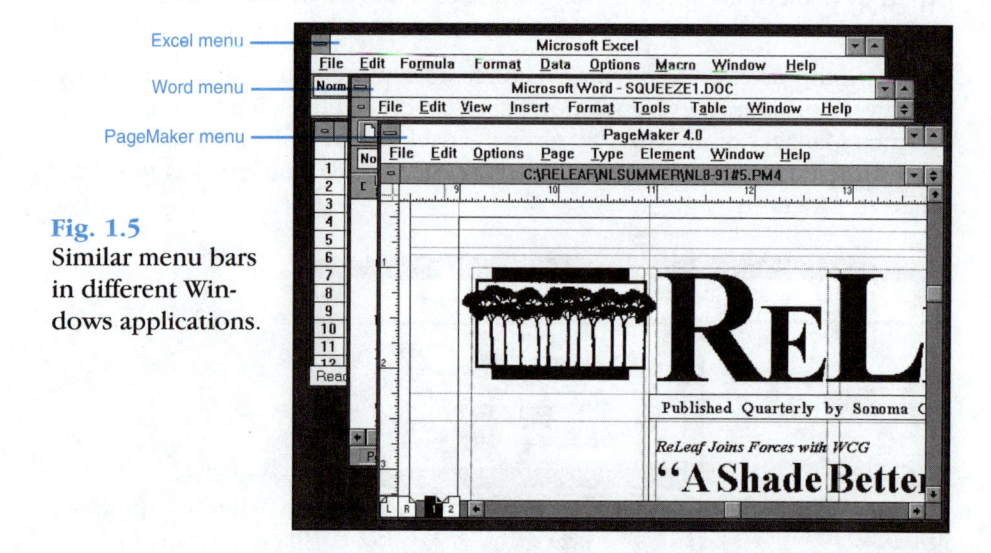

Fig. 1.5
Similar menu bars in different Windows applications.

Using the Windows Desktop

The term *Windows desktop* is a metaphor for the desktop on which you're used to working. You can think of the computer screen, the GUI environment, as your desktop. You run multiple programs on the desktop. Each Windows program can fill the screen or fit into a window. DOS programs fill the screen, unless you are running Windows on an 80386 or 80486 computer.

Running programs in separate windows enables you to see what is happening in other programs and to switch to other programs quickly. This technique is called multitasking.

When you want to save space on the desktop, you can shrink a program's window so that it becomes an icon at the bottom of the desktop (see fig. 1.6).

Running Multiple Programs Simultaneously

You can load multiple programs in Windows and quickly switch from one program to another—even if they are a mix of Windows and DOS programs. If

To Understand the Advantages of Windows

you run Windows on an 80386 or 80486 computer, you can even request that programs in which you aren't currently working continue to run in background windows. For example, you can run WordPerfect for DOS and Microsoft Excel (a Windows program) at the same time (see fig. 1.7).

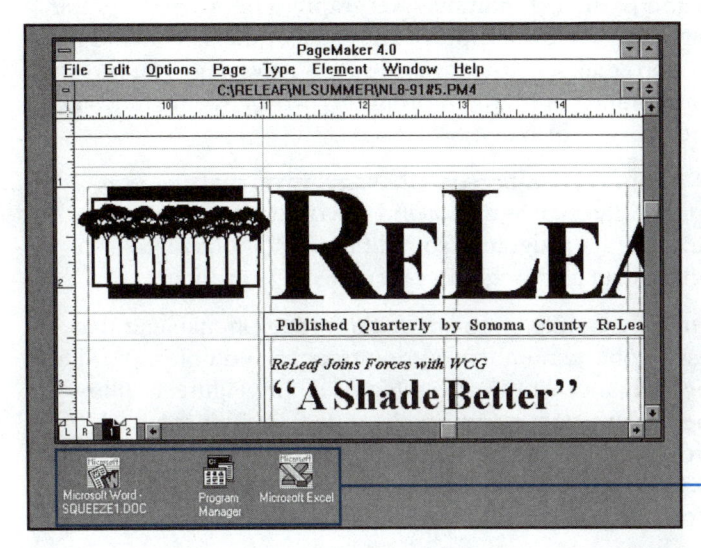

Fig. 1.6 Windows desktop with programs running but not currently being used.

Program icons

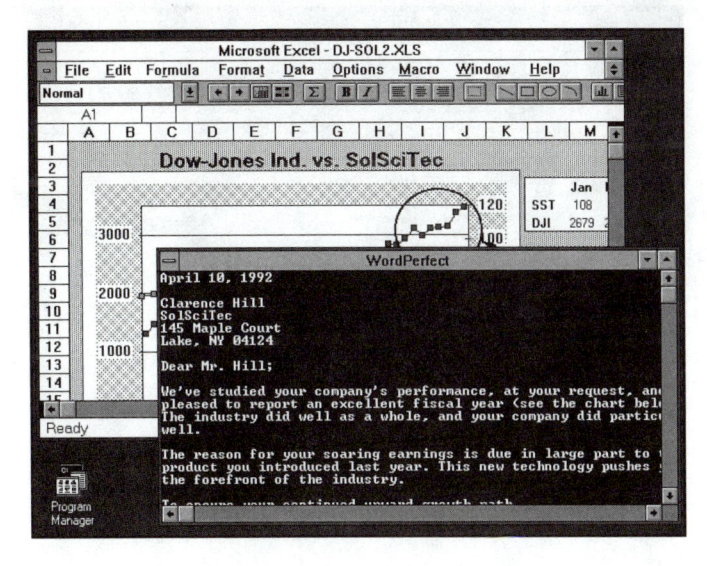

Fig. 1.7 WordPerfect for DOS and Microsoft Excel running simultaneously.

11

An Overview of Windows

1 Copying and Pasting Text and Graphics between Programs

In Windows, you can easily copy text or graphics from one program to another. You can copy and paste text, numbers, or graphics between programs designed for Windows. You can even capture an image of the screen and paste it into other Windows programs. If you are using DOS programs, you can still copy and paste text and numbers between programs, saving typing time and eliminating the chance of typing errors.

You can link many Windows programs so that changes you make to one program's data automatically change the data in the other linked Windows programs. Therefore, separate programs from different manufacturers can work together and share data as though they were a single program.

The program PackRat, for example, is a personal information manager that stores names, addresses, phone numbers, appointments, and notes. Word for Windows is a high-performance word processing program. Figure 1.8 illustrates sharing data between programs written by different companies. Although these two programs are made by different companies, you can write letters in Word for Windows and let PackRat retrieve the name and address from its database of people you contact.

Fig. 1.8
Sharing data between Word and PackRat.

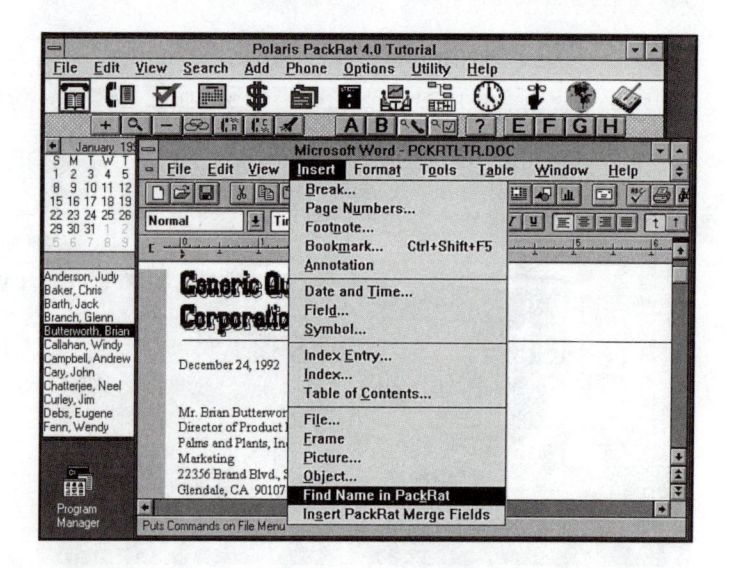

Objective 2: To Run DOS Programs under Windows

You don't have to leave behind DOS programs, such as DOS versions of Lotus 1-2-3 and WordPerfect, when you run Windows. Although these programs were originally designed to run under DOS, Windows adds new capabilities to them. Figure 1.9 shows that you can run WordPerfect for DOS under Windows at the same time other Windows programs are running. You can even copy and paste text and numbers between programs.

Fig. 1.9
Running WordPerfect for DOS with other Windows applications running.

Remember that the active DOS program fills the entire screen—unless you are running Windows on an 80386 or 80486 computer. On an 80386 or 80486 computer, you can run DOS programs so that they fill the screen or fit into a window.

Making Better Use of Memory

Programs designed for DOS 4.0 and earlier were restricted to using no more than 640K of primary memory. Such programs either left out features in order to stay small, or were slow because they continually had to retrieve pieces of the program from disk.

Windows breaks that 640K memory limit. Programs designed for Windows aren't restricted to using 640K. Removing this restriction means faster operation for large programs and almost unlimited memory for data. In fact, if you run Windows on an 80386 or 80486 computer, information that doesn't fit into primary memory (RAM) spills over on to your hard disk—making your hard disk an extension of memory. This technique is called *virtual storage*.

An Overview of Windows

1 Getting Help

Windows programs are easy to use because they offer an extensive Help feature. Word for Windows, for example, includes almost 200 pages of Help information that is on the hard disk and available to you while you work. Chapter 3 discusses the Help facility in greater detail.

Many Windows programs contain help about commands and procedures, such as how to create a form letter (see fig. 1.10). Selecting underlined words or phrases in the Help window displays a definition or opens another Help window.

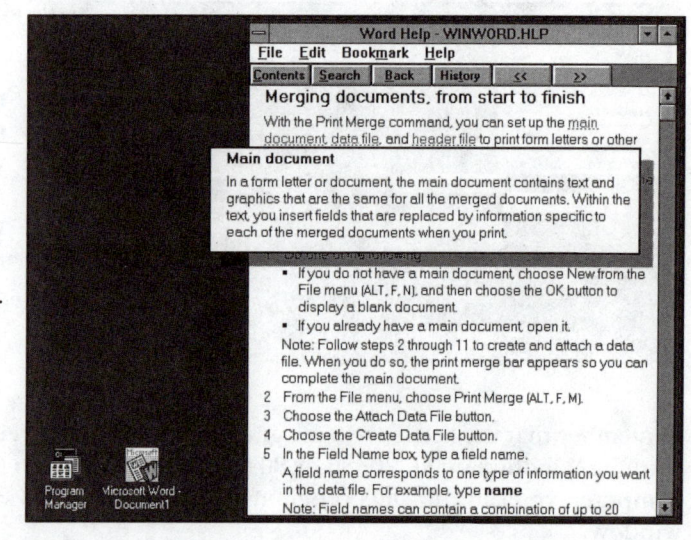

Fig. 1.10
Getting Help in Word for Windows.

Help files in many Windows programs use a feature known as *hypertext*. Hypertext enables you to jump quickly from one Help topic to another. For instance, if you are looking in Word for Windows at a Help file that shows how to build a mailing list, you may see the phrase `Printing form letters or other merged documents` underlined in the explanation. Clicking the underlined phrase takes you immediately to a window that explains File Print Merge. You can also backtrack to an earlier action, search for Help by keywords, and print the Help information.

Objective 3: To Identify Helpful Windows Features

In addition to providing the features already discussed, Windows comes with programs and tools that make using your computer easier. The Program Manager displays icons that represent the programs and data documents with which you work most frequently (see fig. 1.11).

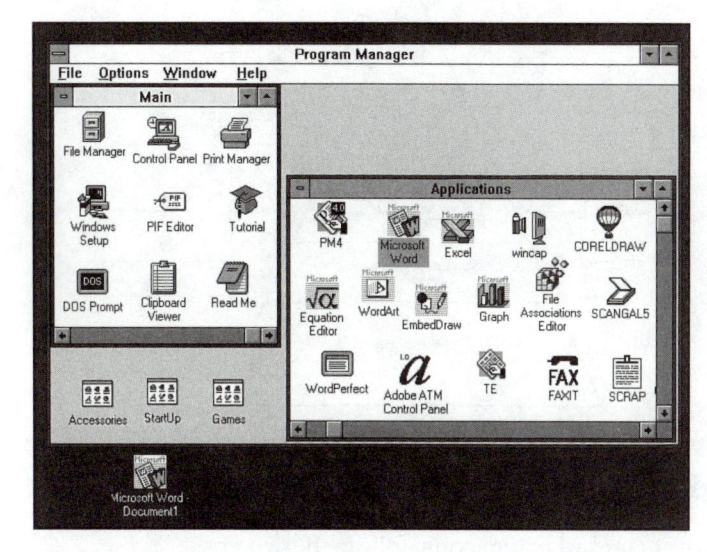

Fig. 1.11
Icons in the Program Manager window.

You can start programs by choosing an icon in the Program Manager instead of typing the program's name. Chapter 2 discusses starting programs.

Exercise 3.1: Exploring the Windows Environment

To understand the specifics of your environment, fill in the blanks beside the pyramid shown in figure 1.12. Follow these steps:

1. Look at your hardware (computer). On the pyramid, write the company name and model you find on the processor box (the same box that houses the floppy drive).

2. Write **DOS** on the lower line in the lines next to the Systems software area. DOS is the operating system that manages the computer's resources.

An Overview of Windows

3. Write **Windows** next to the System software area above *DOS*.
4. Look at your screen. You see a window called Applications. List all the icon names in the application software area of the pyramid.
5. Write either the user's name or user group's name, such as *Intro to Computing Students*, in the top line beside the pyramid. Remember— the user is always on top!

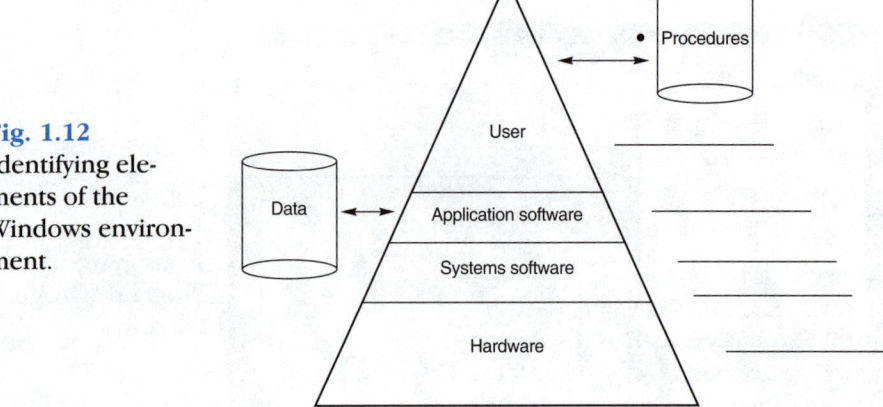

Fig. 1.12
Identifying elements of the Windows environment.

Exercise 3.2: Identifying Icons and Their Uses

To understand the advantages of using icons, follow these steps:

1. Look at each of the icons on your desktop. Make a list of the icons.
2. Try to guess the function of each icon, based on its appearance. Write down your deductions.
3. Notice how the icons are grouped. Notice what window title is used for each grouping. What does that title tell you about the function of the icon?

Another helpful program is the File Manager. Using the File Manager is much easier than using arcane DOS commands for organizing your hard disk and copying, erasing, or moving files (see fig. 1.13). The File Manager displays a tree-like structure that shows how files and subdirectories are arranged on your hard disk. Chapter 5 discusses the File Manager in more detail.

To Identify Helpful Windows Features

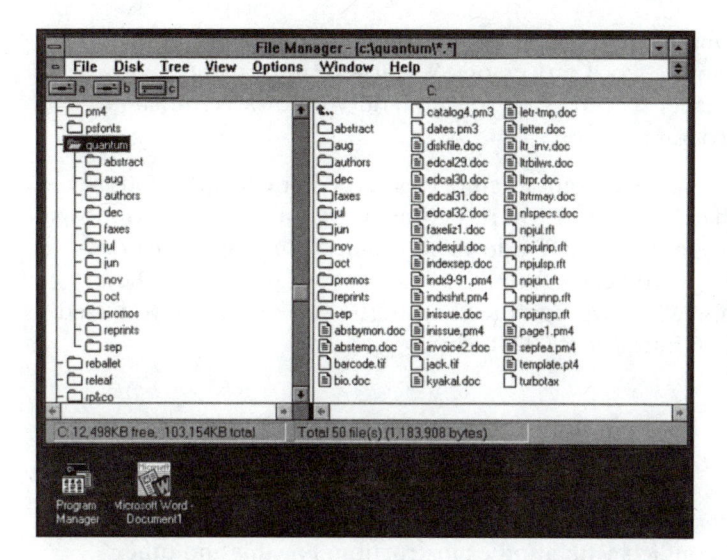

Fig. 1.13
Directories, subdirectories, and files as displayed in the File Manager.

A third program, the Control Panel, enables you to customize many features within Windows, such as the desktop background, colors, printer connections, and mouse operation (see fig. 1.14). Customizing the desktop background and window colors can make your computer a little more friendly and much more personal.

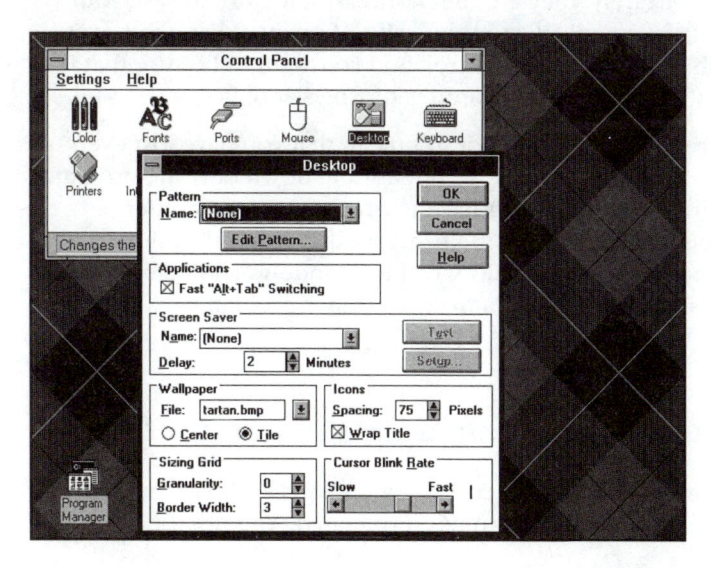

Fig. 1.14
Note the friendly and personal desktop background.

17

An Overview of Windows

Windows provides many other accessory programs. These programs include Windows Write (a simple word processor), Windows Paintbrush (a drawing program), Print Manager (control of printing), and Windows Terminal (a communications program).

In some documents, you may want to embed objects. For example, you may want to embed a chart in a report you're writing using the Word for Windows word processing program. Using Windows' new *object linking and embedding* (OLE) technology, you can embed the chart in your report and then, from within Word for Windows, edit the chart in the same program you used to create it. Chapter 6 introduces OLE technology.

Objective 4: To Recover from a Crash

Your computer occasionally encounters an internal instruction that it doesn't understand or that conflicts with another instruction. For this and other reasons, your program may "crash," or stop working. Another problem can be a "frozen" keyboard. The keyboard doesn't respond to your keystrokes. This problem is another kind of crash. When your computer crashes, you generally see a message on-screen advising you that the program has encountered an unrecoverable error.

Although crashes occur rarely, they are the best reason for you to save your important documents frequently. Get in the habit of saving documents every few minutes. A crash is outside your control, and you want to be sure that if a crash occurs, you will lose only a few minutes of work—not hours.

Fortunately, your program's crashing doesn't mean that you have lost everything. Often you can recover from a crash by shutting down only the program that crashed. In many cases, you won't have to turn off your computer or restart Windows. You lose the data in the program that crashed (unless the program has a file-recovery utility, as do Word for Windows and many other programs), but you shouldn't lose data from any other programs that were running at the same time.

Exercise 4.1: Recovering from a Crash: Soft Boot

Suppose that you have experienced a crash—either your keyboard has frozen, or you get a message that your program has terminated. You may be prompted with a message offering you three alternatives. The first is to press the [Esc] key, which closes the message box. If you don't think that your program really crashed, you can try pressing [Esc] to return to your program. If this step doesn't work (and it probably won't), press [↵Enter] to exit the program and return to Windows. If that step doesn't work, you must reboot your computer. Follow these steps to soft-boot your computer:

1. Press [Ctrl]+[Alt]+[Del]. (Hold down [Ctrl] and [Alt] while you press [Del].) You see a list of options on the screen.
2. Press [Esc] to return to the desktop. You have terminated the soft boot.
3. Press [Ctrl]+[Alt]+[Del] again, and when you see the list of options, press [Ctrl]+[Alt]+[Del] to restart your computer. You have just soft-booted your machine. Watch the screen to see the steps the computer follows during a reboot.

Exercise 4.2: Recovering from a Crash: Hard Boot

Unfortunately, sometimes even a soft boot won't solve the problem. In that case, a hard boot is required. To hard-boot a computer, follow these steps:

1. Save any work you have been working on. Remember that anything not saved to secondary storage will be lost during either a hard or soft boot.
2. Turn off the computer. Leave it off for about 15 seconds.
3. Turn on the computer.

   You have just hard-booted your machine. Watch the screen to see the steps the computer follows during a reboot.

Chapter Summary

Now you know why Windows is causing a revolution in the way people use personal computers. Windows programs—and DOS programs running under Windows—are easier to use, which means that advanced programs are more accessible to everyone. Windows makes your personal computer more enjoyable to use.

Now that you are familiar with what Windows can do for you, put it to work. Chapter 2 shows you how to get started. If you are new to Windows, read Chapter 3, "Operating Windows." What you learn in that chapter applies to all Windows programs.

An Overview of Windows

1 Testing Your Knowledge

True/False Questions

1. Windows provides a graphical user interface environment that takes advantage of the way people are accustomed to working.
2. Many menus and commands of different Windows programs are in the same location and perform the same function.
3. Running more that one program simultaneously is called virtual storage.
4. Programs written for DOS may not run under Windows.
5. DOS is an example of application software.

Multiple Choice Questions

1. To perform a soft boot, you should
   A. simultaneously press Shift + B + S.
   B. simultaneously press Ctrl + Alt + Del.
   C. simultaneously press Enter + Shift.
   D. turn off the computer for 15 seconds and then turn it on.
2. The Windows desktop is representative of
   A. the way computer programmers think.
   B. the use of pull-down menus.
   C. the five-component model pyramid.
   D. the desktop on which you are used to working.
3. A pictorial representation of a command, program, or document is a
   A. window.
   B. icon.
   C. pull-down menu.
   D. document.
4. You can embed objects by using Windows' new
   A. object linking and embedding technology.
   B. desktop technology.
   C. Control Panel.
   D. Windows Terminal technology.

Testing Your Knowledge

5. While using Windows, you can use which of the following input devices?

    A. shortcut keys

    B. keyboard

    C. mouse

    D. all the above

Fill-in-the-Blank Questions

1. _____ enables you to jump quickly from one Help topic to another.
2. The _____ Manager is used to organize your hard disk and to copy, erase, and move files.
3. Programs designed for DOS 4.0 and earlier were restricted to using no more than _____ K of memory.
4. Virtual storage extends primary storage by extending it to _____ storage.
5. A rectangular area on-screen that encloses one specific program or one specific document is called a _____.

Review: Short Projects

1. Getting To Know Your Hardware

   Familiarize yourself further with the hardware components of your environment. Areas to check are the megahertz of the processor, the generation of processors, the kind of graphics card, the amount of primary storage (RAM), the amount of secondary storage (hard disk space), and the number and size of floppy drives.

2. Getting To Know Your Software

   Find out what application programs you will be using in your work. Will you be using DOS programs as well as Windows programs?

3. Getting To Know Your Data Types

   What kind of data do you think you will be copying and pasting between programs? Can you list three scenarios when you would use this capability? Why is the capability to copy and paste helpful?

An Overview of Windows

1

Review: Long Projects

1. Deciding between Windows and DOS

   You are the president and CEO of a new venture called Bella's Ice Cream Parlor. Bella's Ice Cream Parlor is a new kind of ice cream store you have envisioned. It not only sells high-quality ice cream, but serves as a kind of meeting place and hub of social activity. You will initially sell a wide variety of coffee and pastries along with the ice cream, and you hope to expand to a larger menu later. You will be purchasing software for your state-of-the-art, IBM-compatible machine in the next few days. Your decision is whether to buy Windows and Windows applications or use DOS. The system will be used by you and your small staff. What factors will you consider while making this decision?

2. Comparing the Desktop to Your Desktop

   Describe your physical desktop, that is, the desk at which you usually do your work. Do you have folders for your papers? Do you have a place to throw old papers? Do you have stacks of paper on your desk now? How does your desktop compare to the Windows desktop?

Getting Started

If you are new to personal computers or if you are new only to Windows, this chapter will help you get started. If you have any experience with personal computers or with Windows, some of this material may be familiar to you. After you feel comfortable with the parts of the Windows environment, you can move to the next chapter to continue learning basic Windows operations.

Objectives

1. To Start Windows
2. To Start Programs
3. To Understand the Windows Desktop
4. To Understand the Parts of a Window
5. To Use the Mouse and Keyboard
6. To Close Documents, Programs, and Windows

Getting Started

	Key Terms in This Chapter
Pointer	The on-screen symbol you control with the mouse and use to select items and commands.
Mouse button	The button on the mouse that, when pressed, selects the item on which the pointer is located.
Program window	A window that contains a Windows or DOS (non-Windows) program. Multiple program windows can be open at one time.
Document window	A window that contains a document and is displayed within a program window. Some programs enable you to open multiple document windows.
Control menu	A menu that appears as a hyphen or a long bar at the top left corner of each program or document window, enabling keyboard users to move, size, or close windows.
Mouse pointer	An on-screen pointer that moves as you move the mouse on your desk. You use the mouse and mouse pointer to select text or objects; to choose menu commands; and to move, size, or close windows.
Program Manager	A Windows program that helps you group other programs and documents so that you can find and start them easily.
Click	To put the mouse pointer on an item, and press the left mouse button.
Drag	To put the mouse pointer on an item, press and hold down the left mouse button, and move the mouse.
Double-click	To point to an item, and rapidly press and release the mouse button twice.
⇧Shift+click Ctrl+click	Hold down ⇧Shift or Ctrl as you click. You use ⇧Shift+click in many Windows programs to select more than one item. You use Ctrl+click to select multiple nonadjacent file names in a list.

Objective 1: To Start Windows

This section shows you how to start Windows from your hard disk. Before you start Windows, you must install it. Refer to your Windows manual or ask your instructor for instructions on how to install Windows.

Exercise 1.1: Starting Windows

Follow these steps to start Windows from the hard disk in your computer:

1. Make sure that the drive door of each floppy drive is open.
2. Turn on your computer.
3. If necessary, respond to the prompts for the date and time.
4. When the C:\> prompt appears, type **win**, and press ⏎Enter.

Notes

1. If you have followed the Windows on-screen installation instructions and let the installation process modify your AUTOEXEC.BAT file, you can use the preceding instructions to start Windows from any directory on your hard disk.
2. You cannot run Windows from a floppy-disk-only system unless that system is on a network.
3. If you have less than two megabytes of primary memory, see your Windows documentation for instructions on how to start Windows.

Objective 2: To Start Programs

Programs in Windows share many common features. They operate similarly, supporting both the mouse and the keyboard. They look alike, with features in one program window similar to those in another program window. Programs in Windows are represented as *program item icons*, which are contained in program windows in the Program Manager. And you start them all the same way—directly from an icon in the Program Manager (see fig. 2.1). You can use either the mouse or the keyboard to start a program.

25

Getting Started

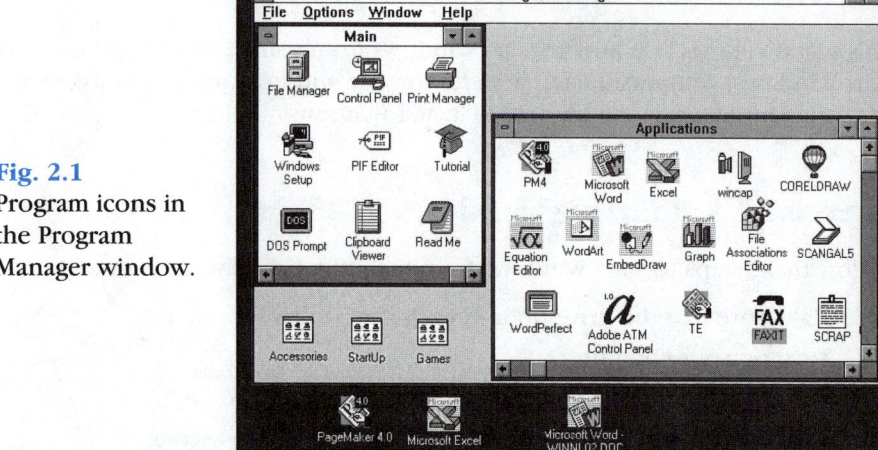

Fig. 2.1
Program icons in the Program Manager window.

Exercise 2.1: Starting Programs

To use your mouse to start (or invoke) a program, follow these steps:

1. Start Windows. The Program Manager window should now be open on your screen. If the Program Manager window is not on-screen, double-click the Program Manager icon to open it.

   Don't worry if the first time you double-click nothing seems to happen. Try pressing a little harder as you double-click. Sometimes people are somewhat nervous at first and double-click so fast and lightly that the signal isn't received. Relax and try again.

2. Click the program window containing your word processor, probably the Windows Application window. (If the program window appears as an icon, double-click the icon to open the program window.)

3. Double-click the word processing program item icon.

4. To exit the word processor, double-click the Control menu in the uppermost left-hand screen. You have now left Word for Windows.

5. Exit Windows by double-clicking the Exit icon in the lower left-hand part of the screen. The Exit icon is a picture of a door with an EXIT sign hanging on the top. The icon should make you think of the way to leave Windows, as the EXIT sign in a theater gives you a clue as to how to get out.

Exercise 2.2: Starting a Program and Windows Simultaneously

You can start a program when you start Windows. For instance, to start Windows and simultaneously start Word for Windows, follow these steps:

1. At the DOS prompt, type **win winword**, and press ⏎Enter.

   The *win* portion of this command starts Windows, and the rest of the command tells Windows which program to run. If you are using another word processing program, substitute the command for that program.

2. To exit Word for Windows, double-click the Control menu in the uppermost left-hand screen. You have now left Word for Windows.

If this technique does not work, Windows cannot find the program; therefore, you must type the program's complete path. For example, if the program you want to start is Word for Windows and its command file, WINWORD.EXE, is located on drive C in the WINWORD directory, you type **win c:\winword\winword.exe** at the DOS prompt.

You can start a Windows program and also load one of its documents when you start Windows. For example, to start Windows and to start Microsoft Excel with the worksheet BUDGET.XLS loaded, type the following line at the DOS prompt:

   win c:\excel\budget.xls

In this example, the BUDGET.XLS worksheet is located in the C:\EXCEL directory. Because files ending with XLS are *associated* with Microsoft Excel, the Microsoft Excel program starts and then loads the BUDGET.XLS file. Every program provides its own file extension; files with this extension are automatically associated with the program. In Chapter 5, "Managing Files," the discussion of the File Manager describes how to associate other data files.

Objective 3: To Understand the Windows Desktop

Windows programs run on a screen background known as the *desktop*. The programs and their documents appear on-screen, like reports lying on your desktop. Your Windows desktop may contain multiple Windows or DOS (non-Windows) programs. Each program appears in its own window or fills the screen.

Getting Started

Two types of windows appear on the desktop (see fig. 2.2). A *program window* contains the program itself. The menu bar that controls the Windows program is always at the top of the program window and below the title bar. In Windows, you can have several program windows open at one time. (A DOS program must fill the screen when Windows is in Standard mode.) A *document window* may appear within some program windows. Document windows contain the data or document on which the program works. Programs like Word for Windows and Microsoft Excel can have more than one document window, enabling you to work on multiple letters, worksheets, charts, or databases at once.

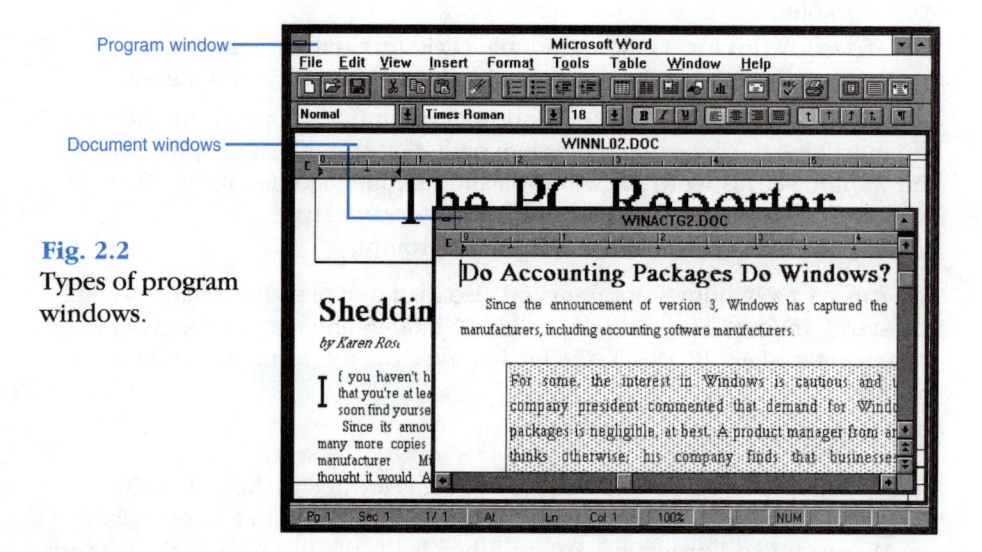

Fig. 2.2
Types of program windows.

Understanding the Program Manager

When Windows starts, it displays the Program Manager, which contains group windows and group icons (see fig. 2.3). Each group contains a collection of programs or data you use to get a specific type of work done. If you group work-related programs and data, starting programs and their associated data documents is easier. You can start a program by choosing the icon that represents the program.

The Main group consists of programs that come with Windows. Inside the Main group window are program item icons, each of which represents a program or a program and its associated data document. Activating a program item icon, as just done in Exercise 2.2, starts the program for that icon and loads an associated data document if you have defined one.

To Understand the Windows Desktop

Fig. 2.3
The Windows Program Manager.

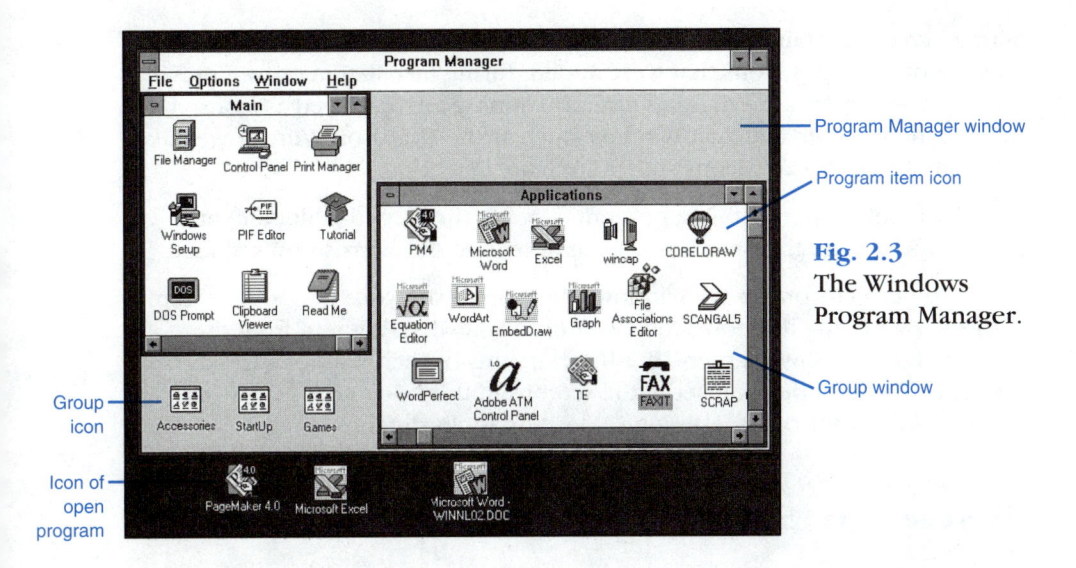

Windows programs already running are displayed in their own windows or as icons at the bottom of the screen (refer to fig. 2.3). Table 2.1 describes the Program Manager window parts.

Table 2.1 Program Manager Window Parts

Window Part	Description
Program Manager window	A program window containing group windows and group icons
Group window	A window, within the Program Manager, that contains program item icons
Group icon	A small representation of a closed group window
Program item icon	An icon that starts a Windows or DOS program and possibly an associated data document
Icon of open program	An icon representing a running program that has been minimized to an icon

Other groups that come with Windows are shown as group icons at the bottom of the Program Manager window. The Accessories group contains small desktop programs, including an executive word processing program, a calculator, a clock, and a calendar. The Games group contains two games. The

Getting Started

StartUp group contains programs that start whenever you start Windows. You may see other group icons that were added during installation or by a previous Windows operator. Programs already running are displayed as icons outside the Program Manager window, such as the Microsoft Word, PageMaker 4.0, and Microsoft Excel icons shown in figure 2.3.

If a document is open within a program already running, that document's name appears with the program icon, as shown in the Microsoft Word icon.

Note: You can customize the Windows desktop to suit your needs. As a result, your own Windows desktop probably looks somewhat different from the screens shown in this chapter—but the elements of each Windows desktop are the same. So don't be confused if the screens in this book look somewhat different from your own—everyone's desktop looks different.

Exercise 3.1: Understanding the Windows Desktop

To investigate your desktop, follow these steps:

1. Look at your screen. Although it may be slightly different from figure 2.3, find the program icons on your screen that are also seen in figure 2.3.
2. Find the Group icons Accessories, Games, and StartUp on your screen. Where are they in comparison to figure 2.3?
3. How many windows are currently opened on your screen?
4. Double-click the Word for Windows (or other word processor) icon. What information does your word processor give you as it starts?

Objective 4: To Understand the Parts of a Window

A window is built from parts that enable you to change the window by moving, sizing, or scrolling it. To understand the directions given in this book, you must be able to identify the various parts of a window.

Illustrated in this section are the different parts of a program (or document) window (see fig. 2.4). The window elements are the same for all Windows programs. In this example, Word for Windows is on the upper portion of the Windows desktop in a program window. The smaller document window, inside the Word for Windows window, contains a single document. The small icons—miniature pictures—at the bottom of the screen represent programs that are not in windows.

To Understand the Parts of a Window

Fig. 2.4 Parts of a window.

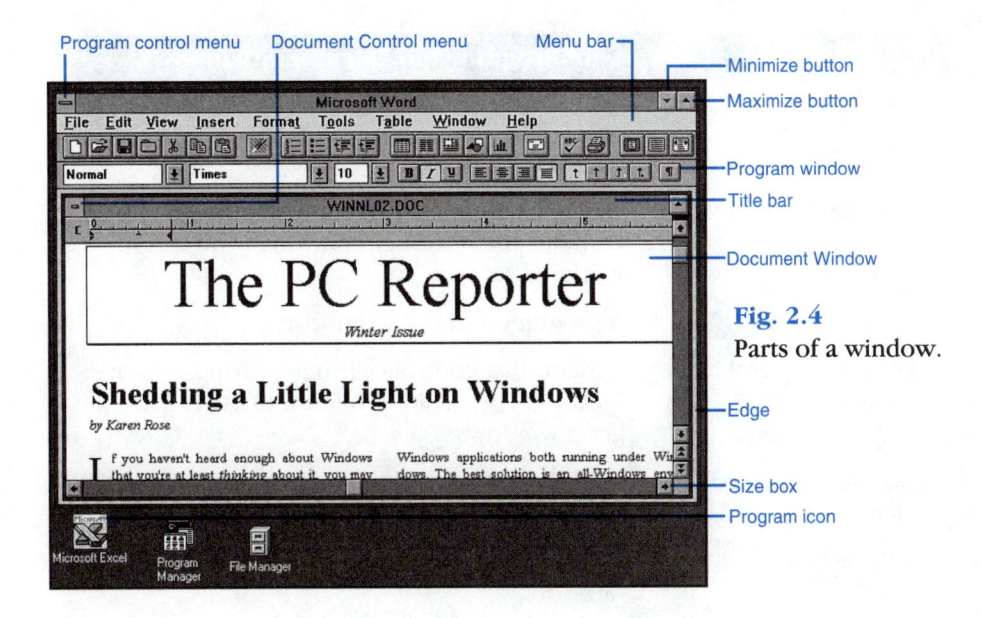

Table 2.2 describes the parts of the window shown in the illustration.

If a document window fills the inside of a program window or if a program window fills the screen, a different icon appears at the top right corner of the program window (see fig. 2.5). The Restore icon restores a full-screen program or document into the window it previously occupied. Chapter 3 illustrates this concept further.

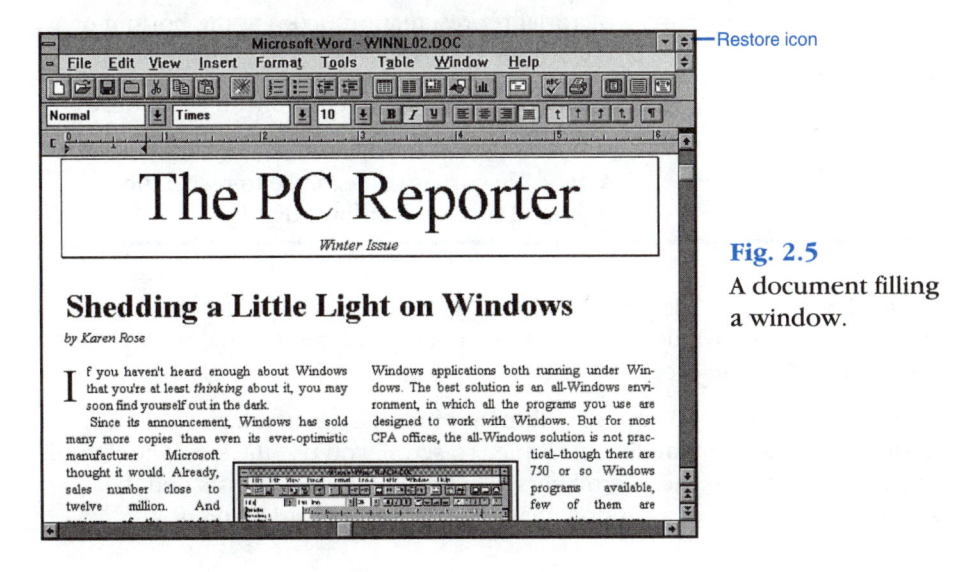

Fig. 2.5 A document filling a window.

31

Getting Started

Table 2.2 The Parts of Program and Document Windows

Window Part	Description
Program window	A window that contains a program
Document window	A window within a program window, that contains the document on which you are working
Program icon	A program reduced to an icon
Program Control menu	A menu that controls a program window's size, location, and position relative to other program windows
Document Control menu	A menu that controls a document window's size and location
Title bar	A bar containing a program or document title, or both
Menu bar	A bar containing a program's pull-down menus
Status bar	A bar containing menu descriptions, prompts to action, or document status
Maximize button	An icon that increases a window to a full screen
Minimize button	An icon that shrinks a program window to a pictorial representation (icon) at the bottom of the screen
Edge	A window edge you can move with the mouse to resize a window
Size box	A movable corner you can use to resize the right and bottom window edges

Figure 2.5 shows the same document as figure 2.4; however, the Word for Windows program window fills the screen here, and the document window fills the inside of the program window.

You can scroll a data document within its window so that you can see more information than is immediately visible. To scroll, you use the scroll boxes and the horizontal and vertical scroll bars (see fig. 2.6). Table 2.3 lists and describes the elements of a window that you use to scroll a document.

To Understand the Parts of a Window

Fig. 2.6

Windows elements used for scrolling.

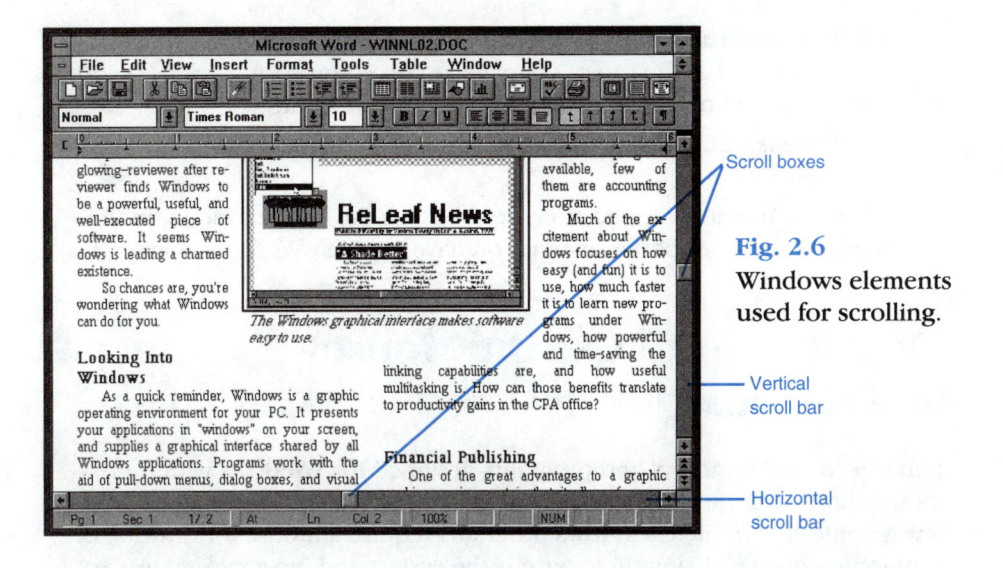

Table 2.3 Window Elements Used for Scrolling

Window Part	Description
Horizontal scroll bar	Scrolls data sideways through the window and document
Vertical scroll bar	Scrolls data vertically through the window and document
Scroll box	Shows the horizontal or vertical position of the data displayed in the document window, relative to the entire document

Exercise 4.1: Using the Scroll Bars

To use the scroll bar, follow these steps:

1. Find the scroll bars on your screen.
2. On the vertical scroll bar, click the down arrow. You see the scroll box jump to the bottom of the bar.
3. To go back to the top of the document, click the up arrow of the vertical scroll bar.

33

Getting Started

4. Click the right arrow of the horizontal scroll bar. Watch the numbers on the ruler near the top of the page as you continue to click. How do they change? You can see the page scroll to the right.
5. Click the left arrow until the scroll box is back at the starting (far left) position.
6. To exit a Windows application, double-click the Control menu, in the upper left corner of the screen. You have now left Word for Windows.

Objective 5: To Use the Mouse and Keyboard

You can control Windows and programs designed for Windows with the mouse, keyboard, function keys, shortcut keys, or a combination of these. A few graphically oriented Windows programs require a mouse for drawing or positioning objects. Using the mouse is the easiest and most natural way to learn Windows and Windows programs. If you are new to Windows, begin by using the mouse; later, if you want, you can make a transition to touch-typing your commands or pressing shortcut keys (key combinations).

Note: Do not feel that you must use either the mouse or the keyboard exclusively. Use them together for more efficiency and productivity.

The mouse you are using has two or three buttons; you can use either type of mouse with Windows. The mouse serves two purposes: to make selections from pull-down menus and pop-up dialog boxes, and to select text or objects you want to delete, move, or modify.

Using the Mouse

For most tasks, you use the left mouse button. The mouse pointer changes appearance on-screen. Usually, the mouse pointer appears as an arrow or an I-beam. Other pointer shapes are described throughout the chapter. The basic shapes of the mouse pointer are summarized in table 2.4.

34

To Use the Mouse and Keyboard

Table 2.4   Mouse Shapes and Functions

Mouse Shape	Function
Arrow	Chooses menus, commands, or options
Two-headed arrow	Resizes windows and selected objects or borders in some programs
Four-headed arrow	Moves selected objects in some programs
Cross hair	Draws graphics objects in graphics programs
Hourglass	Waits while the program works
I-beam	Moves the insertion point (cursor) or selects text you want to edit

Exercise 5.1: Using the Mouse: To Click or Not To Click

To use the mouse, follow these steps:

1. Hold the mouse in a relaxed but firm grip with two fingers resting on the buttons, the head under your palm, and the tail (wire) pointing in the same direction as your fingers. When you press a mouse button, do not move the mouse.

2. Relax and comfortably click the button.

   Do not choke the mouse. Relax!

3. Without clicking the buttons, move the mouse on your desktop. Notice that a pointer on the Windows screen moves accordingly.

   The pointer is often shaped like an arrowhead but may change shape depending on the pointer's location on-screen. Chapter 3 discusses the shapes and functions of the pointer in greater detail. If you find that you aren't moving the pointer accurately when you use the mouse, check the way you are holding it. Make sure that the tips of your fingers are on the buttons and that the wire runs parallel to your fingers.

Getting Started

4. Practice moving the mouse so that the pointer goes to the desired location. Pick up and lift the mouse when you need to move farther than a few inches. Some people, when they are first learning to use a mouse, don't think that the desk area is big enough. But remember that when the mouse is not touching a surface, the pointer does not move.
5. Practice lifting the mouse from the surface of your desktop, putting the mouse in a different location on your desktop, and continuing to move the cursor.
6. Move the mouse so that the tip of the mouse pointer (usually an arrow) is on the menu name, command, dialog box option, graphics object, or text you want to select. In this exercise, point to any icon on the screen.
7. Quickly press and release the mouse button. You see that the object is now highlighted. To remove the highlighting, click anywhere else on the screen.

Exercise 5.2: Using the Mouse To Drag

To drag across text or to drag a graphics object, follow these steps:

1. Move the mouse so that the tip of the mouse pointer is on the Exit icon. It is the icon in the lower left corner of the screen with an EXIT sign over an open door (see fig. 2.7).
2. Press and hold down the mouse button.
3. While holding down the mouse button, move the mouse. Because you are dragging a movable graphics object, as all icons are, the object moves. Move the Exit Windows icon anywhere on the screen.
4. Release the mouse button. You have moved the Exit Windows icon by dragging it!

Using the Keyboard

With Windows and Windows programs, you can use the keyboard for typing, choosing menus and commands, and selecting options from pop-up dialog boxes. In addition, many Windows programs have shortcut keys (key combinations) that reduce multiple-keystroke or mouse-keystroke combinations.

To Use the Mouse and Keyboard

Fig. 2.7
The Exit Windows icon.

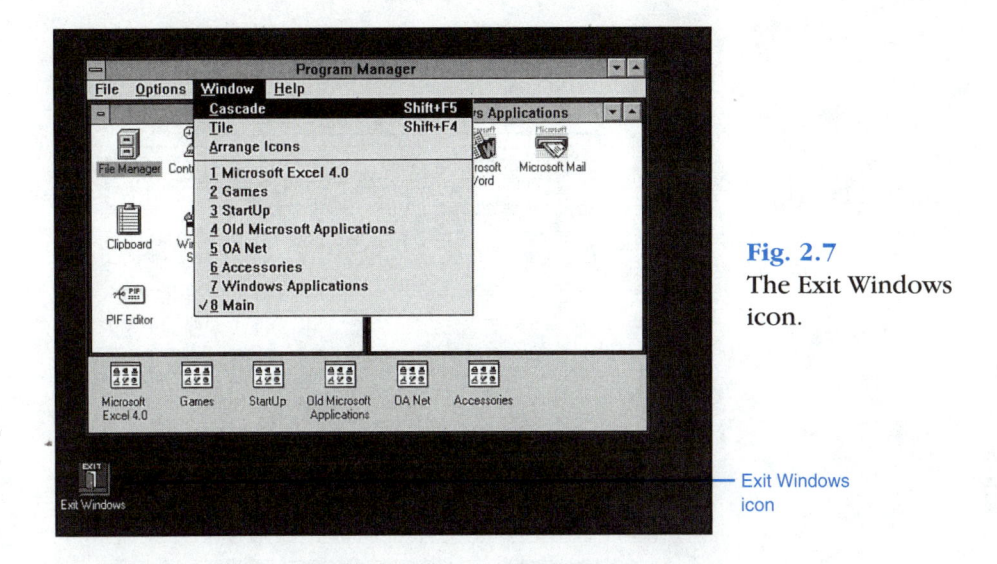

Windows uses the following areas of the keyboard (you may find slight variations on your keyboard):

- The function keys, labeled F1 to F12 at the top of the IBM Enhanced Keyboard (or F1 to F10 at the left of the IBM Personal Computer AT keyboard)
- The alphanumeric, or "typing," keys, located in the center of the keyboard (These keys are most familiar to you from your experience with typewriter keyboards.)
- The numeric and cursor-movement keys, found at the right side of the keyboard

Figure 2.8 shows the IBM PC AT keyboard, figure 2.9 shows the IBM Enhanced keyboard.

Function Keys

Many Windows programs use function keys in combination with other keys. In some programs, each function key can perform as many as four tasks depending on whether you use it by itself or with another key. In Windows, the function keys or their combinations provide shortcuts for commands you can choose from the menu. You should use the menus to select commands as you are learning, or if the command you want to select is one you use infrequently. Use shortcut keys after you become experienced.

Getting Started

Fig. 2.8
The IBM PC AT keyboard.

Fig. 2.9
The IBM Enhanced keyboard.

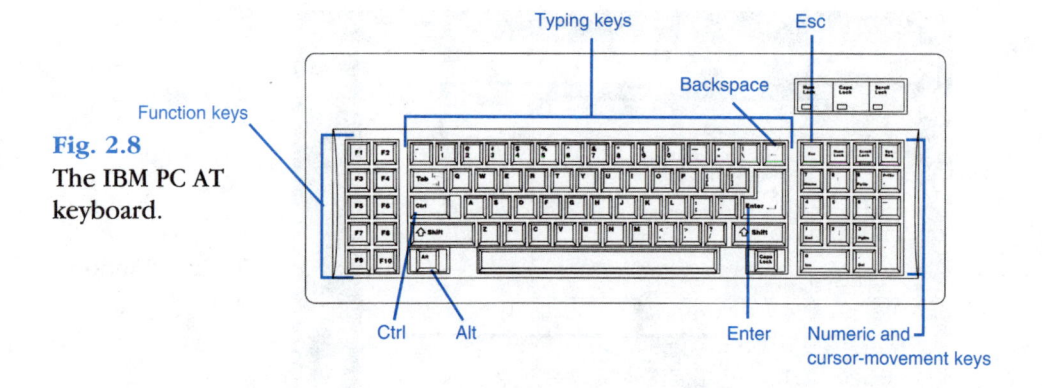

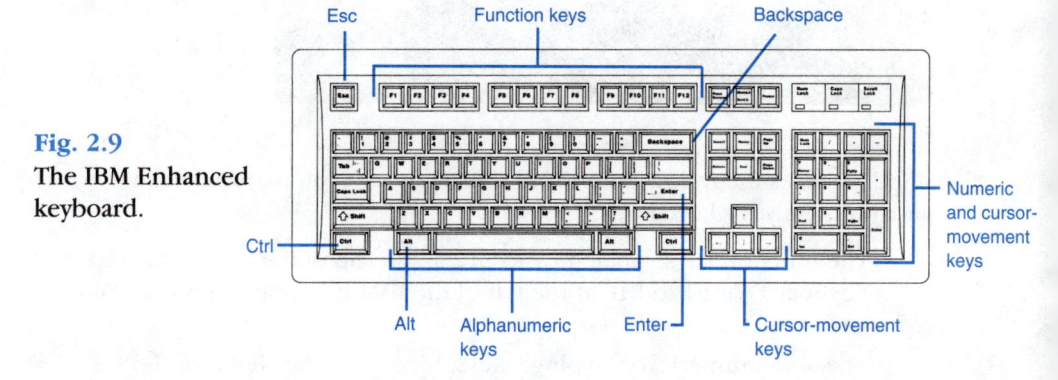

You use the following keys in combination with the function keys:

⇧Shift

Alt

Ctrl

To use the Alt + F4 combination, for example, you press and hold down the Alt key and then press the F4 function key. After you press the function key, release both keys.

Alphanumeric Keys

The alphanumeric keys work similarly to those on a typewriter. A critical but easily overlooked difference between typing with a typewriter and typing in a

38

computer program is that you do not need to press [↵Enter] to end lines at the right margin. When you type text and reach the end of a line, the text automatically "wraps" to the next line.

You can use the [↵Enter] key as a carriage return at the end of a paragraph. You press [↵Enter] to insert blank lines into your text, such as the lines that separate paragraphs. You can also use [↵Enter] to complete commands or dialog boxes you have selected in Windows programs.

The [⇧Shift], [Alt], and [Ctrl] keys are part of the alphanumeric keyboard. The [⇧Shift] key creates uppercase letters and other special characters, just as it does on a typewriter keyboard. You can also use [⇧Shift], [Alt], and [Ctrl] with the function keys as shortcut key combinations that duplicate menu commands. Pressing [Alt] by itself activates the menu bar.

Cursor-Movement Keys

The *insertion point* is the blinking vertical line in Windows programs that marks the location on-screen where the next character you type will appear. In DOS programs, the insertion point is called a *cursor* and appears as a blinking underline character or a reverse-video (highlighted) character.

Use the keys marked with arrows, located at the right side of the keyboard, to control the movement of the insertion point or cursor. When you press an arrow key, the insertion point or cursor moves, if possible, in the direction indicated by the arrow on the key. Most programs also enable you to use the [Home], [End], [PgUp], and [PgDn] keys to move around in the document.

Arrow keys are also located on the number keys on the numeric keypad at the far right side of the keyboard (duplicating the arrow keys on the Enhanced Keyboard). When you activate the [Num Lock] key (as indicated by a light on some keyboards), pressing keys on the numeric keypad produces numbers. You press [Num Lock] to alternate between numbers and arrow keys on the numeric pad.

Exercise 5.3: Using the Keyboard

To understand your keyboard, work through these steps:

1. Look at your keyboard, and compare it to figures 2.8 and 2.9. Which keyboard are you using?
2. Find the [Esc] key on your keyboard.
3. Find the [↵Enter] key on your keyboard.

39

Getting Started

4. Find the function keys on your keyboard.
5. Find the cursor-movement keys on your keyboard.
6. Are there any keys on your keyboard that aren't shown in the figures?

Objective 6: To Close Documents, Programs, and Windows

When you close a document window, program window, or Windows itself, you clear the open data documents from the computer's primary memory. If you need to use these documents again, you must save them on *secondary memory*, which makes a magnetic recording of your documents on a floppy disk or your hard disk. (Later, you can open these magnetic recordings, called *files*, and your documents will reappear on-screen.)

Note: When working with a Windows program, if you close a document window, the program asks whether you want to save the changes you made to the document. When working with DOS programs, be careful; some programs close immediately, without asking whether you want to save changes to the document. In these DOS programs, you must remember to save the document before exiting the program.

Exercise 6.1: Closing a Document Window

To close a document window, follow these steps:

1. Open your word processor by double-clicking the program's icon.
2. Open the File menu, and then click the Close command (see fig. 2.10).

   If you have changed the document since you opened it, a dialog box appears before the document closes. You have four choices: Yes, No, Cancel, and Help. Click the Yes button to save and then close the document, the No button to close without saving, or the Cancel button to ignore the Close command.
3. Click the Yes button.

   If you have previously saved the document, the program saves it under the same name.

To Close Documents, Programs, and Windows

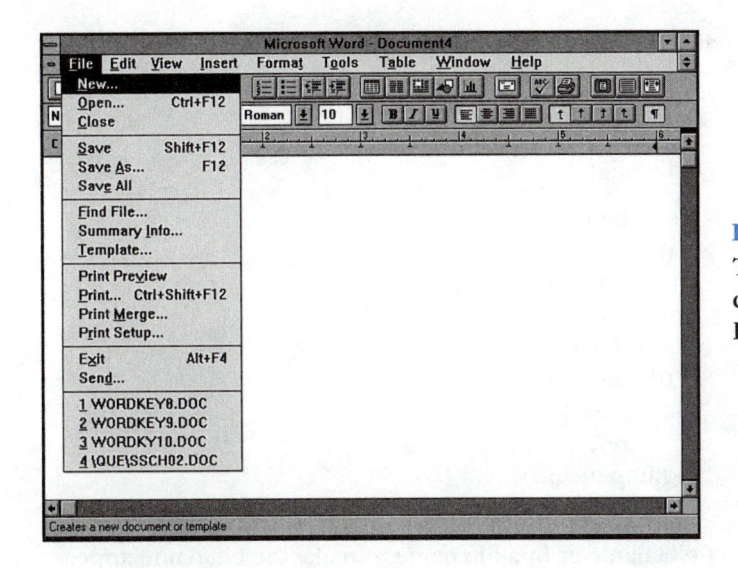

Fig. 2.10
The Close command on the File menu.

If you have not yet saved the document, another dialog box appears, prompting you to type a file name.

Now you create a new file name. Use the Del (Delete) or Backspace key to correct errors in typing. If a blank file name box appears, simply type the file name in the box.

4. Type **closeit** in the box below File Name. You have just named your file CLOSEIT.DOC.

A file name consists of a root name of one to eight characters. When you name a file, you must observe the file-naming guidelines of your operating system (MS-DOS, DR DOS, or PC DOS). For example, MS-DOS file names can be one to eight characters long, with no spaces, periods, or other punctuation marks (although symbols such as the pound sign or ampersand are allowed). After you name and save a file, the file name appears in the title bar of the document's window.

Many programs add their own three-character extensions to your file name. You can add your own extension if you prefer, separating it from the root name by a period (.). When you later open a file, however, most Windows programs list only the files that contain their own extensions; therefore, letting your program assign the extension is better than adding your own. In this case, DOC was added as the extension because that is the convention used by Word for Windows.

41

Getting Started

File names can contain the following characters:

Letters	a through z
	A through Z
Numbers	0 through 9
Symbols	- (hyphen)
	_ (underscore)
	! (exclamation point)
	@ (at)
	# (pound)
	$ (dollar)
	% (percent)
	^ (caret)
	& (ampersand)

Use a symbol as the first character in a file name to make the file name appear first in a list of file names.

File names cannot contain the following elements:

Blank spaces (use a valid symbol instead)

The symbols *, +, and =

More than one period

The following file names are valid:

BDGT_JUN.XLS

!PROPSL.DOC

LTR08#12.DOC

The following file names are invalid:

BDGT JUN.XLS (blank space used)

\PROPSL.DOC (backslash used)

LTR08.12.DOC (extra period used)

A second way to close a document window is to activate the Document Control menu ([Alt], -), and choose the Close command. You can also press [Ctrl]+[F4] to close the active document window.

To Close Documents, Programs, and Windows

Exercise 6.2: Closing a Program Window

When you close a program's window, you also close the document windows within it. When you close a Windows program, you are prompted to save documents that you have changed.

Note: Closing the Program Manager window exits Windows.

Word for Windows is used in the following illustrations to show how to close a program window. In nearly every Windows program, the **F**ile menu contains a command for exiting the program. Follow these steps to close Word for Windows:

1. Open the **F**ile menu, and click the E**x**it command (see fig. 2.11).

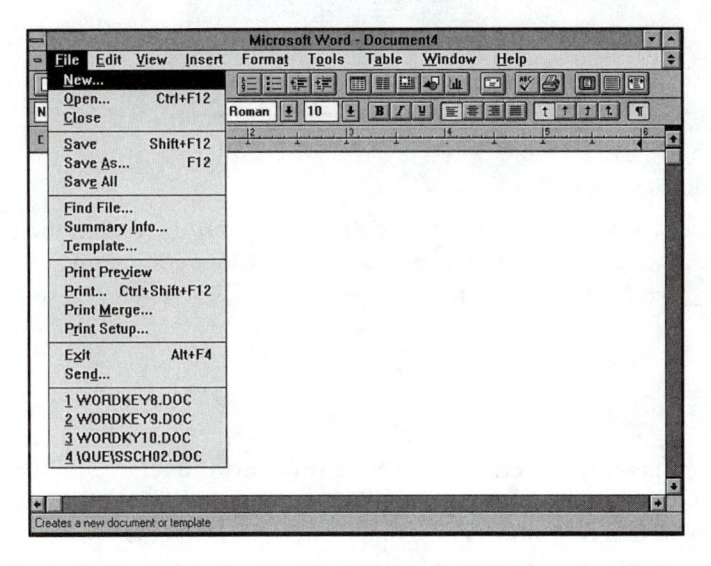

Fig. 2.11
The Word for Windows File menu.

2. Double-click the Word for Windows icon to open the program again.
3. Activate the Program Control menu (Alt , **space bar**), and choose the **C**lose command.
4. Double-click the Word for Windows icon to open the program again.
5. Press Alt + F4 to close the program window.

You now know a number of ways to close a program window.

You close windows containing DOS programs by saving any documents you have changed and then exiting the DOS program. When you exit the DOS program, its window closes.

43

Getting Started

Exercise 6.3: Exiting Windows

Windows is under the control of the Program Manager. When you close the Program Manager window, you exit Windows.

Follow these steps to exit Windows:

1. Make sure that the Program Manager window is now visible.
2. Click the **F**ile menu, and then click the E**x**it Windows command.

    The Exit Windows dialog box appears. You can click OK or press ⏎Enter to exit Windows; you can click Cancel or press Esc to return to Windows (see fig. 2.12).

Fig. 2.12
The Exit Windows dialog box.

3. Click OK to exit Windows.

A second way to close Windows is to activate the Program Control menu in the Program Manager (press Alt, **space bar**), and choose the **C**lose command. You can also press Alt+F4 to close Windows.

Chapter Summary

This chapter helps you get acquainted with the Windows environment. Learning these Windows basics is valuable because once you understand them, you can use them in any Windows programs. These fundamentals—starting Windows and programs, understanding the desktop and parts of a window, and defining the input devices—have now prepared you to begin Chapter 3.

Testing Your Knowledge

True/False Questions

1. **WIN** is the command to start Windows.
2. You cannot start both Windows and an application program with the same command.
3. A status bar is an icon that increases a window to a full screen.
4. A scroll box shows the horizontal or vertical position of the data displayed in the document window, relative to the entire document.
5. Cursor keys are keys that you use when you feel like exclaiming an expletive.

Multiple Choice Questions

1. Which of the following names is invalid according to the MS-DOS conventions?
    A. TESTIT.PLS
    B. GOFORITNOW.DOC
    C. NO
    D. YES_NO.DOC
2. If the Program Manager is topmost on the screen, which command will exit Windows?
    A. [Alt]+[Ctrl]
    B. [Esc]
    C. [Alt], [F], [X]
    D. [Alt], [F], [D]
3. A menu that controls a program window's size, location, and position relative to other program windows is called a(n)
    A. edge.
    B. Program Window.
    C. Document Control menu.
    D. Program Control menu.

Getting Started

4. A movable corner you can use to resize the right and bottom window edges is called a(n)
   A. size box.
   B. Minimize button.
   C. Shrink It box.
   D. edge.
5. What is the three-character extension that Word for Windows automatically adds to document names?
   A. XLS
   B. PIC
   C. DOC
   D. WFW

Fill-in-the-Blank Questions

1. Windows programs that are already running but not currently used are displayed in their own windows or as icons at the _____ of the screen.
2. The _____ point is the blinking vertical line in Windows programs that marks the location on-screen where the next character you type will appear.
3. Windows programs run on a screen background known as the _____.
4. A _____ scroll bar moves data sideways through the window.
5. MS-DOS file names can be one to _____ characters long.

Review: Short Projects

1. Starting Windows and Applications

   Practice starting Windows and simultaneously starting applications. Start Windows with each application you plan to use. Is it faster to do it this way? If you have any documents in those applications, try starting Windows and the application and opening the document at the same time. Is that faster?

Testing Your Knowledge

2. Using the Mouse

    Practice moving your mouse around the desktop. Practice double-clicking program icons to start them and then double-clicking the Control menu in the upper left corner of the application screen to exit. Become proficient at using the mouse—getting it where you want it to be and double-clicking.

3. Learning the Keyboard

    Close your eyes and see whether you can find each of the following keys by touch: Enter, Esc, Shift, Ctrl, Del. With your eyes closed, do you know where the function keys are, if you have them? Can you find the cursor-movement keys with your eyes closed? The more comfortable you are with the keyboard, the more easily you can use it!

Review: Long Projects

1. Reviewing the Basics

    Continuing with Bella's Ice Cream Parlor, you have decided to use Windows. Explain the desktop metaphor to your staff. Explain program and document windows, icons, scroll bars, and the keyboard and mouse. Keep your explanation simple but clear. Remember, you are trying to familiarize your staff with the environment so that they can be productive and help Bella's Ice Cream Parlor satisfy its customers. Prepare a written summary of the explanation.

2. Reviewing Windows Conventions

    The GUI (Graphical User Interface) of Windows uses some conventions about the location of icons, menus, scroll bars, and so on. Knowing these conventions will help you in all your work in Windows because they provide a common environment that is transferable to all Windows programs. Make a list of the conventions you have now seen, both from this chapter and Chapter 1. For example, programs running but not currently in use are where on the screen? Where is the menu bar? What is the first menu choice? Prepare a summary of these conventions.

Operating Windows

3

Compared with most DOS character-based programs, Windows programs are easier and more natural to learn and operate. With Windows programs, you benefit from decreased learning time, fewer mistakes, and an easier transition from one Windows program to another. In fact, studies show that people who use graphical interfaces, such as Windows, use three times as many programs in their daily work as people who use character-based programs. Windows programs can make you more efficient, more productive, and more valuable at work.

What you learn in this chapter will help you operate any Windows program. The skills you learn here carry over to other programs.

Objectives

1. To Control Menus and Use Dialog Boxes
2. To Control Window Positions and Sizes
3. To Switch between Programs
4. To Get Help

Operating Windows

Key Terms in This Chapter	
Dialog box	A window containing options, that appears when a command needs additional information before it can be executed.
Choose	To activate a menu or a command or to complete a dialog box. Click the menu name and then the command, or press [Alt], *letter*, *letter*. To specify an option you want to use, click the option name, or type its underlined letter.
Select	To indicate on-screen the item you want to affect or to highlight text.
Deselect	To remove the highlighting from an item on-screen. Click anywhere outside the selection, or press any arrow key.

Objective 1: To Control Menus and Use Dialog Boxes

Learning how to operate one Windows program puts you well on your way to operating other Windows programs. The menus, commands, and dialog boxes in all Windows programs operate similarly; and many commands—such as **F**ile, **E**dit, Forma**t**, **W**indow, and **H**elp—are exactly the same in different programs. This similarity means that learning one program helps you over and over again with other programs. These skills are *transferable*.

Before you work with menus and dialog boxes, you should understand the terms explained in the "Key Terms in This Chapter."

Some commands need additional information before they can perform an operation. On a pull-down menu, the names of these commands are followed by an ellipsis (...). A dialog box appears after you choose one of these commands. A dialog box enables you to see every available option. Dialog boxes require a response.

Dialog boxes contain different items designed to help you enter data or select options for a command. Table 3.1 lists the kinds of items in a dialog box and summarizes their uses.

To Control Menus and Use Dialog Boxes

Table 3.1 Dialog Box Elements

Element	Description
Text box	A data-entry area for text, data, or numbers
List box	A list of predefined data-entry items, options, or existing files or directories
Option button	A round button that specifies an option. You can select only one button from a group; the selected button is filled.
Check box	A square box that specifies an option. You can select more than one check box; an X in the check box indicates that the option is selected.
Command button	A large rectangular button that executes or cancels a dialog box. Some command buttons display another dialog box.

A drop-down list box conserves space by not showing the full list until you request it. With the mouse, you can display the drop-down list box by clicking the drop-down icon at the right end of the text box. When the scrolling list appears, you choose the item you want by clicking it. You can make large jumps through the list by clicking in the gray area of the scroll bar. You drag the white square (*scroll box*) in the scroll bar to new locations for long moves.

Command buttons complete or cancel a dialog box or display an additional dialog box. Choosing OK completes the dialog box, accepting all the selections you have made; choosing Cancel backs out of the dialog box, canceling your selections.

Many Windows programs have an Edit Undo command. Undo "undoes" the last command you executed. With the mouse, you can back out of a menu by clicking the menu name a second time. To back out of a dialog box, click Cancel.

Exercise 1.1: Selecting Text

You can select text in a word processing document or in a spreadsheet. To select text in a spreadsheet, follow these steps:

51

Operating Windows

1. Open your spreadsheet program by double-clicking the program icon.
2. Type 1 and press ⏎Enter. You have now put the number *1* into cell A1.
3. Press the right arrow. Type 2 and press ⏎Enter. You have now put the number *2* into cell B1.
4. To select both cells, click B1, hold down the mouse button, and drag the cursor to cell A1. You have now highlighted cells A1 and B1.

Do not close the spreadsheet. You will start at this point in Exercise 1.2.

Hint: In all Windows programs, you make changes by first selecting text, worksheet cells, or graphics objects, and then doing something to them with a command or shortcut key combination. Remember

Select; then do.

Exercise 1.2: Choosing Menus and Commands by Using the Mouse

Menus display the commands available in the program. A command that is available displays in black, and commands that are not available—usually because you first need to do something like select—is gray (see fig. 3.1).

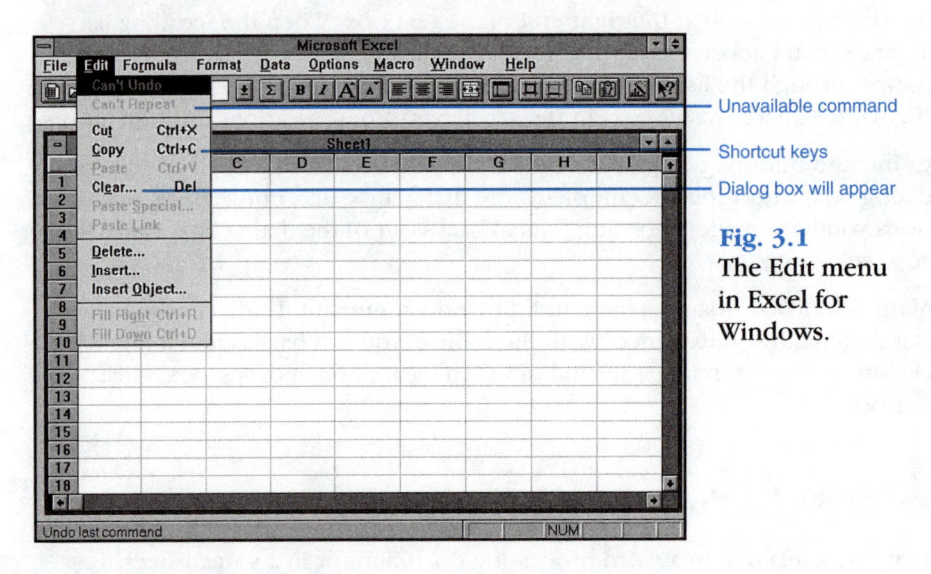

Fig. 3.1
The Edit menu in Excel for Windows.

52

To Control Menus and Use Dialog Boxes

Menu names always appear in a menu bar at the top of each program window. To choose a menu and then choose a command with the mouse, follow these steps:

1. Put the tip of the mouse pointer on the Edit menu name, and click the mouse button. Choosing the menu name, Edit, displays a list of Edit commands (refer to fig. 3.1).
2. Put the tip of the mouse pointer on the Copy command, and click the mouse button. You have now copied the cells you selected in Exercise 1.1 to the Clipboard (a holding place).
3. Move the mouse pointer to cell A5. Click the mouse.
4. Select the Edit menu name with the mouse, and click the mouse button. Choose the Paste command. You have now pasted the contents of the Clipboard into cell A5.

Exercise 1.3: Choosing Menus and Commands by Using the Keyboard

In addition to typing text and numbers, you can use the keyboard in Windows programs to choose menus, commands, and options from dialog boxes.

Shortcut keys can save you steps by bypassing menus, commands, and actions and immediately producing a result. Shortcut keys usually combine the ⇧Shift, Alt, and Ctrl keys with a function key (F1 through F12) or an alphanumeric key. Many programs display the most frequently used shortcut keys on the right side of the pull-down menus (refer to fig. 3.1).

Two other keys have important uses. The ↵Enter key executes the selected command or dialog box. The Esc key backs out of the current menu or dialog box without executing the command.

To choose a menu and then a command with the keyboard, follow these steps:

1. Select cells A1 and B1 with the mouse.
2. Press and release Alt to activate the menu bar.
3. Type the underlined letter in the menu name you want to choose. In this exercise, type e for Edit.
4. Type the underlined letter in the command you want to select. In this exercise, type c for Copy. You have now copied the selected cells to the Clipboard, this time using the keyboard.

Operating Windows

5. Move to cell A10 by pressing the arrow keys.
6. Press and release [Alt] to activate the menu bar.
7. Type the underlined letter in the menu name you want to choose. In this exercise, type **e** for **E**dit.
8. Type the underlined letter in the command you want to select. In this exercise, type **p** for **P**aste. You have now copied the selected cells to cell A10, this time using the keyboard.

Exercise 1.4: Selecting Options from Dialog Boxes

The Microsoft Excel worksheet's Edit Paste Special dialog box illustrates two groups of option buttons and individual check boxes that enable you to indicate how you want pasted numbers to interact with numbers already in the worksheet.

You must have completed Exercise 1.1 in order to perform this exercise. To select options from the Edit Paste Special dialog box, follow these steps:

1. Open the **E**dit menu, and select Paste **S**pecial. You see the Edit Paste Special dialog box (see fig. 3.2).

   The **A**ll option button is selected from the Paste group, and the **N**one option is selected from the Operation group.

Fig. 3.2
The Edit Paste Special dialog box in Excel.

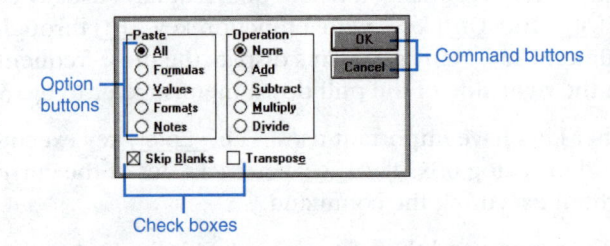

Option buttons — Check boxes — Command buttons

2. Click A**d**d under Operation.
3. With the keyboard, press [Alt]+[R] to choose Fo**r**mulas. A dashed line surrounds the active option button. Select another button in the same group by pressing any arrow key. Press [↓] once to select **V**alues.

   In this dialog box, the Transpos**e** check box is empty, which means that this option is deselected.

4. With the mouse, click the Transpos**e** check box to select it. Click the check box a second time to remove the X and deselect the check box.

54

To Control Menus and Use Dialog Boxes

5. With the keyboard, press Alt+B to select the Skip **B**lanks check box. Each time you press Alt+B, you toggle the check box between selected and deselected.

6. To exit the dialog box, click Cancel to remove the changes, or click OK to apply the changes. In this exercise, click Cancel.

7. To reduce Excel to an icon, open the Program Control menu, and choose minimize. This menu provides one way to shrink a window. See "Reducing a Window to an Icon and Restoring an Icon to a Window" in this chapter for alternative ways.

Exercise 1.5: Using a Drop-Down List Box

A special type of list box, a *drop-down list box*, is a text box with a down arrow (the drop-down icon) at the right end of the text box. Follow these steps to use a drop-down list:

1. Open Word for Windows or your word processor by double-clicking the program icon.

2. Open the Forma**t** menu.

3. Choose the **C**haracter command.

4. Click the drop-down icon (down arrow) at the right end of the font box (see fig. 3.3). A scrolling list box displays a list of possible entries from which you can choose (see fig. 3.4).

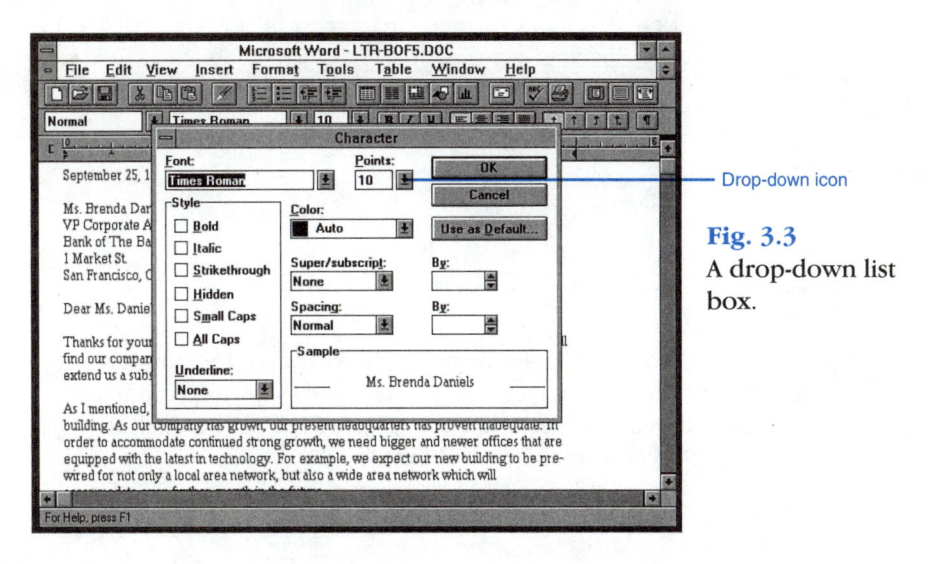

Fig. 3.3
A drop-down list box.

Operating Windows

Fig. 3.4
A drop-down list box.

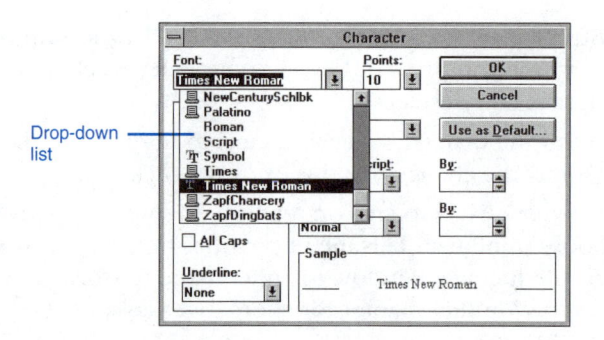

5. Scroll through the list by clicking the up or down arrow at the right side of the scroll bar. Click the item you want to select. The selected item in the list is highlighted.

6. Choose a typeface by clicking it. The selected item in the list is highlighted.

7. Choose 12-point type size from the **P**oints box to the right of the font box (see fig. 3.5). Just as in all drop-down list boxes, you click the down arrow at the right end of the box and then scroll through the list until you find your choice. Alternatively, you can just click in the box and type **12**.

8. Click the OK command button.

Fig. 3.5
The Points drop-down list box.

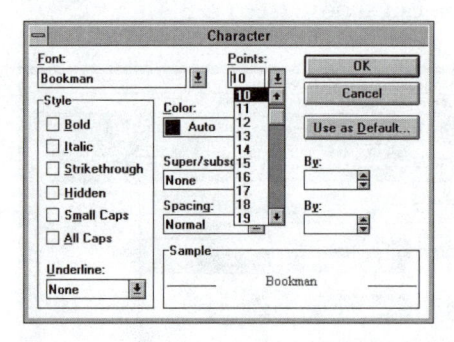

9. Repeat steps 2 through 7, this time using the keyboard to complete the dialog box. With the keyboard, press ⏎Enter to choose the command button enclosed in a bold rectangle (usually the OK command button). Press Esc to choose the Cancel button.

Objective 2: To Control Window Positions and Sizes

Just as you move papers on your desk, you can move and reorder program windows on your screen. In fact, you can resize windows, expand them to full size, shrink them to small icons to save space, and restore them to original size.

The topmost program window is the active window. It contains the program in which you are currently working, just as the topmost paper on your desk is the paper you are working on. This section shows you how to make a program window the active window and how to work with your windows.

If you can see several windows on-screen, you can use the mouse to activate a window by clicking the window. You can double-click an icon to open it into a window.

Exercise 2.1: Moving a Window

You can move a window to any location on-screen. By moving a program window or document window, you can arrange your work on-screen just as you arrange papers on your desk.

To move a window with the mouse, follow these steps:

1. Activate the window by clicking its title bar or edge.

   Note: You cannot move a window that is maximized to occupy the full screen. To move a maximized window, first restore it to a smaller size by clicking the two-headed arrow in the upper right hand corner of the screen (see Exercise 2.3).
2. Point to the window's title bar.
3. Press and hold down the mouse button.
4. Drag the window to its new location by moving the mouse as you continue to hold down the mouse button.
5. Release the mouse button when the window is where you want it.

Exercise 2.2: Changing the Size of a Window

Changing the size of a window enables you to position and size program and document windows so that you can see more than one data area. Copying and

Operating Windows

pasting data between programs is therefore much easier. To change the size of a window, drag one or more window edges to a new position. When you drag an edge of a window, one side moves. When you drag the corner of a window, two sides move.

With the mouse, change the size of a window by following these steps:

1. Activate the Word for Windows window by clicking its title bar or edge.
2. Move the pointer to the edge or corner of the window you want to size. When the pointer is correctly positioned, it changes to a two-headed arrow.
3. Press and hold down the mouse button, and drag the two-headed arrow to move the edge of the window.
4. Release the mouse button.

Exercise 2.3: Filling and Restoring Screens into Windows by Using the Mouse

Sometimes you will want the program to fill the entire screen, especially when you are working with only one program. In programs that contain multiple document windows, such as Microsoft Excel and Word for Windows, you can make a document fill the entire area within the program window. This feature is useful if you want to see the largest area of a worksheet or letter. To use the mouse to make a window fill the screen, follow these steps:

1. Click the up-arrow button at the top right corner of the program or document window. This up-arrow button is known as the *Maximize button*. In this exercise, click the Maximize button of the word processing window to maximize the window (see fig. 3.6).

   Note: Some Windows programs contain a single document. In these programs, you cannot maximize the document because it already fills the major portion of the program's window.

2. To use the mouse to restore a full-screen program into a sizable, movable window, click the two-headed arrow located at the top right corner of the program window. This two-headed arrow is the *program restore button*. It reduces a full-screen Windows program into a smaller window. In this exercise, click the two-headed arrow of the Word for Windows program (see fig. 3.7).

To Control Window Positions and Sizes

Document Maximize button

Fig. 3.6
The Maximize button.

Restore buttons

Fig. 3.7
The Windows Restore buttons.

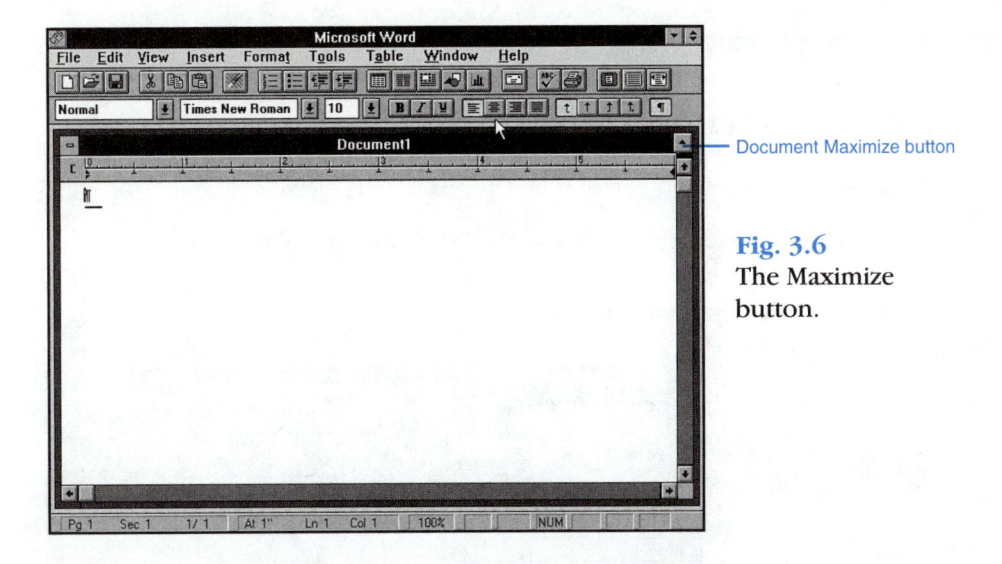

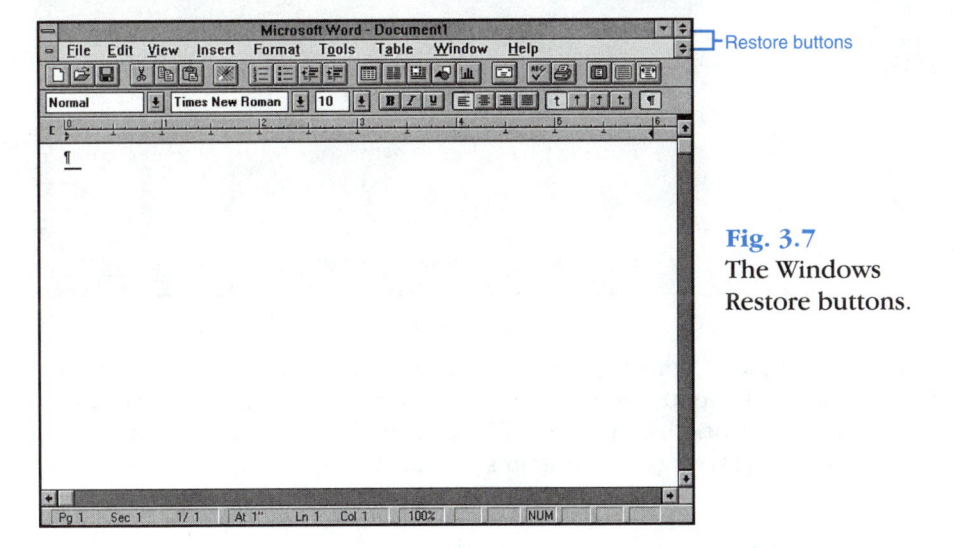

Exercise 2.4: Filling and Restoring Screens into Windows by Using the Keyboard

To use the keyboard to make a window fill the screen, follow these steps:

Operating Windows

1. Press [Alt], **space bar** to choose the Program Control menu.
   Or press [Alt], [-] to choose the Document Control menu.
2. Choose the Ma**x**imize command.

To use the keyboard to restore a full-screen program into a smaller window, follow these steps:

1. Press [Alt], **space bar** to choose the Program Control menu (see fig. 3.8).
2. Choose the **R**estore command.

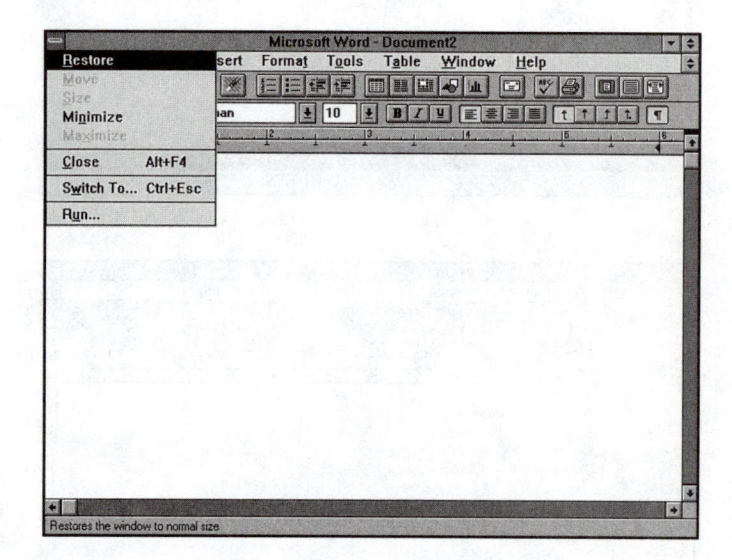

Fig. 3.8
The Program Control menu.

Note: The Program Control menu may change position. When the document is in a window, its Control menu is at the top left of the document window. When the document is maximized to fill the inside of a program, the Document Control menu for some programs appears to the left of the File menu.

Exercise 2.5: Reducing a Window to an Icon and Restoring an Icon to a Window

When you need to work with a large number of programs at one time, you may want to reduce some of them to icons. A program icon contains the program and its document; however, program icons require less space on-screen, and you can quickly open an icon into a window or full screen.

60

To Switch between Programs

You can shrink programs such as Microsoft Excel, Word for Windows, and Aldus PageMaker and arrange them as icons. Follow these steps:

1. With the mouse, shrink a window to an icon by clicking the down-arrow button located on the right side of the program's title bar. This arrow is known as the *Minimize button*. Click the Word for Windows Minimize button. You now see Word for Windows as an icon at the bottom of the screen as in figure 3.9.

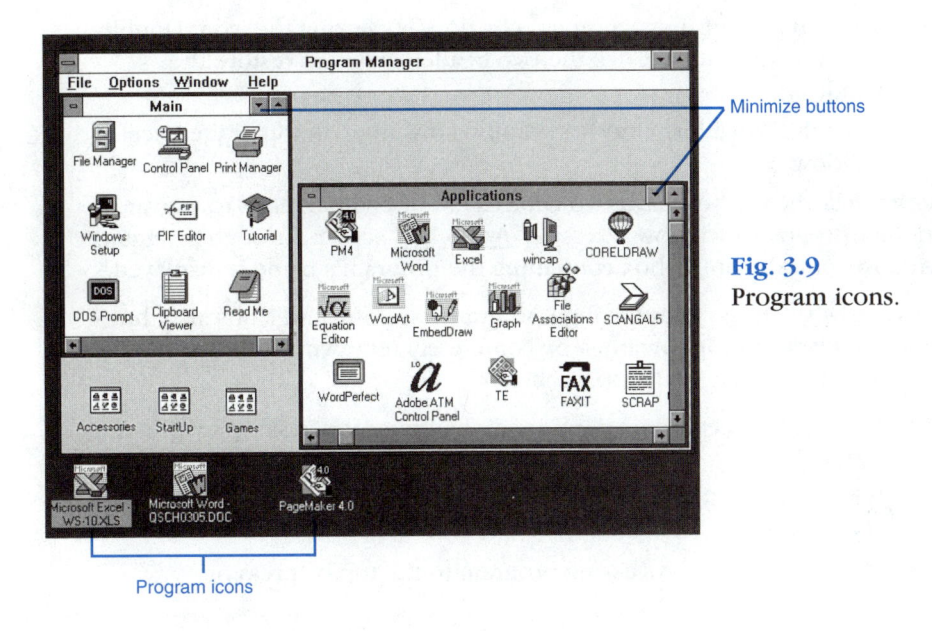

Fig. 3.9
Program icons.

2. Restore an icon to a window by double-clicking the icon. Double-click the Word for Windows icon.

Objective 3: To Switch between Programs

When you have many programs running, you need an easy way to switch from one program to another. Remember that the topmost program window with a solid title bar is the active window, the one in which you are working.

61

Operating Windows

Exercise 3.1: Switching with the Mouse or the Keyboard

To switch between programs by using the mouse, follow these steps:

1. Activate a window, or bring it to the top, by clicking that window. Be careful not to click a part of the program's window that will issue a command.

   You can activate a program icon by double-clicking the icon. Double-click the Excel icon. Click the two-headed arrow to restore the window.

2. Click the Word for Windows window. It is now on top of the Excel window.

With the keyboard, you have two choices of key combinations to activate another program's window. Pressing Alt+Tab cycles through program windows quickly; only a box containing the program's name is displayed.

Pressing Alt+Esc cycles through program windows and icons also, but more slowly; each window must be completely redrawn before the next window appears. Try both approaches:

1. Bring your spreadsheet window to the top of the desktop by pressing Alt+Tab.

2. When you see the name of the program you want, release the Alt and Tab keys.

3. Bring your word processing program to the top by pressing Alt+Tab.

Objective 4: To Get Help

Windows programs have Help information to guide you through new commands and procedures. In some programs, the Help files are quite extensive. They tell you about parts of the screen, the actions of commands, and the step-by-step procedures to complete specific tasks.

To get help in Windows programs, choose the **Help** menu by clicking **Help** or pressing Alt, H (see fig. 3.10). Then choose one of the Help commands.

From the **Help** menu, you can select commands that provide help with using the Help feature or the operating procedures, that provide an index of specific topics, and that enable you to search for information about a specific topic. Choosing one of these commands displays a Help window.

To Get Help

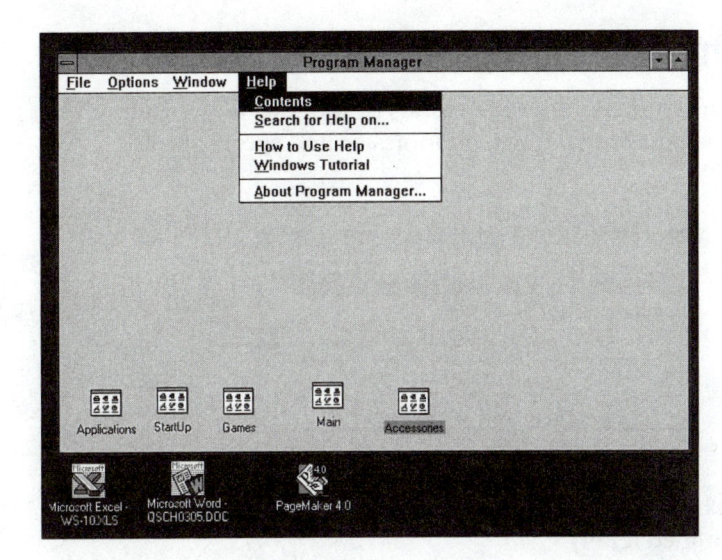

Fig. 3.10
The Help menu.

Help programs may differ slightly from one Windows program to another and between older and newer versions, but most Windows programs contain variations on three methods of controlling the Help program. These methods are summarized in table 3.2.

Table 3.2	Controlling Help
Method	*Description*
Menus	At the top of the Help window are the menus to control the Help program.
Buttons	Under the menus are buttons for listing the contents of the Help file, searching for a specific subject, going back to the preceding subject or help screen, and choosing from a list of the Help subjects you have most recently viewed.
Hypertext words	The text in a Help screen contains underlined words or phrases. Choosing a word or phrase with a solid underline moves you to that topic so that you can learn more about it. Choosing a word or phrase with a dotted underline pops up a window containing a short definition.

Operating Windows

Locating a Help Topic

Command buttons are located under the menus of some Windows Help programs, enabling you to browse through topics or find specific topics quickly (see fig. 3.11).

Fig. 3.11
A Help screen.

Choose a command button by clicking it or pressing Alt+*letter* (where *letter* is the button's underlined letter).

Table 3.3 describes the Help buttons displayed in the Program Manager Help screen and two buttons (<< and >>) that many other Help programs use.

Table 3.3 Common Help Buttons	
Button	Description
Contents	Displays the contents of the program's Help file. Choose one of the listed subjects to jump to that subject.
Search	Displays a list of key words and phrases in the program's Help file. You can type or select a word or phrase to jump to that subject.
Back	Displays the most recent subject you viewed. You can continue choosing **Back** to review subjects you have already viewed, until you get to the Contents screen.
History	Displays the last 40 subjects you have viewed, with the most recently viewed subject at the top of the list. You can return to a subject by double-clicking it.
Glossary	Displays an alphabetized list (glossary) of terms used in the Help program. You can select a term to display its definition. (Not all Help programs use this button.)

To Get Help

Button	Description
<<	Displays the preceding subject in a series of related subjects. You can continue choosing this button until you reach the first subject in the series. The button is dimmed if no previous subjects exist.
>>	Displays the next subject in a series of related subjects. You can continue choosing this button until you reach the final subject in the series. The button is dimmed if no more subjects exist.

Viewing Help's Contents

To get an overview of your program or to see what subjects are contained in the Help file, you can list the Help file's contents. To view the contents, choose the Contents button.

In the Program Manager's list of contents, subjects are divided into three categories: How To, Commands, and Keyboard (see fig. 3.12).

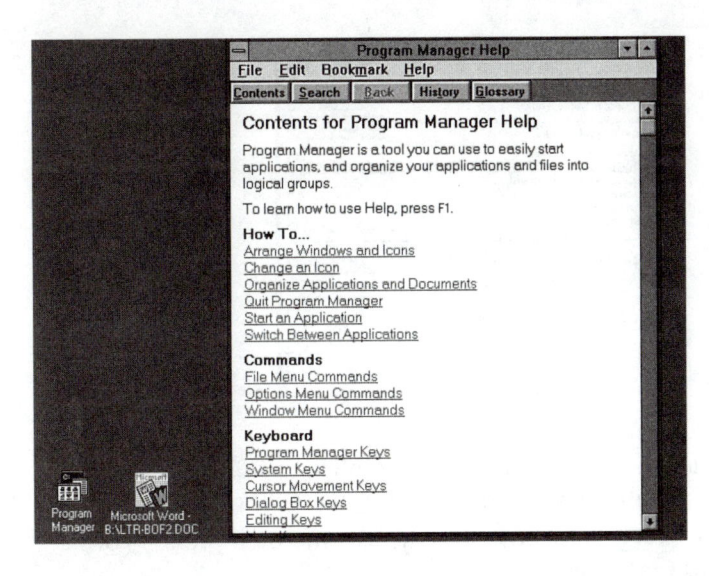

Fig. 3.12 The contents of a Help file.

Operating Windows

The subjects listed in the How To category describe how to perform functions in the Program Manager. The subjects listed in the Commands category describe how the commands in the Program Manager's three menus work. The subjects in the Keyboard category describe how to use key combinations and specific keys. To jump to any of these subjects, click the subject, or press the `Tab` key to select the subject you want to display, and then press `Enter`.

Exercise 4.1: Searching for Help on Specific Topics

In the Help program, you can select the **S**earch button when you want to search for help on a specific topic. In the Program Manager, for example, you can follow these steps to search for topics related to starting applications:

1. Open the **H**elp menu.

    Note: In many Windows programs, pressing `F1` immediately displays the Help window.

2. Click the **S**earch button to display the Search dialog box.

    Alternatively, press `Alt`+`S` to display the Search dialog box.

3. In the Type a **W**ord text box, type **applications, starting** (see fig. 3.13).

Fig. 3.13
The Search dialog box of the Help program.

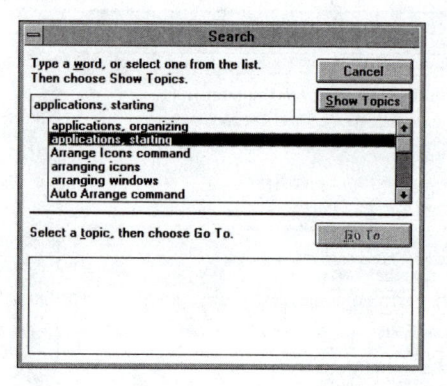

Alternatively, click the down arrow in the scroll bar until `applications, starting` appears in the list; then click that phrase.

Alternatively, press `Tab` to move into the list, and then press `↑` or `↓` to select `applications, starting`.

4. Click the **S**how Topics button at the top right corner of the dialog box.

    Alternatively, press `Alt`+`S` to show the topics (or press `Enter`).

To Get Help

All topics found that are related to the word or phrase you typed appear in the topic list at the bottom of the dialog box (see fig. 3.14).

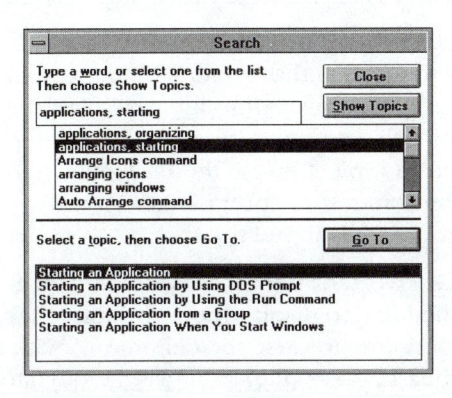

Fig. 3.14
A list of related help topics.

5. In the Select a **T**opic text box, click the topic you want to read.

   Or press ↑ or ↓ to select the topic you want to read.

6. Click the **G**o To button to go to the topic.

   Or press Alt + G to go to the topic (or press ↵Enter).

Pressing ⇧Shift + F1 displays context-sensitive help in some Windows programs. Pressing ⇧Shift + F1 when a dialog box or error box appears gives you help about that box. In some Windows programs, pressing ⇧Shift + F1 first changes the mouse pointer into a question mark. If you then click a command or a particular part of the screen, the program displays information about that command or that portion of the screen.

Jumping to Another Help Topic

Within the Help text are underlined *hypertext* words or phrases that enable you to jump quickly to related information. Two kinds of underlines are used for hypertext words and phrases in Help text. These kinds are explained in table 3.4.

Operating Windows

Table 3.4 Hypertext Actions

Underline	Action You Take
Solid underline	Click the word or phrase underlined with a solid line to jump to that topic. With the keyboard, press [Tab⇆] or [⇧Shift]+[Tab⇆] to select the word or phrase, and then press [↵Enter] to jump to the selected topic. Choose the **B**ack button (or the << button in some programs) to return to the previously displayed topic.
Dashed underline	Click a word or phrase underlined with a dashed line to display the definition (click a second time to close the definition). With the keyboard, press [Tab⇆] or [⇧Shift]+[Tab⇆] to select the word or phrase, and then press [↵Enter] to display the definition. Press [↵Enter] a second time to close the definition.

Exercise 4.2: Marking Help Locations for Easy Reference

In some Windows programs, when you find a Help topic that you may want to return to again, you can put a bookmark on it, just as you use a bookmark to mark a location in a book. You can then return to a topic that has your bookmark. You can use more than one bookmark in a Help file.

To put a bookmark on a Help topic, follow these steps:

1. Display the Help topic on which you want to put a bookmark.
2. Open the Book**m**ark menu, and choose the **D**efine command. The Bookmark Define dialog box appears (see fig. 3.15).

Fig. 3.15
The Bookmark Define dialog box.

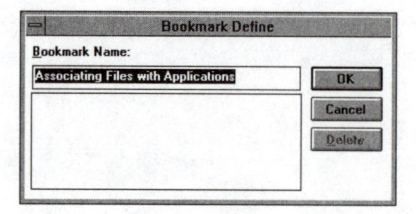

To Get Help

3. Select the **B**ookmark Name text box (if it isn't already selected), and type a bookmark name of your choice. Notice that the bookmark name that first appears in the text box is the title of the current topic; you can accept this title as your bookmark name.
4. Choose OK, or press `↵Enter` to attach your bookmark to the specified topic.

To return to a bookmark in a Help file, use these steps:

1. Choose the **H**elp command in the Windows program.
2. Open the Book**m**ark menu by clicking it or by pressing `Alt`+`M`. The list of bookmarks shows that several topics have bookmarks (see fig. 3.16).

Fig. 3.16
List of topics that have bookmarks.

3. Click, or type the number of, the bookmark to which you want to return.
4. If more than nine bookmarks are shown, click **M**ore at the bottom of the menu, or press `M`. From the Go To Bookmark list that appears, select the bookmark you want to go to, and then choose OK.

The Help window displays the topic containing your bookmark.

To remove a bookmark, follow these steps:

1. Choose the Book**m**ark menu.
2. Choose the **D**efine command.
3. Click the bookmark's name in the list, or press `Tab⇥` to move to the list.
4. Press `↑` or `↓` to select the name.
5. Choose the **D**elete button to delete the bookmark, and then choose OK or press `↵Enter`.

69

Chapter Summary

This chapter covers the most important information you need to operate Windows and Windows programs. You have learned how to use both the mouse and the keyboard to choose menus, commands, and options from dialog boxes. You have seen how to switch between programs and how to change the size and position of windows on-screen—all under mouse or keyboard control. Finally, you learned how to get help information about using menus and commands.

Testing Your Knowledge

True/False Questions

1. For most functions, you press the right mouse button.
2. The `Enter` key executes the selected command in a dialog box.
3. On pull-down menus, the names of commands that have additional information are followed by question marks (???).
4. You can double-click an icon to open it into a window.
5. The arrow that shrinks a window to an icon is called the Maximize button.

Multiple Choice Questions

1. When a command needs additional information before it can be executed, a window appears containing options. This window is called a
    - A. pointed.
    - B. dialog box.
    - C. mouse button.
    - D. drag.
2. When you want to select more than one adjacent item from a list, you use
    - A. `Shift`+click.
    - B. click.

Testing Your Knowledge

   C. double-click.

   D. `Ctrl`+click.

3. A special type of list box that has a down arrow at the right end of the box is called a

   A. drop-down list.

   B. dialog box.

   C. controlling menu.

   D. check box.

4. To get help in Windows programs, you can

   A. press `Alt`, `H`.

   B. choose the Help menu by clicking **H**elp.

   C. press `F1`.

   D. all the above.

5. What key is pressed to back out of menus or dialog boxes or to return to your document from the menu bar?

   A. `↵Enter`

   B. `Ctrl`

   C. `Esc`

   D. `Home`

Fill-in-the-Blank Questions

1. When in a dialog box, each time you press `Alt`+*letter*, you _____ the check box between selected and deselected.

2. To choose a menu from the current Windows program, you press _____ and the underlined _____ in the name of the menu you want.

3. To use the mouse to make a window fill the screen, click the _____ button at the top right corner of the program or document window.

4. A _____ is an alphabetized list of terms used in the Help program.

5. When the mouse pointer is shaped like a _____, you can resize windows and selected objects or borders in some programs.

Operating Windows

Review: Short Projects

1. Learning the Windows Menu System

    Investigate the menus in your Windows environment by opening every menu and every icon. Note how the menus are organized—for example, what applications each menu contains and what the theme of the menu is.

2. Reorganizing the Desktop

    Rearrange the windows on the desktop, and decide which arrangement is best for your needs. Play with different alternatives until you are satisfied with the best desktop for you.

3. Minimizing and Maximizing Programs

    Minimize the Program Manager, and then maximize it. You can see that it is also an application that can be reduced to an icon on your screen.

Review: Long Projects

1. Using Windows Applications

    Continuing with Bella's Ice Cream Parlor, develop a list of software packages that you might use in your job as CEO. How do you think the Windows environment will serve your role? List several components of your job that would be aided by the Windows software. Write up your findings as an executive summary.

2. Increasing Productivity with Windows

    You have accepted a job as a training consultant for a large Fortune 500 company. Your first assignment is to prepare a list of five bulleted points explaining why the Windows 3.1 environment will increase productivity in comparison to a DOS environment. What are the points you will make?

Editing, Copying, and Moving in Windows

4

One of the greatest advantages of working with Windows is that all Windows programs work in a similar way. Every program has a title bar that tells you the name of the program and the name of the document you're working on; every program has a menu bar; and every program displays in a window that works in a predictable manner.

But the similarities go even deeper. Not only do all Windows programs have a menu bar, all menu bars contain certain commands that are the same in every Windows program. And in all programs that include typed text, the basic techniques for editing text are identical. Selecting text you want to copy or cut is one of the most important skills you can learn. In this chapter, you learn common Windows commands, and you learn how to select and edit text in any Windows program.

Editing, Copying, and Moving in Windows

Objectives

1. To Edit Text
2. To Copy and Move Text in Windows Programs
3. To Copy and Paste in DOS Programs
4. To View and Save Cut or Copied Data

Key Terms in This Chapter	
Clipboard	An area of memory reserved to hold text or graphics you cut or copy.
Copy	An operation that stores in the Clipboard a duplicate of selected text or graphics from a program.
Paste	An operation that inserts information in the Clipboard into the active program at the current insertion point or cursor.
Cut (Move)	An operation that removes selected text or graphics from a program and stores it in the Clipboard. You can also use the Cut operation to move text or graphics.

Objective 1: To Edit Text

With the exception of some shortcut keys, the text-editing techniques described in this section work in all Windows programs and in the text boxes in the dialog boxes these programs display.

When you position the mouse pointer over an area of text that can be edited, the pointer appears as an *I-beam* (see fig. 4.1). This shape indicates that you can edit this text if necessary. The *insertion point* is the flashing vertical line in text, indicating where text editing or typing will occur.

Exercise 1.1: Editing Single Characters

Editing documents is tedious work, but with Windows programs, editing can be easier and almost fun. You can edit single characters with the mouse or

To Edit Text

with the mouse and the keyboard. After you have had some practice, you may find that using a combination of the mouse and keyboard is the fastest method.

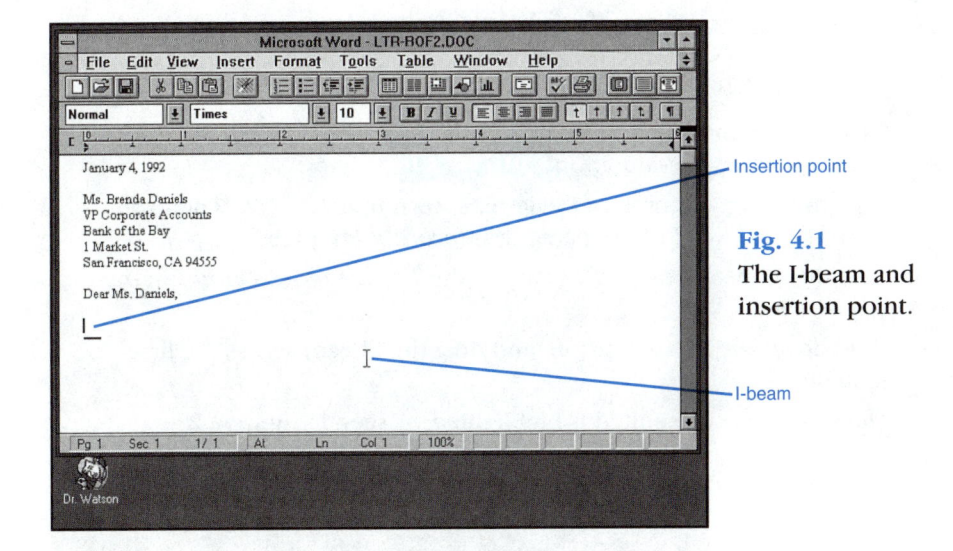

Fig. 4.1
The I-beam and insertion point.

With the mouse, you edit single characters in text by following these steps:

1. Open your word processing program by double-clicking its icon.
2. Enter the date, address, and salutation as seen in figure 4.1 by typing the letters and pressing [Enter] at the end of each line. To add an extra line, simply press [Enter] again. For example, after you type the date, *January 4, 1992*, press [Enter] twice to put a blank line between the date and the inside address. Continue entering the data in this manner.
3. With the mouse, place the I-beam between the two *c*'s in *Accounts*.
4. Click the mouse to position the flashing insertion point between the characters.
5. Press [Del] to delete a character to the right.
6. Press [Backspace] to delete a character to the left.
7. Type **cc** at the insertion point.

With the keyboard, you edit single characters in text by following these steps:

1. Press the down-arrow key ([↓]) twice to move the flashing insertion point to the end of the word *St*.

75

Editing, Copying, and Moving in Windows

2. Press [Del] to delete the period.
3. Type **reet** at the insertion point to spell out the word *Street*.

Exercise 1.2: Editing Multiple Characters

With the mouse, you edit multiple characters by following these steps:

1. Press [PgDn] to move to the bottom of the page. Press [↵Enter] to insert a blank line after the salutation.
2. Type the first paragraph of the letter shown in figure 4.2. When you reach the last word of the paragraph (*profitable*), press [↵Enter].
3. With the mouse, move the I-beam to the *T* in the word *Thanks* in the first sentence.
4. Hold down the mouse button, and drag the I-beam across the first sentence.

   The sentence to be edited is highlighted, as seen in figure 4.2.

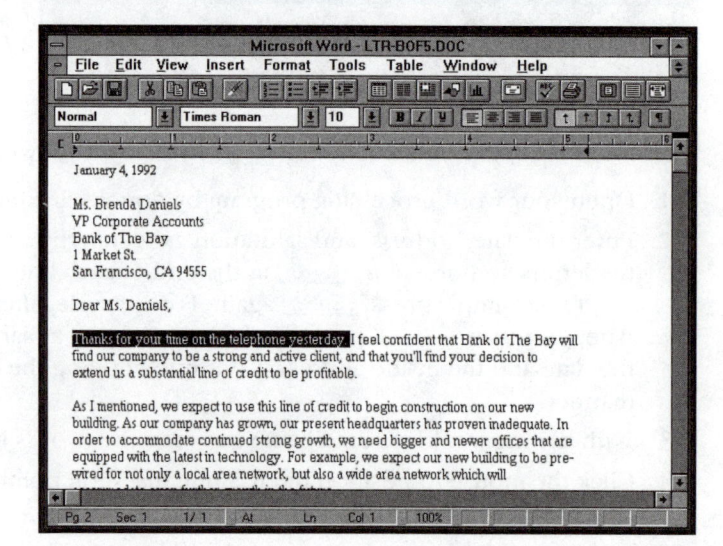

Fig. 4.2
Text highlighted with the I-beam.

5. Press [←Backspace] to delete the selected characters.
6. To replace the selected sentence, type **Thanks for your letter of 11/19/91.**

To Edit Text

With the keyboard, you edit multiple characters by following these steps:

1. Using the arrow keys, move the flashing insertion point to the beginning of the word *active*.
2. Hold down `Shift` and `Ctrl` together as you press the right arrow (`→`) to select the whole word *active*.
3. Type **aggressive** to replace *active*, and press the **space bar** to insert a blank space after *aggressive*, and then delete the word.

To deselect text with the mouse, click anywhere in the text. To deselect text with the keyboard, press `PgUp`, `PgDn`, or an arrow key.

Some Windows programs include shortcuts for editing text. These shortcuts may work in some parts of the program, such as body copy or a formula bar, but not in other parts, such as a dialog box. Experiment to find the shortcuts that help you. Table 4.1 lists shortcuts you can use for editing in many Windows programs.

Table 4.1 Common Windows Editing Shortcuts

Action	Result
Double-click	Selects the word under the I-beam
Click, `Shift`+click	Selects all text between the first click and the `Shift`+click
`Shift`+`←` or `→`	Selects the next character to the left or right, respectively
`Shift`+`↑` or `↓`	Selects the preceding or next line, respectively
`Shift`+`PgUp` or `PgDn`	Selects text from the insertion point to the top or bottom of the page or screen, respectively
`Shift`+`Home`	Selects text from the insertion point to the beginning of the line
`Shift`+`End`	Selects text from the insertion point to the end of the line
`Ctrl`+`Shift`+`←` or `→`	Selects a word each time you press `←` or `→`

Editing, Copying, and Moving in Windows

Objective 2: To Copy and Move Text in Windows Programs

Nearly all Windows programs contain the commands **Cut**, **C**opy, and **P**aste on the **E**dit menu. These commands enable you to cut or copy information you have selected in one place and paste the information somewhere else. You can use these techniques to copy and move information either within a document, between documents, or between programs.

Because copying information between programs is fairly new, you may not think of many ways to use the feature at first. But as you work more with multiple programs, you will find that copying and pasting between programs saves you time, eliminates typing errors, and gives you the chance to use programs together, as though they were part of a single program.

An important part of the copying and moving process is the *Clipboard*. Like a writer's clipboard, the Clipboard is a Windows program that temporarily holds information so that you can copy or move it from one place to another—within *and* between programs.

To refresh your memory about switching between programs, refer to Chapter 3, "Operating Windows."

Exercise 2.1: Copying and Moving Text

You can copy or cut text from a Windows program and paste the text into any other Windows or DOS program that accepts your keystrokes. You can use the same technique to copy or move text within a Windows document or between Windows documents.

To copy and move text between Windows documents or programs, or within a document, follow these steps:

1. Select the first paragraph of the letter you have been typing (see fig. 4.3).
2. Open the **E**dit menu, and choose the **C**opy command.
3. Open a new document by choosing **F**ile and then selecting **N**ew from the menu bar. You will copy the first paragraph to this new document.
4. Position the insertion point at the beginning of the first line of the new document (the default position).
5. Open the **E**dit menu, and choose the **P**aste command.

To Copy and Paste in DOS Programs

You have now copied text from one document into another. You use the same procedure for copying text between applications.

6. Choose **F**ile and then **E**xit to leave your program. Choose **Y** in the dialog box to save the document. Type **baybank** underneath File Name.

Copying and moving graphics within and between Windows programs is basically the same as copying and moving text.

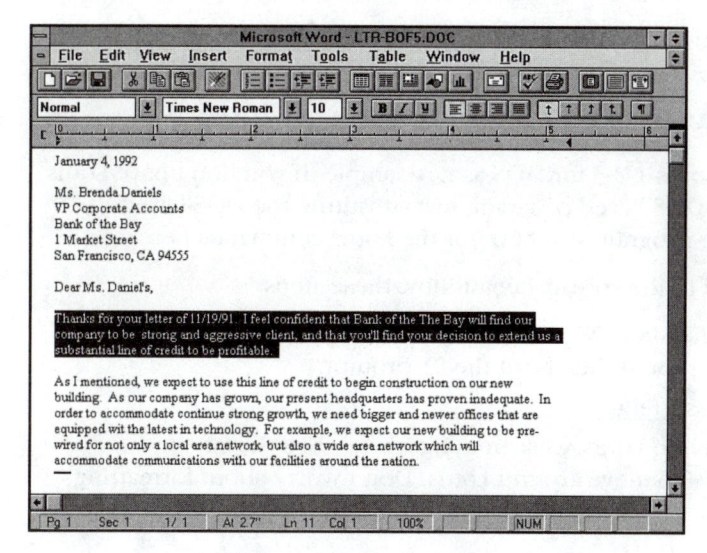

Fig. 4.3
Paragraph highlighted to be copied.

Objective 3: To Copy and Paste in DOS Programs

DOS programs can use the copy and paste capabilities provided by Windows with some limitations. For example, you cannot paste graphics into a DOS program. And if you are running Windows in Standard mode, you can capture only a full screen of text, not a selected portion of text.

Moving text and objects in DOS programs is different from moving them in Windows programs. To move within a DOS document, use the program's own techniques. In many DOS programs running under Windows, you don't have a Cut command, as you do in Windows programs. To move text from a DOS program running under Windows, you must copy and paste it using the Windows technique, and then delete the text from the DOS program using the program's own technique.

79

Editing, Copying, and Moving in Windows

Copying in 386-Enhanced Mode

In 386-Enhanced mode, you can run a DOS program in a window rather than the full screen. Running a DOS program in a window enables you to see multiple programs and copy selected text from the screen. Or you can copy the entire graphics screen. You can use either the mouse or the keyboard to copy in a DOS program that is running in a window. (Remember, the DOS program must be running in a window—not full-screen—to copy selected text.)

Exercise 3.1: Copying in 386-Enhanced Mode

This exercise uses Lotus 1-2-3 for DOS as its example. If you don't have Lotus 1-2-3 but do have a DOS-based program, just substitute the DOS-based commands from the program you have for the Lotus commands here.

To prepare material in the spreadsheet, follow these steps:

1. Double-click the MS-DOS prompt icon (usually part of the Main window). You should then be at the C: prompt.
2. Type **123**. Press [↵Enter].
3. Enter the data into Lotus, as seen in figure 4.4. Use the cursor-movement keys to move around Lotus. Don't worry about formatting the text and numbers.

Fig. 4.4
Entering data into a Lotus 1-2-3 spreadsheet.

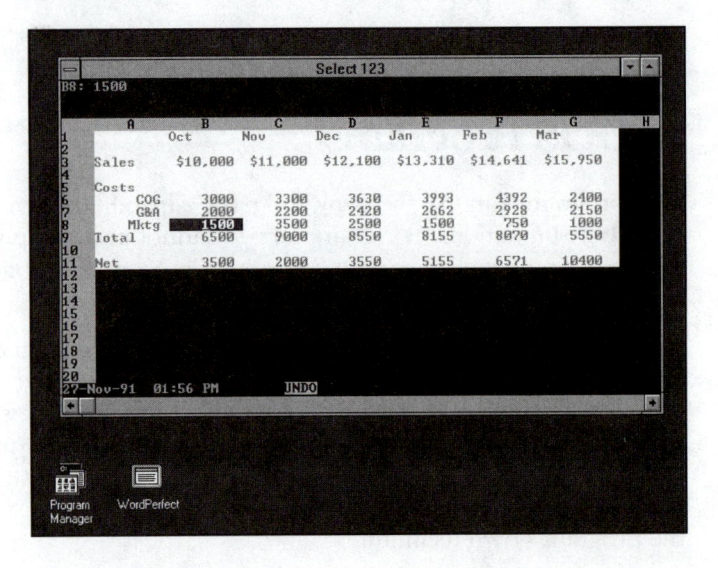

80

To View and Save Cut or Copied Data

With the mouse, copy selected text from a DOS program by following these steps:

1. Put Lotus in a window by pressing [Alt]+[↵Enter]. (Pressing [Alt]+[↵Enter] a second time restores the DOS program to full screen.)
2. Click the Control menu icon in the upper left corner of the window, and choose the Edit command.
3. Choose the Mark command.
4. Select the row of sales data by pointing to the word *Sales*, clicking and holding the mouse button, and dragging across the row to include all six sales numbers for October through March. The selected text appears in reverse video.
5. Click the right mouse button to copy the selected text to the Clipboard.
6. Press [Alt]+[↵Enter] to restore the DOS program to full screen.
7. Press [/] in Lotus to see the menu at the top of the screen. Then press [Q] for Quit and [Y] to end session and [Y] to end without saving the data.
8. Type **exit** at the DOS prompt to leave DOS and go back to Windows.
9. Double-click your word processor's icon.
10. Open the Edit menu, and choose the Paste command to paste the Sales numbers from the Clipboard to the document in your word processor.
11. Exit your word processor.

Note: While you are selecting text or graphics with the mouse, the title bar of the program changes to show the word `Select`. You cannot paste or use the program while you are selecting. Press [Esc] to return to program control.

Objective 4: To View and Save Cut or Copied Data

Another feature shared by Windows programs is the Clipboard—a temporary storage area that holds text you copy or cut. Because the Clipboard is shared by all Windows programs, you can duplicate or move text in many ways: within a single document, between different documents in the same program, and between different programs. You can even copy and move text between Windows programs and DOS programs (such as Lotus 1-2-3 and WordPerfect) running in Windows.

81

Editing, Copying, and Moving in Windows

When you cut or copy information, Windows stores it in the Clipboard. The information stays in the Clipboard until you clear it or until you cut or copy new information. You therefore can repeatedly paste the same item until you clear or change the Clipboard.

With the Clipboard Viewer program, located in the Main group window, you can view the Clipboard's contents, clear the Clipboard, or save and retrieve Clipboard contents (see fig. 4.5). This last feature is convenient because you can make a library of different clippings you want to use repeatedly, or a set of clippings you want to send to someone on a disk or by electronic mail.

Fig. 4.5
A clipping in the Clipboard window.

Exercise 4.1: Viewing Clipboard Contents

To see the contents of the Clipboard, follow these steps:

1. You should be at the desktop. If you are not, exit the application you are using.

2. Double-click the Clipboard Viewer icon from the Main group in the Program Manager.

You can see the current clipping in the Clipboard's window. Because the last editing command was to copy the sales data from Lotus 1-2-3, you should see that data in the Clipboard. Use the scroll bars to move the window's contents if you want to see more. The contents may look out of proportion, but items adjust after you paste them.

Exercise 4.2: Saving and Retrieving Clipboard Contents

You can save and retrieve Clipboard contents to use later or on a different computer. You can also create libraries of files on-disk that contain clippings you use frequently.

To save the contents of the Clipboard to a file, follow these steps:

1. Open the **F**ile menu, and choose the Save **A**s command.
2. Type **sales** as the file name in the File **N**ame text box. The Clipboard saves the file with the extension CLP.
3. Choose OK, or press ↵Enter.

To retrieve Clipboard contents saved to a file, follow these steps:

1. Open the **F**ile menu, and choose the **O**pen command.
2. Select SALES from the **F**ile Name list box, or type the word in the File **N**ame text box.
3. Choose OK, or press ↵Enter.

Clearing the Clipboard To Regain Available Memory

Large clippings may take up a great deal of memory. To delete the Clipboard's contents and regain memory, display the Clipboard Viewer window, open the Edit menu, and choose the **D**elete command.

Chapter Summary

This chapter describes one of the most important features of Windows: copying and moving data within and between programs. When you use only Windows programs, you find that you can use programs together as though they were a single program. Even if you use DOS programs, you can reduce the amount of retyping you do and the number of typing errors you introduce into the transferred data.

The next chapter, Chapter 5, "Managing Files," describes your Windows tool to manage your work environment. This information will enable you to organize and control your work in a way that is both fast and easy to use.

Editing, Copying, and Moving in Windows

Testing Your Knowledge

True/False Questions

1. To deselect text with the mouse, click anywhere in the text.
2. Text and graphics that are copied to the Clipboard are lost as soon as you leave a program.
3. You can view the contents of the Clipboard with the Clipboard Viewer program.
4. All Windows programs work in a similar way.
5. Information can be copied or moved both within and between programs in Windows.

Multiple Choice Questions

1. Which of the following keystrokes selects an entire word?
   A. `Shift`+`Ctrl` as you press an arrow key
   B. `Alt`+`Ctrl` as you press an arrow key
   C. `Enter`+`Ctrl` as you press an arrow key
   D. `Tab`+`Ctrl` as you press an arrow key
2. An operation that stores in the Clipboard a duplicate of selected text or graphics from a program is the
   A. **S**tore command.
   B. **P**aste command.
   C. **C**opy command.
   D. Cu**t** command.
3. An operation that inserts the information in the Clipboard into the active program at the current insertion point or cursor is the
   A. **S**tore command.
   B. **P**aste command.
   C. **C**opy command.
   D. Cu**t** command.

Testing Your Knowledge

4. What keystrokes select text from the insertion point to the end of the line?

   A. `Ctrl` + `End`
   B. `Shift` + `PgDn`
   C. `Shift` + `Home`
   D. `Shift` + `End`

5. What action positions the mouse pointer at the flashing insertion point?

   A. triple-click
   B. double-click
   C. click
   D. point and drag

Fill-in-the-Blank Questions

1. The _____ is an area of memory reserved to hold text or graphics that you cut or copy, within or between programs.

2. When you position the mouse pointer over an area of text to be edited, the pointer appears as a(n) _____.

3. The _____ point is the flashing vertical line in text, indicating where text editing or typing will occur.

4. Characters that are selected appear _____ on the screen.

5. Either the _____ key or the `Del` key may be used to remove selected characters.

Review: Short Projects

1. Using the Clipboard

   While in your word processor, choose **O**pen from the **F**ile menu, and open BAYBANK.DOC. Copy the address to the Clipboard. Go to the Clipboard, and save the contents. Then open the BAYBANK.CLP while in the Clipboard. Now go back to your word processor, and paste the contents into the document. Open a new document, and paste the address from the Clipboard.

2. Working with a DOS-Based Program

   If you are using a DOS-based program, practice opening it and putting it into a window. Practice copying data between the DOS-based program and a Windows program. Become familiar with the keystrokes to put a program into a window and to return to full-screen editing.

3. Using the Mouse and the Keyboard

   Using your word processor, create a list of the keystrokes for editing shortcuts that you use most often. Think about when you might use the mouse instead of keystrokes. What are the reasons you would use one or the other in editing? Does the length of the document make a difference? Does your choice depend on whether you are writing the first draft or making corrections? Think about a situation in which you use word processing editing. Do your needs change depending on the project?

Review: Long Projects

1. Considering DOS and Windows Applications

   Continuing with Bella's Ice Cream Parlor, make a list of all the application needs you will have in running the Ice Cream Parlor. Are some of the applications DOS-based? If so, what kinds of data will you need to share between DOS- and Windows-based programs? What kinds of data will you want to save as Clipboard files? Which employees in the organization will use which applications? Write a summary of your decisions.

2. Displaying More Than One Program On-Screen

   Suppose that you need to use a spreadsheet and a word processor at the same time. Open both programs, and size them so that they both fit on the screen at once. Think about the most convenient way to display them on the screen. Suppose that in the spreadsheet you will be creating what-if analyses to be pasted into a document in the word processor. What size should the screens be? Try doing this, and experiment to find the "best" way for you.

Managing Files

5

The File Manager in Windows is a well-designed tool that acts as an office manager. The File Manager helps you organize your files, manage your disks, copy and erase files, and start programs.

You can maintain your files and directories more easily with the File Manager than with DOS commands. For example, with the mouse, you can copy all the files in a directory to a floppy disk by dragging the directory's icon on to the disk drive icon and releasing the mouse button.

Objectives

1. To Understand the File Manager
2. To Select and Open Files and Directories
3. To Control File Manager Windows and Displays
4. To Manage Files and Directories
5. To Manage Disks

Managing Files

5

Key Terms in This Chapter	
Primary storage (electronic memory) RAM	The electronic part of your computer, where work and calculations are done on programs and data. The contents of the memory disappears when you turn off the power.
Disk	A hard or floppy disk device that magnetically stores programs and data. Data and programs on disk do not disappear when you turn off the power. A hard disk is inside your computer and stores tens of millions of characters. A floppy disk is a flexible plastic disk that stores approximately one million characters.
Data	The information you create with the help of a computer program. Each type of program has its own unique way of saving data. Data for Windows programs is often referred to as a document. Data stored on-disk is stored in a file.
Program or application	Instructions that tell the computer how to operate and what to do when you give a command. For example, one program tells a computer to do word processing, and another program tells the computer to do accounting.
Secondary Storage	A mechanical part of your computer system where data and programs are stored magnetically for long periods while the computer is off. Storage places also are referred to as disk drives, hard disks, or floppy disks.
File	A collection of data or program information stored magnetically on a disk. A file is similar to a letter or report within a filing cabinet.
File name	A name by which you can find, open, or manage a file.
Directory	A method of segmenting a disk so that files and programs can be grouped together by type or category. Directories are similar to the drawers of a filing cabinet.

88

Subdirectory	A directory within another directory. Subdirectories are similar to folders in a drawer of a filing cabinet.
Directory tree	A diagram showing how directories and subdirectories are related.

Objective 1: To Understand the File Manager

Before you can understand the File Manager, you should understand how a computer keeps data while you work on it and how a computer stores data for long periods of time. After you understand the File Manager, managing your disks and the files they contain is much easier.

Understanding Storage, Memory, Files, and Directories

Your computer does all its calculations and work in primary storage, also called electronic memory. Electronic memory is called *RAM—random access memory*. RAM is where the computer program and Windows reside as they work; RAM is also where the data you are working on resides. If the computer loses electrical power, the data, program, and windows are lost from memory. Because electronic memory is limited in size and is volatile, the computer needs a way to store large amounts of data and programs for long periods of time.

Computers use magnetic (secondary) storage to store programs and data for long periods of time or during times when the power is off. Magnetic-storage media can be *floppy disks*, which are removable and don't contain much space, or *hard disks*, which are inside the computer and have large amounts of space. A *disk drive* reads data from a disk and writes data to a disk. Floppy disks are identified by the drive letters A and B. Hard disks may be identified by the drive letters C, D, and so on. When you load a program or a data file, the computer places into electronic (primary) memory a copy of the information stored on-disk. If power is lost, the disk copy on secondary storage is still available.

Managing Files

You save your work in magnetic files, which store the data on a floppy disk or the hard disk. Over time, you may have hundreds or even thousands of files. Searching for a specific file among the thousands of file names that the File Manager displays can be very time-consuming.

To make the job of finding files easier, hard disks are usually organized into *directories*. If you think of your hard disk as a filing cabinet, directories are like the drawers in the filing cabinet. In a filing cabinet, each drawer can hold a different category of documents. In a hard disk, each directory can hold a different category of files. The files in a directory can be programs or documents.

Within a filing-cabinet drawer, you can put hanging folders to further divide the drawer. Within a hard disk, you can subdivide a directory by putting *subdirectories* under it. Subdirectories also can hold files.

The process of organizing your hard disk is the same as organizing a filing cabinet. Using File Manager commands, you can create, name, and delete directories and subdirectories. (Some networks may prevent you from altering directory structures.) For example, you may want a WINWORD directory for word processing jobs. Within the WINWORD directory, you may want subdirectories with names such as BUDGETS, SCHEDULE, LETTERS, and REPORTS.

Exercise 1.1: Starting the File Manager

To start the File Manager, you activate the Program Manager and open the Main group window (see fig. 5.1).

The File Manager is located within the Main group window. Appropriately enough, the File Manager icon looks like a filing cabinet.

Follow these steps to start the File Manager:

1. Start Windows.
2. Activate the Program Manager if it is minimized to an icon by double-clicking the icon.
3. Activate the Main group window by clicking it.
4. Open the File Manager by double-clicking its icon.

You are now in the File Manager.

To Understand the File Manager

Fig. 5.1
The Windows Program Manager.

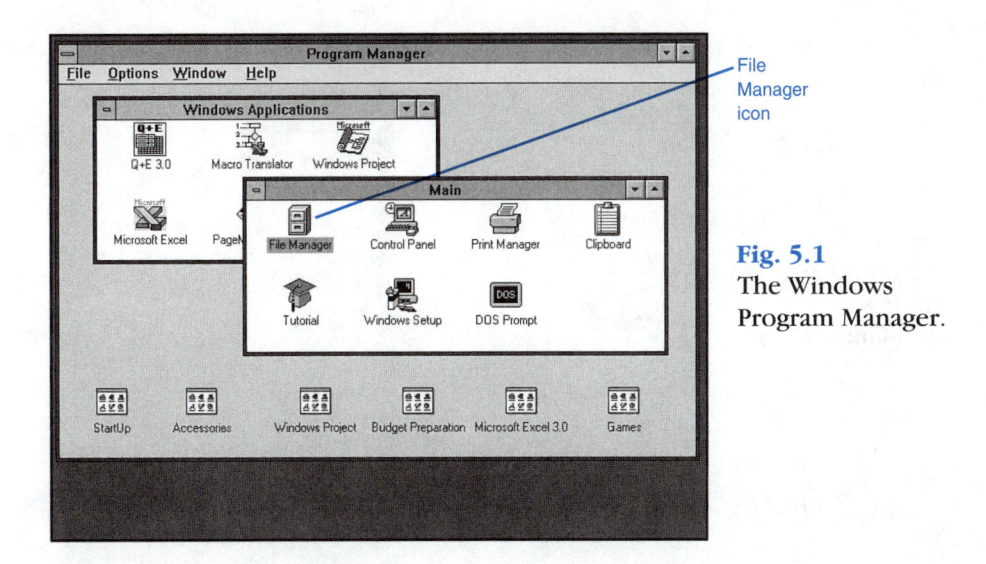

Understanding the File Manager's Display

The File Manager displays all important disk and file information in one window. When you first start the File Manager, the directory window is divided into two parts. The *directory tree,* with the expanded structure of directories and subdirectories on drive C, occupies the left portion of the window. The *contents list* occupies the right portion of the window, showing the files in the selected directory (see fig. 5.2).

At the top of the directory window is the *drive bar*, which displays icons that represent the available disk drives. Drives A and B are floppy disk drives; their icons look a little different from the icon for drive C, a hard disk drive (your own computer may have more or fewer drives). The *title bar* shows the directory path for the selected directory.

Notice the *status bar* at the bottom of the File Manager (refer to fig. 5.2). At the right, the bar always displays the number and aggregate size of the files in the selected directory or subdirectory. When the directory tree portion of the window is active, the left portion of the bar shows the available storage on the active disk. When the contents list is active, this area shows the total size in bytes of the selected files. Scroll bars appear on the right and bottom sides of the directory tree and at the bottom of the contents list. If either part contains more information than can be shown at once, the scroll bar is shaded.

91

Managing Files

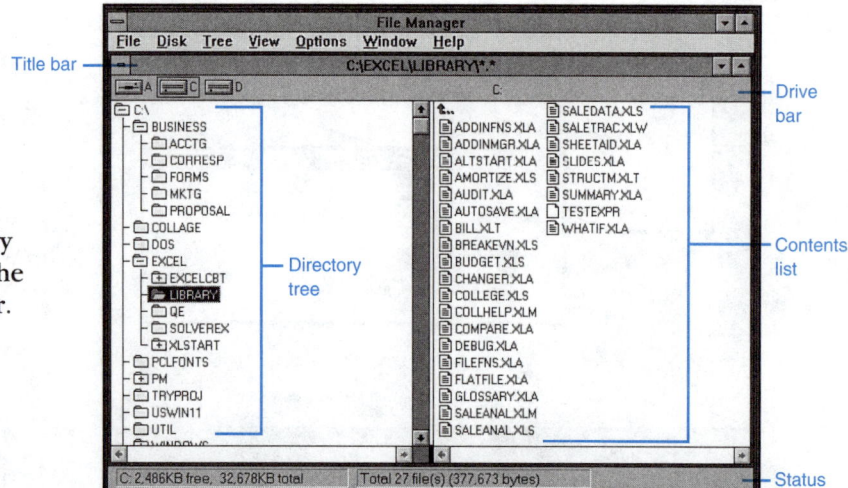

Fig. 5.2
The directory window of the File Manager.

The directory tree shows miniature folder icons, which represent directories and subdirectories, and the contents list shows files as icons that look like miniature documents. The first time you start the File Manager, a plus sign (+) in a directory or subdirectory icon indicates that additional subdirectories are inside the icon (see fig. 5.3). A minus sign (–) in a subdirectory icon indicates that you can collapse the directory so that its directories do not show. An option in the **T**ree menu enables you to turn the plus and minus signs off and on. When the plus and minus signs are displayed, a folder icon without a plus or minus sign contains no subdirectories. When a directory or subdirectory icon is expanded, you can see the subdirectories beneath it. Notice the vertical lines and indentations that show how directories and subdirectories are related.

Exercise 1.2: Understanding the File Manager's Display

To turn the plus and minus signs on and off, follow these steps:

1. Choose the **T**ree menu.
2. Notice whether the menu shows a check next to the menu item **I**ndicate Expandable Branches.
3. Choose **I**ndicate Expandable Branches, and watch how the directory folders on the left side of the screen either add pluses and minuses (if they weren't there before) or remove them (if they were there before).
4. Leave the directories with the **I**ndicate Expandable Branches on so that you can see pluses and minuses on the icons.

To Select and Open Files and Directories

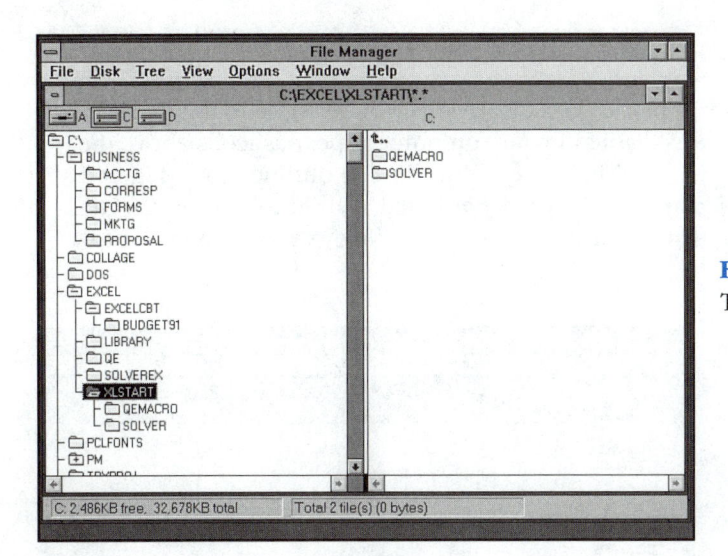

Fig. 5.3
The directory tree.

Open folder icons indicate that the directory's contents are shown in the contents list.

At any given time, only one area of the File Manager is active: the drive bar, the directory tree, or the contents list. The active area contains a *selection* with a dark background or with a dashed border called the *selection cursor*. In the active area, you can use the arrow keys to move the selection. Press Tab to activate different areas. You can also use the mouse to activate different areas by clicking the area you want.

The File Manager can display multiple windows at one time to show the file contents of any drive, directory, or subdirectory you select. Opening multiple directory windows on different disks and in different directories makes comparing disk contents or copying or deleting files easy.

Objective 2: To Select and Open Files and Directories

The File Manager follows the primary rule of all Windows programs: *Select, then do*. If you want to affect a file or directory in the File Manager, you must first find and select that file or directory. After you select a file, you can display information about it, open it, copy it, move it, or delete it. After you select a directory, you can find information about the directory contents, copy or move the directory, or open the directory to see the subdirectories or files it contains.

Managing Files

Selecting a New Disk Drive

Before you can work with files and directories, you must be in the correct disk drive. The disk drives available in your computer appear as icons above the directory tree (see fig. 5.4). The current drive has an outline around it, and also has a dark background if the drive bar is active and the drive is selected. To change to a new drive with the mouse, click the drive icon you want to activate.

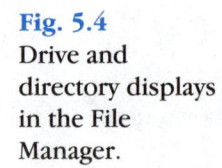

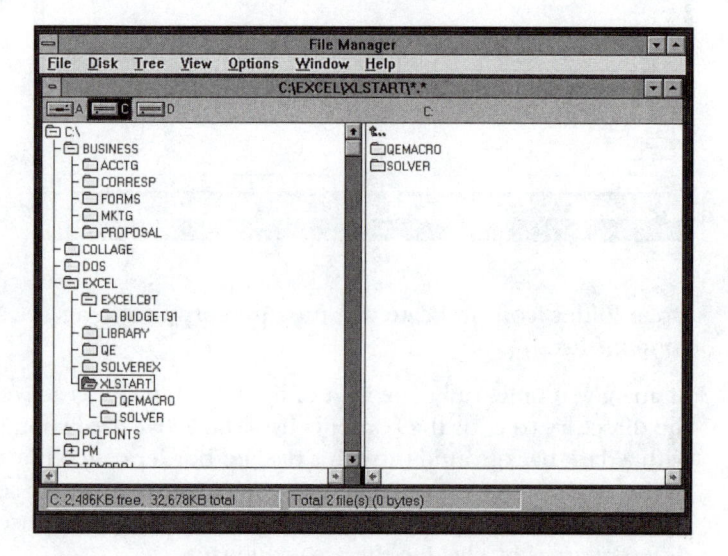

Fig. 5.4
Drive and directory displays in the File Manager.

To change to a new drive with the keyboard, you must first notice which area is active. If the drive icon bar is active, change to a new drive by pressing the left- or right-arrow key to move the selection cursor to a different drive; then press the space bar. The dark background moves behind the drive you selected. If the directory-tree area or contents-list area of the window is active, you press Ctrl+*letter* to change to a different drive, where *letter* is the drive's letter.

Working with Networks

If your computer is connected to a local area network (LAN), you may have access to more than one hard disk drive. You can access those drives through Windows if you're logged on to a LAN (see fig. 5.5).

To Select and Open Files and Directories

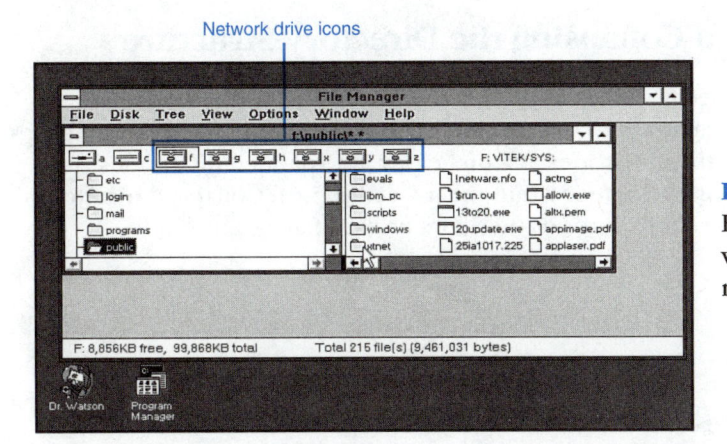

Fig. 5.5
File Manager window for a network.

Each drive on the network shows up in the File Manager window as a disk icon different from the local-drive icons. When you select a network-drive icon, the path to that drive displays in the status bar at the bottom of the File Manager window. In a LAN environment your computer is referred to as a *workstation*.

If you want to use network drives with Windows, you must log on to the network before you start Windows. See your network administrator for the procedure on how to log on to your network. When you connect your computer to a network, additional disk drives are available. You can use these additional drives with Windows if you know the path name to the drive and the password.

Note: If you log on to the network before starting Windows in 386-Enhanced mode, you may not be able to log off from the network while you are in Windows. To log off from the network, exit Windows, and then type **logout**, or whatever command has been specified as the Exit command by the network administrator.

Note: If you want to use network drives with Windows, you must connect to the network before you start Windows. When you connect to the network and then start Windows, the Windows network commands are available. If you start Windows without first connecting to the network, the network commands are gray and therefore unavailable.

Note: If you connect a DOS program to a network while that program is running in Windows, disconnect from the network before quitting the program.

95

Managing Files

Expanding and Collapsing the Directory Structure

After you select a specific directory, you may want to see the subdirectories beneath it, or you may want to collapse the fully expanded directory structure so that you can see the directories at a higher level. Expanded directories show the subdirectories located within them (see fig. 5.6). Collapsed directories do not show the subdirectories they contain (see fig. 5.7).

Fig. 5.6
Expanded directories.

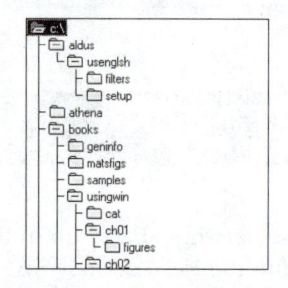

Fig. 5.7
Collapsed directories.

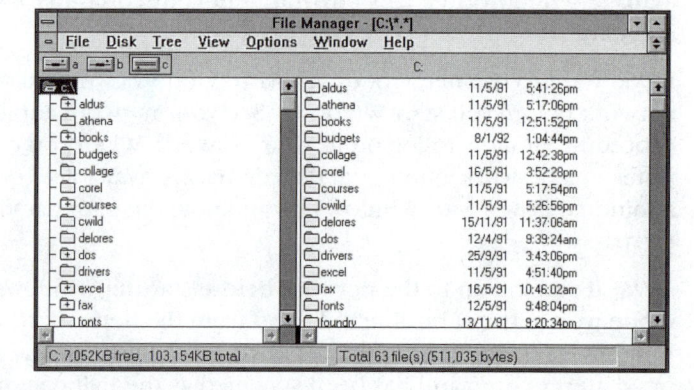

Exercise 2.1: Expanding and Collapsing Directories

To expand or collapse a directory or subdirectory with the mouse, use the following mouse actions:

1. Double-click the plus (+) on directory SYS. This action expands the directory one level, and you can now see the directories and files under the SYS directory. (If you don't have the directories referred to in this exercise, use these actions to find the Windows files. *Hint:* Windows files begin with WIN.)

To Select and Open Files and Directories

2. Double-click the plus (+) on WIN to see all the windows subdirectories and files.
3. Collapse the WIN directory by double-clicking SYS.

To expand or collapse directories with the menu commands, follow these steps:

1. Select the SYS directory.
2. Choose **T**ree and then E**x**pand One Level. Notice the additional directories and files.
3. Choose **T**ree and then Expand **B**ranch. Again, you see more directories and files.
4. Choose **T**ree and then Expand **A**ll. Now you can see all the subdirectories in all the directories of the drive.
5. Select the C: folder icon, and choose **T**ree and then **C**ollapse Branch. Now all the directories and files have been collapsed in the icon.
6. Choose **T**ree and then E**x**pand One Level to return to the start position.

Table 5.1 gives a summary of the **Tree** menu commands.

Table 5.1 Tree Menu Commands	
Command	*Action*
Expand One Level	Expands the selected directory to show all subdirectories at the next lower level
Expand **B**ranch	Expands the selected directory to show all lower subdirectories
Expand All	Expands all subdirectories in the drive
Collapse Branch	Collapses the lower-level subdirectories into the selected directory

Selecting Directories

The directory window always displays in the File Manager window. The directory window may be in its own window or in an icon at the bottom of the File Manager window. The directory tree (in the left half of the File Manager) shows the hierarchical structure of the area of the disk you are currently examining (see fig. 5.8).

97

Managing Files

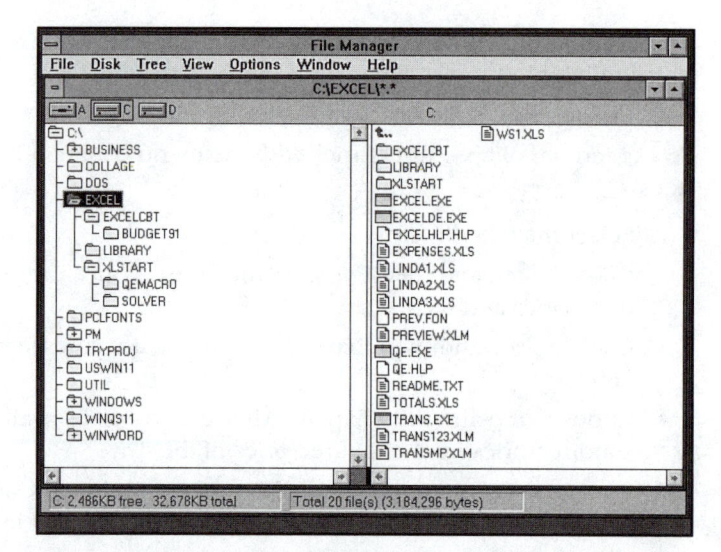

Fig. 5.8
A directory window.

In this directory window, drive C contains an Excel directory containing three subdirectories: EXCELCBT, LIBRARY, and XLSTART. The EXCELCBT and XLSTART subdirectories contain additional subdirectories.

You can select only one directory at a time in a given directory window; however, you can open multiple directories so that each appears in its own directory window. Open more than one directory when you want to see the contents of multiple directories at one time. Also, copying files between directories is easier when you open a source-directory window and a destination-directory window.

To select a directory using the mouse, click the directory or subdirectory you want. If you cannot see the directory, use the vertical scroll bar in the directory tree to scroll it into sight before clicking. If you need files in a subdirectory, first open the directory above the desired subdirectory, as described later in this section.

Understanding File Icons

Each file within a directory window displays an icon that helps identify the type of file it is. Table 5.2 shows and defines these file icon shapes.

To Select and Open Files and Directories

Table 5.2　File Icons

Icon	Type of File
📂	Open directory or subdirectory
📁	Closed directory or subdirectory
▭	Program or batch file with the extension EXE, COM, PIF, or BAT (choosing one of these files may start a program)
📄	Document file associated with a program (choosing one of these files starts the program that created the file)
▯	Other files

Exercise 2.2: Selecting Files

Files are listed on the right side of the directory window in the contents list. Before you can work on a file, you must select it. In some cases—when copying or deleting files, for example—you may want to select multiple files before giving a single command.

To select a single file with the mouse, click the file name. To select multiple adjacent files, follow these steps:

1. Expand a directory so that you can see many files on the right side of the directory window in the contents list.
2. Select the first file by clicking its name.
3. Press and hold the ⇧Shift key, and click another file name eight lines below the first file name. All files between the two files you clicked are selected (see fig. 5.9).

To select nonadjacent files, follow these steps:

1. Click the first file name, and hold down Ctrl as you click the next four file names (see fig. 5.10).
2. If you want to retain current selections but deselect a file, press and hold Ctrl as you click the last of the four files you just selected. You have now deselected that file.

99

Managing Files

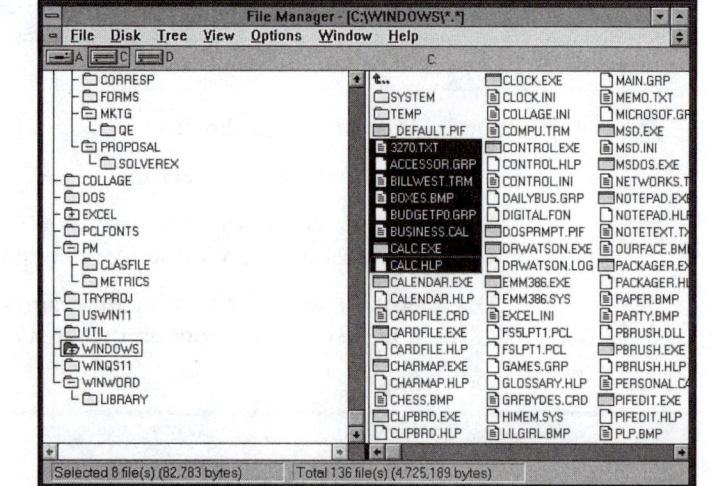

Fig. 5.9
Adjacent files selected.

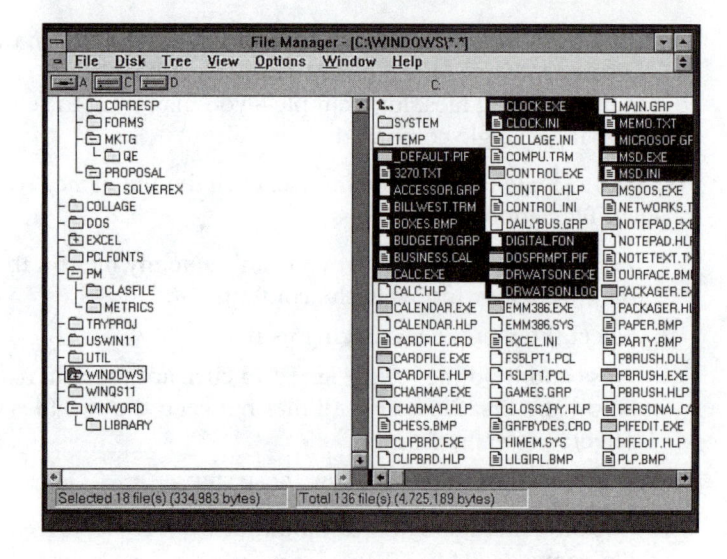

Fig. 5.10
Selected nonadjacent files.

If you want to select all files with a given extension in a directory window, choose the **F**ile menu, and select the **S**elect Files command. In the Select Files dialog box, you can type a specific extension and use DOS wild cards to select a particular group of files (see fig. 5.11).

To Control File Manager Windows and Displays

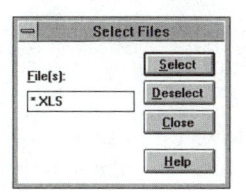

Fig. 5.11
The Select Files dialog box.

Note: To select all files in the window, choose the **Select** button while the Files box displays *.*. If you then want to deselect certain files, change the Files parameter, and choose **Deselect**. Choose **Close** when you have finished making your selections.

Objective 3: To Control File Manager Windows and Displays

You will want to arrange your windows and files in a way that enables you to get your work done efficiently. Whether you are copying files between directories, making backup copies to a floppy disk, or deleting files, the display should provide easy access to your files. The following sections explain how to manipulate the appearance of the Windows display screen.

Exercise 3.1: Opening and Selecting Directory Windows

You can have many directory windows that show the contents of individual directories (see fig. 5.12). Each directory window can display a different directory—and even different disks.

Displaying multiple directory windows is a convenient way to move or copy files with the mouse.

To open a new directory window, follow these steps:

1. Open the **W**indow menu, and choose the **N**ew Window command. The new window will display the path name of the previously active window in the title bar, followed by a colon and the number *2*, which indicates that this window is the second window associated with that directory. If you choose another directory, the path name in the new window changes.

101

Managing Files

2. Open the **W**indow menu, and choose the **N**ew Window command again. You have now opened a third window, a third version of the same window.

You now have multiple directory windows open and want a specific window active. Click a portion of the third window to make it active.

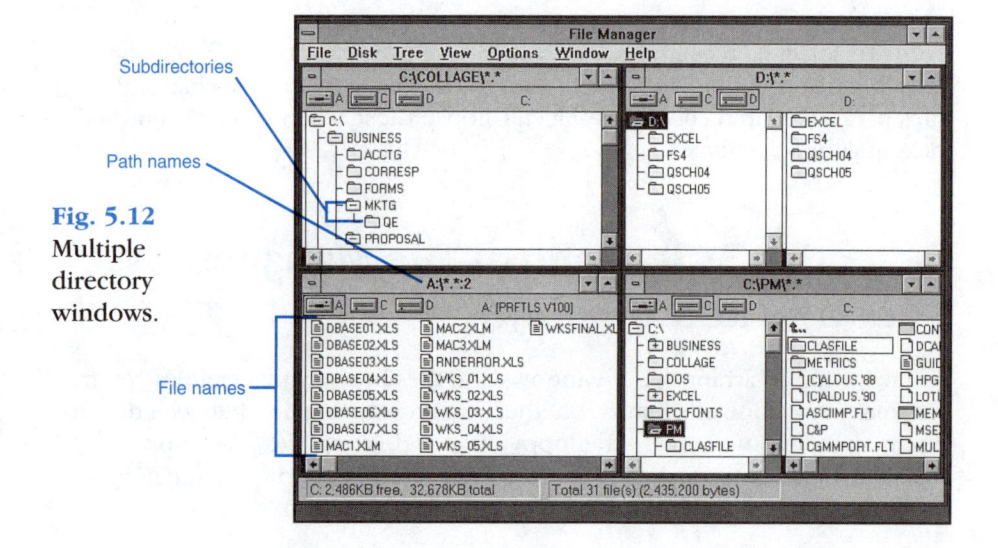

Fig. 5.12
Multiple directory windows.

Exercise 3.2: Arranging Directory Windows and Icons

You can arrange directory windows and icons in three ways. You can arrange them by manually positioning them, by cascading them to show all the window titles, or by placing them in tiles to show each window's contents. To try each arrangement, follow these steps:

1. To arrange directory windows in a cascade, open the **W**indow menu, and choose the **C**ascade command. The active window becomes the top window in the cascade (see fig. 5.13).

2. To arrange directory windows in tiles so that the screen is evenly divided by the windows, open the **W**indow menu, and choose the **T**ile command. The active window becomes the window at the top left in the File Manager (see fig. 5.14).

   When windows are arranged by cascading or by tiling, you can still use the mouse or each directory window's Control menu to move a window manually. Chapter 3 describes how to move or size a window.

To Control File Manager Windows and Displays

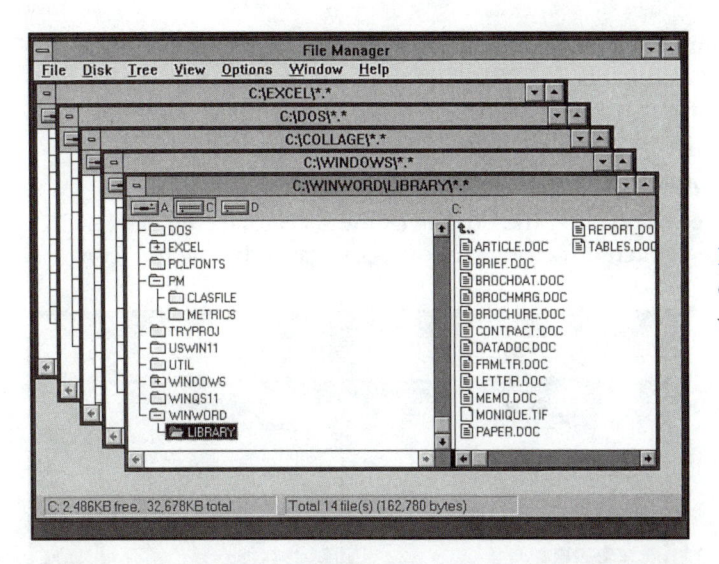

Fig. 5.13 Cascaded windows.

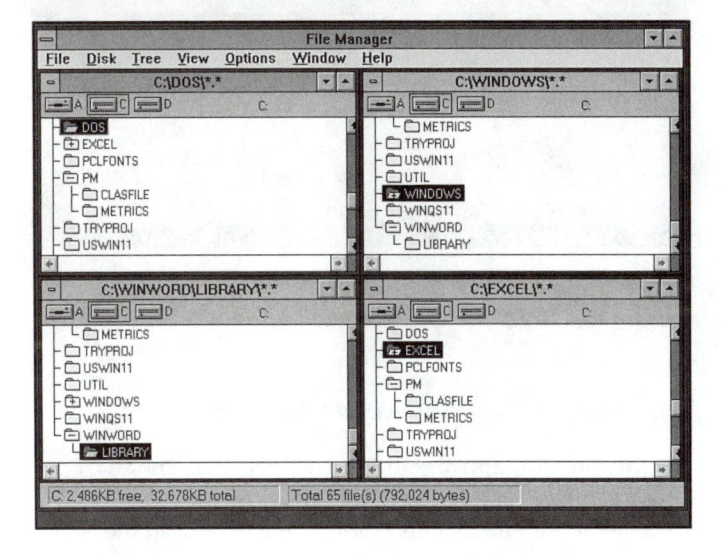

Fig. 5.14 Directory windows arranged in tiles.

3. Move the mouse pointer to the edge of the middle window until the pointer becomes a two-headed arrow. Now drag the window to a smaller size. You have just manually resized the window.

   You reduce directory windows to icons inside the File Manager window

103

Managing Files

4. Click the Minimize button (the down arrow) at the right end of the bottom window's title bar (C:\EXCEL in the figures). (If a window is maximized, restore it to display the Minimize button by clicking the Restore icon, a two-headed arrow.)

5. Minimize two other directory windows.

   You can now see the icon at the bottom of the screen (see fig. 5.15). The path name of each directory window is displayed below the icon.

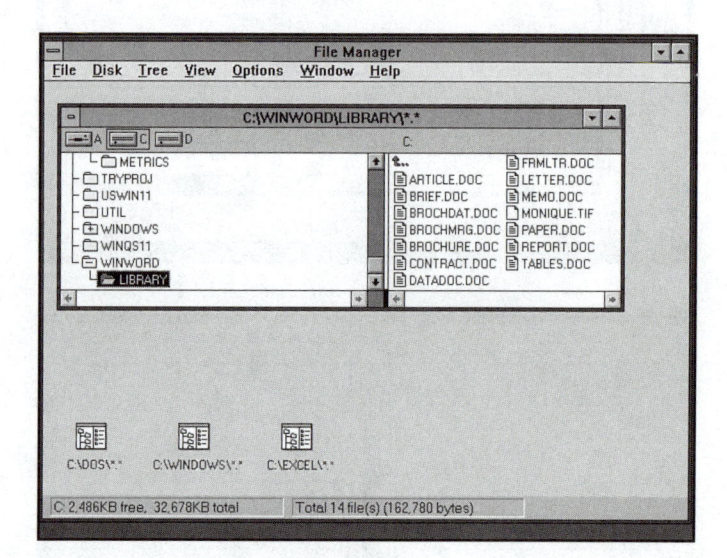

Fig. 5.15
Directory window and directory window icons.

6. Maximize the directory icon by double-clicking it.

Exercise 3.3: Specifying File-Display Formats

You can specify what file information appears in the contents list. The two most common displays use the **View Name** command to show only the file names and extensions and **View All File Details** command to show all file information.

To display file information, follow these steps:

1. Activate the directory window nearest the top on your screen.

2. Choose **V**iew and then **N**ame. Now only names and directories are displayed (see fig. 5.16).

To Control File Manager Windows and Displays

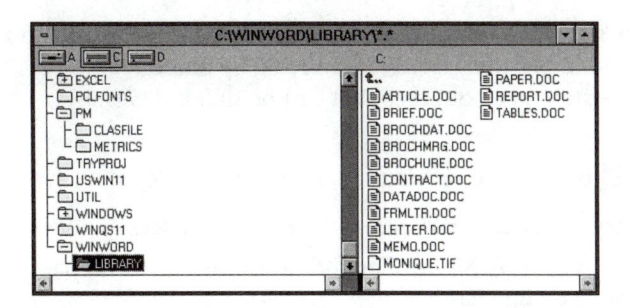

Fig. 5.16
Directory window displaying only file names and directories.

3. Choose **V**iew, and then choose **A**ll File Details.

   The contents list displays all file details: the name, size, date, and time that each file was last saved (attributes are displayed, but hidden by the right edge of the window). This information can be very helpful when looking for a file (see fig. 5.17).

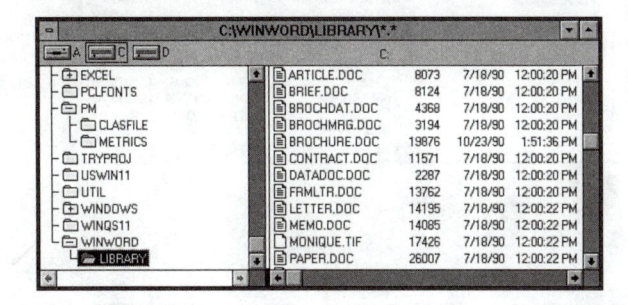

Fig. 5.17
Directory window displaying file information.

From the **V**iew menu, you can also choose **P**artial Details, selecting the details you want to view; or you can view by File **T**ype, selecting only certain types of files to view.

Note: Some programs may not automatically update the information in the File Manager. As a result, you may activate the File Manager and not see a file you have just saved. Update the window manually with the **W**indow **R**efresh command.

Exercise 3.4: Sorting the Display of Files and Directories

Finding files or directories can be easier when you reorganize the contents of a directory window. By default, the File Manager lists files alphabetically by

Managing Files

name, but you can order the window contents alphabetically by file extension, by file size, or by the date the file was last saved. Sorting by name makes files easier to find. Sorting by date makes old files that can be deleted easier to find.

To sort a window's contents by name or file type, follow these steps:

1. Activate the directory window that contains your word processing files.
2. Choose **V**iew and then **S**ort by Name. The files are now sorted alphabetically by file name (see fig. 5.18).

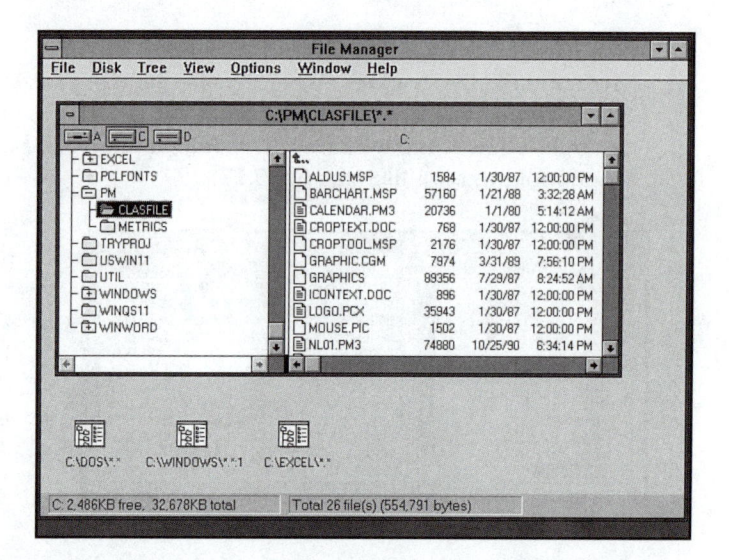

Fig. 5.18
Files sorted alphabetically by file name.

3. Choose **V**iew and then Sort **b**y Type. The files are now sorted alphabetically by file extension and then by file name.
4. Choose **V**iew and then Sort by Si**z**e. The files are now sorted by file size, from largest to smallest.
5. Choose **V**iew and then Sort by **D**ate. The files are now sorted by last date saved, from newest to oldest (see fig. 5.19).

You can decide for yourself the best way to view your data. You may change how you display the data depending on your needs. Play around with this useful feature, and decide how you would like to see the data.

Note: You do not have to display the file date or size in the directory window to sort by those attributes. If you want to see the file's date and size in the directory window, choose the View menu, and choose **A**ll File Details or **P**artial Details.

106

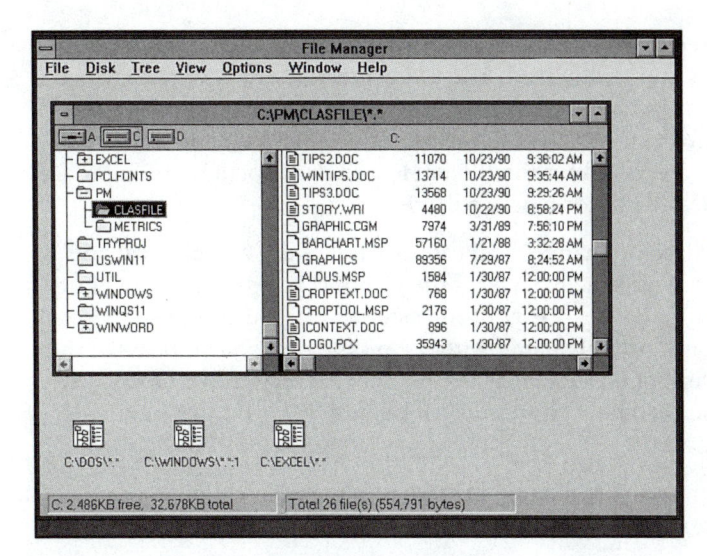

Fig. 5.19
Files sorted by date.

Objective 4: To Manage Files and Directories

Working without a hard disk can be difficult, but working *with* one can be confusing. Problems arise if people do not erase unnecessary files or do not make backup copies of files in case the hard disk fails.

This section shows how easily you can erase unwanted files, copy files to other disks, or move files between directories. You also learn how to make your own directories so that you can organize your disk to fit your work and data.

Understanding File Names and Wild Cards

File names and directory names have rules you must follow if you want to find your data again. If you do not name a file or directory correctly, you may not be able to find it later, or the system may not accept the name.

File names and directory names have three parts: the file name, the separator, and the file extension.

filename.ext

File name — Separator — File extension

107

Managing Files

The file name or directory name can contain from one through eight characters. The separator is always a period. The file extension can have as many as three characters. In most cases, Windows programs add their own file extensions to the file names you type. Therefore, you don't need to add a file extension when you are asked for the file name of a data document. If you do not type a file extension, do not type a period.

For file names and directory names, you can use any of the alphabetical and numerical characters. You can also use all the symbols across the top of your keyboard (! @ # $ % ^ & ( ) _ -) except the asterisk (*), plus sign (+), and equal sign (=). If you start a file name with a symbol, the name appears at the top of alphabetical lists of files (such as the list that appears in the Open dialog box)—this idea can be a good trick for naming files you use frequently and want to find quickly.

Note: Never use a space in a file name or directory name. Include a period only if you are using a file extension.

Exercise 4.1: Searching for Files or Directories

Losing a file is frustrating and wastes time. With Windows, you can search disks or directories for file names similar to the file you have misplaced.

To search for a file by its name or part of its name, follow these steps:

1. Choose disk drive C to search.
2. Choose the directory of your word processor.
3. Open the **F**ile menu, and choose the Searc**h** command.

    The Search dialog box appears (see fig. 5.20).

Fig. 5.20
The Search dialog box.

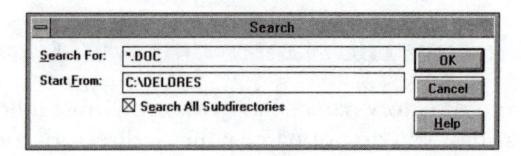

4. Suppose that you are searching for a file you created in your word processor, but you can't remember the exact name. You are certain, however, that the file names starts with *S*. In the **S**earch For text box, type **D*.doc** to retrieve all files with names starting with D and having *DOC* has an extension. (If you don't have any files that begin with *D*, make the search command relevant for you.)

To Manage Files and Directories

5. Type **c:** in the Start **F**rom text box to search all directories on the current disk, beginning with the root directory.

   By default, Windows searches all subdirectories beneath the directory you specify. To search only the specified directory, turn off the S**e**arch All Subdirectories option.

6. Choose OK or press ↵Enter. You see a listing of all files that meet the search criterion. The Search Results window displays the paths and file names of all files that match the pattern for which you were looking (see fig. 5.21).

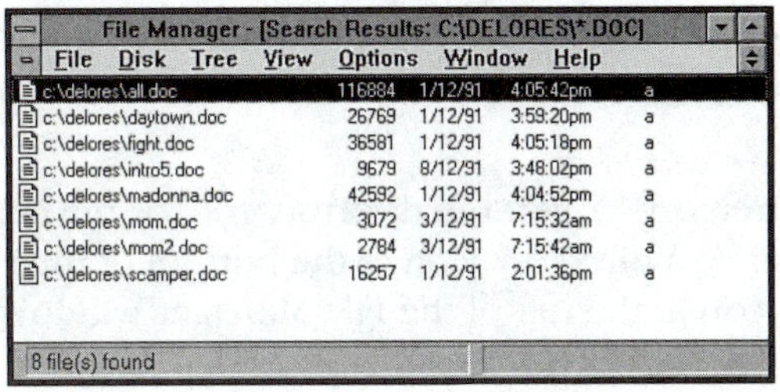

Fig. 5.21
The Search Results window.

When you use wild cards in a name pattern, remember that the * wild-card character finds any number of characters in the same or following positions, without regard to case. The ? wild-card character matches any single character in the same position. For example, use the pattern *E*.XLS* to search for all file names beginning with *E* and ending with the three-letter extension *XLS*. Use the pattern *BDGT???.** to search for file names that start with *BDGT* and are followed by exactly three characters. Any file extension will match the *.

If you know the directory in which a file is located and the date or time when the file was last saved but don't know the file name, you can display the time and date of all the files in the directory window to help you locate the file. Open the **V**iew menu, and choose the **A**ll File Details command to show the time and date on which files were last saved. This command also indicates file attributes at the right.

Copying Files or Directories

Copying files is an important part of keeping your work organized and secure. When organizing files, you may have to copy a file to make it accessible in two locations. A more important reason for copying files is security. The hard disk on which you store files is a mechanical device and has one of the highest

109

Managing Files

failure rates among computer components. If your hard disk fails, the cost of replacing the disk is insignificant compared to the cost of the hours you worked accumulating data on the disk. One way to prevent the loss of this data is to make a set of duplicate files.

If you have ever used DOS commands to copy files, you will find that copying files and directories is much easier with Windows and a mouse. All you do is drag the files you want to copy from one location in the directory window to another.

When you copy or move files, you have a source and a destination. The *source* is the item you want to copy. It can be a file icon in the contents list; a directory icon from the contents list or the directory tree; a directory window; a directory icon; or a disk-drive icon. In this exercise, the source is the file you have highlighted.

The *destination* can be a directory icon in the directory tree or the contents list. The destination can also be a directory icon at the bottom of the File Manager window or a disk icon at the top of the File Manager window. In this exercise, the destination is another directory on the C drive.

In the directory tree, you can select only a single directory or subdirectory to copy. In the contents list, however, you can select multiple files or subdirectories to copy simultaneously. When you copy a directory or subdirectory, you copy all the files and subdirectories it contains.

Exercise 4.2: Copying Files

Follow these steps to copy files with a mouse:

1. Open a new window in the File Manager.
2. Select a file by using the Search command (see fig. 5.22). You will copy that file to another location on the C drive.
3. Make sure that both the source and destination are visible, by using either **T**ile or **C**ascade in the Window menu.
4. Drag the file to the destination. Press and hold Ctrl because the destination is on the same disk as the source files (see fig. 5.23). (If you do not press and hold Ctrl, you *move* the files rather than copy them.)

To Manage Files and Directories

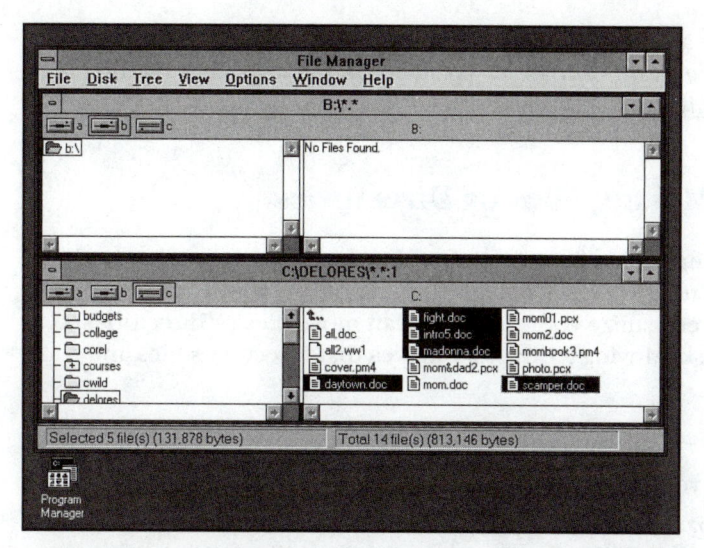

Fig. 5.22
Preparing to copy a file.

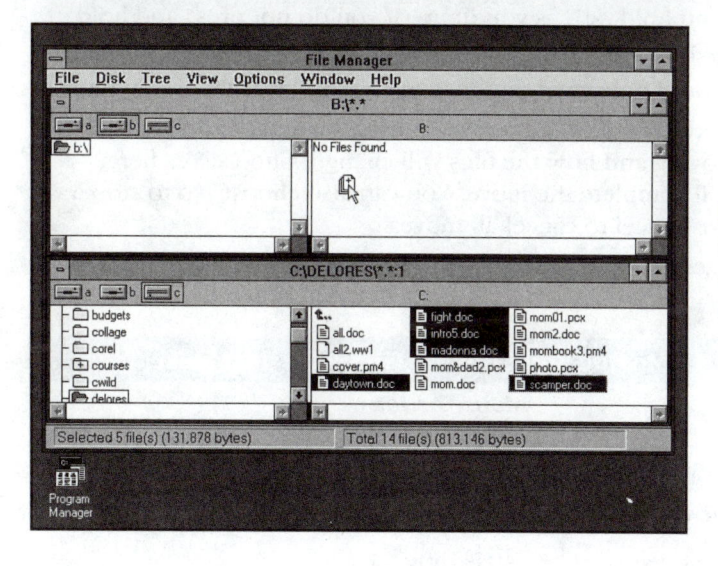

Fig. 5.23
Selected files dragged to a destination window.

5. When the file icon is over the destination, release the mouse button; release `Ctrl` if you were using it.

   If the destination has a file with the same name as the file you are copying, you are asked to confirm that the destination file can be replaced by the copy.

111

Managing Files

Note: You can copy all the files from a directory by selecting them all before you drag them to the new destination. To select all the files, click the first file, press and hold ⇧Shift, and click the last file. Alternatively, press Ctrl+/.

Exercise 4.3: Moving Files or Directories

You can move files just as easily as you can copy them. Moving a file puts it in a new location and removes the original from the old location. You move files when you need to reorganize your disk. You can move files or directories to a new directory or disk. Moving a directory moves that directory's files and subdirectories.

To move files or directories with the mouse, follow these steps:

1. Select the file you just copied.
2. Drag the file back to the directory from which you copied it in the preceding exercise. If the destination were on a different disk, you would press and hold Alt as you drag. (If you do not press and hold Alt, you *copy* the files rather than move them.)
3. Release the mouse button when the icon or file is over the destination.
4. If you are asked to confirm the move, consider whether you are copying or moving and how the files will change. Choose **Y**es here. This action will complete the move. You can also choose **N**o to stop a single move or Cancel to cancel all moves.

Table 5.3 summarizes the mouse actions you take to move or copy files with the mouse.

Table 5.3 Moving and Copying Files with the Mouse	
Desired Action	*Mouse Action*
Copy to a different disk	Drag
Copy to the same disk	Ctrl+drag
Move to a different disk	Alt+drag
Move to the same disk	Drag

To Manage Files and Directories

Exercise 4.4: Creating New Directories

Creating new directories on your disk is like adding new drawers to a filing cabinet. Creating new directories is an excellent way to reorganize or restructure your disk for new categories. After you build directories and subdirectories, you can put existing files in them with the **File Move** and **File Copy** commands.

To make new directories or files, follow these steps:

1. Activate the directory tree area. (This step is not necessary if you want to put the new subdirectory under the currently selected directory.)
2. Select the directory of your word processor. You will practice putting a new subdirectory under it.
3. Open the **F**ile menu, and choose the Cr**e**ate Directory command. The Create Directory dialog box appears (see fig. 5.24).

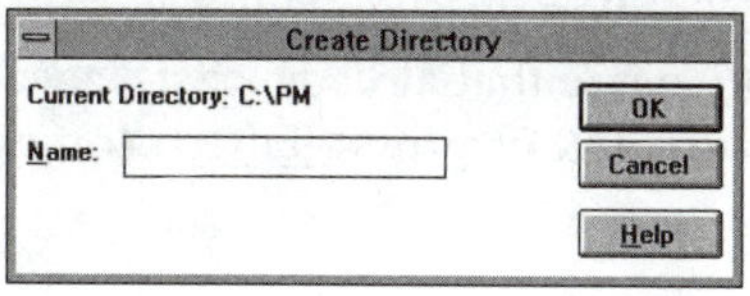

Fig. 5.24
The Create Directory dialog box.

4. Type **classwrk** in the **N**ame text box. The name can be from one to eight characters long.
5. Choose OK, or press Enter. You have now added a subdirectory, CLASSWRK, under your word processing directory.

Adding new subdirectories is like growing new branches on a tree. New subdirectories must sprout from existing directories or subdirectories. If you want to create multiple layers of subdirectories, first create the directories or subdirectories that precede the ones you want to add.

Exercise 4.5: Renaming Files or Directories

Unless you do everything perfectly the first time, you will find times when you want to rename a file or directory. You follow the same procedure for renaming files and renaming directories.

113

Managing Files

To rename a directory, follow these steps:

1. Select the directory CLASSWRK, which you just created.
2. Open the **F**ile menu, and choose the Re**n**ame command. The Rename dialog box appears (see fig. 5.25).

Fig. 5.25
The Rename dialog box.

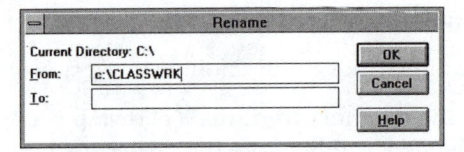

3. In the **T**o text box, type **fall93**.
4. Choose OK, or press ⏎Enter. You have just renamed a directory to FALL93.

These are the same steps you would follow to rename a file.

Note: If you enter a file or directory name that already exists, a warning message box appears after you choose OK or press ⏎Enter. You can then type a unique file name.

Exercise 4.6: Deleting Files or Directories

You delete files or directories when you want to remove old work from your disk. Deleting files makes more storage space available on-disk. Deleting directories that don't contain any files makes little difference in storage space but does unclutter your directory tree.

Unless you have prepared your hard disk with special software, you cannot recover files or directories after you delete them. So be very careful to select only the files or directories you want to delete. If you aren't sure about deleting files or directories, turn on the warning messages by choosing the **O**ptions **C**onfirmation command and selecting the File Delete and Directory Delete boxes.

Note: Be careful that you do not accidentally select a directory when selecting files you want to delete. If you select a directory and choose **F**ile **D**elete, you delete all the files in the directory and the directory itself. Deleting entire directories can be convenient, but it also can be a real surprise if it is not what you wanted to do.

To Manage Files and Directories

To delete a subdirectory, follow these steps:

1. Activate the directory tree area.
2. Select directory FALL93 to delete. (Alternatively, you can use wild cards in step 4. These can be very useful and save time.)
3. Open the **F**ile menu, and choose the **D**elete command, or press [Del]. The Delete dialog box appears.
4. The name of the directory and its root appear in the window (see fig. 5.26). Look at the window carefully, and verify that the name is the directory, FALL93, that you want to delete.

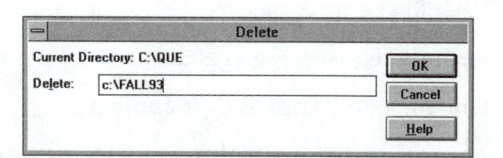

Fig. 5.26
The Delete dialog box.

5. Choose OK, or press [↵Enter]. If you are asked to confirm deletions, choose **Y**es after the Confirm File Delete dialog box appears, or choose Yes to **A**ll to confirm deletion of several files at once.

Displaying Warning Messages

During some File Manager operations, you see a warning message that asks you to confirm the action about to take place. For example, if you select a directory and choose **F**ile **D**elete, you are asked to confirm the deletion of each file and the removal of the directory. If you find the confirmation messages annoying, you can turn them off. Be aware, however, that these warning messages can prevent you from making mistakes; if you turn off the messages, you have no warning for potentially hazardous actions.

You turn off warning messages by first choosing the **O**ptions menu and then selecting the **C**onfirmation command. After the Confirmation dialog box appears, you can deselect the type of warning message you want to turn off (see fig. 5.27).

Table 5.4 gives a list of the options in the Confirmation dialog box and the actions their messages confirm.

115

Managing Files

Fig. 5.27
The Confirmation dialog box.

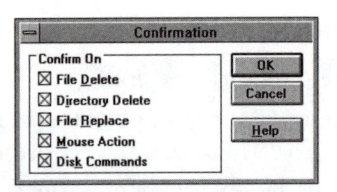

Table 5.4 Options in the Confirmation Dialog Box

Option	Action Confirmed by Message
File **D**elete	Each file being erased
Directory Delete	Each directory being erased
File **R**eplace	One file being copied over another
Mouse Action	Any mouse action involving moving or copying
Dis**k** Commands	Each disk being copied over or formatted

As you gain more experience and confidence with your computer, you may want to turn off these messages. If you are a beginner or have difficulty accurately positioning the mouse, you may want to leave these messages on.

Objective 5: To Manage Disks

The File Manager includes commands not only for copying files, but also for copying entire floppy disks. You can copy the contents of one floppy disk to another—even if you have only one disk drive. You can also use the File Manager to format new disks.

Exercise 5.1: Formatting Floppy Disks

When you buy new disks for storing data and files, you cannot use them until you format them. (Some disks come already formatted.) Formatting prepares disks for use by a specific type of computer. Formatting is like preparing a new, blank book for use by adding page numbers and making a blank table of contents. Part of the process of formatting is checking for bad areas on the disk's magnetic surface. Any bad areas found are identified so that data is not recorded there.

To Manage Disks

Note: If a disk has data on it, formatting completely erases all existing data, which you cannot retrieve. Never format a program disk.

To format a floppy disk, follow these steps:

1. Put the disk you want to format into the correct disk drive.
2. Open the **D**isk menu, and choose the **F**ormat Disk command. The Format Disk dialog box appears (see fig. 5.28).

Fig. 5.28
The Format Disk dialog box.

3. In the **D**isk In list box, select the disk drive containing the disk you want to format.
4. Select the appropriate disk size in the **C**apacity list box.
5. Type the label, **SmartStart1**, in the **L**abel text box. A label can be any name up to 11 characters, in both upper- and lowercase letters. Creating a label is entirely optional.
6. Choose OK, or press ⏎Enter. A message box warns you that formatting will erase all data on the disk. If you're sure that you want to format this disk, choose **Y**es.
7. After this disk is formatted, you are given the chance to format additional disks. If you have more than one disk, go ahead and format the rest. It's nice to get this task out of the way so that when you need a disk, you can use it.

For your information, the other two disk formatting options that can be helpful are

- **Make System Disk.** Choose this option if you want to use the disk to start your computer. Do not use this option unless you need it, because the system files use storage space that can otherwise be used for data.
- **Quick Format.** Choose this option if you want to save time and you're reasonably sure that the disk does not have bad areas.

A good practice is to format an entire box of disks at one time and put a paper label on each formatted disk. With this system, you can know that open boxes contain formatted disks; paper labels also confirm that the disks are formatted.

Managing Files

Exercise 5.2: Copying Disks

Make duplicate copies of disks when you need to store disk information off-site in a secure location or when you need duplicates of original program disks. You should get into the habit of making duplicate copies of your work. This practice is well worth the small amount of time invested if something happens to your disk. And your disk can malfunction with no error on your part. Suddenly, your data can become garbled. You need to have a copy of it on hand in that case.

To duplicate a disk, follow these steps:

1. Protect the original disk by attaching a write-protect tab (5 1/4-inch disks) or sliding open the protect notch (3 1/2-inch disks).
2. Insert the original disk (the *source* disk) into the source disk drive.
3. Insert the disk to receive the copy (the *destination* disk) into the second disk drive. If you don't have a second disk drive, don't be concerned.
4. Open the **D**isk menu, and choose the **C**opy Disk command.

   If you have only one disk drive, the Confirm Copy Disk dialog box appears, warning you that all information will be lost from the destination disk.

   Choose **Y**es, or press ⏎Enter in the Confirm Copy Disk dialog box (see fig. 5.29). You are prompted to switch the source disk and destination disk in and out of the single drive. Windows prompts you to exchange disks.

Fig. 5.29
The Confirm Copy Disk dialog box.

If you have two disk drives, the Copy Disk dialog box appears. Proceed with the following steps.

5. In the **S**ource In list in the Copy Disk dialog box, select the drive letter for the source drive (see fig. 5.30).

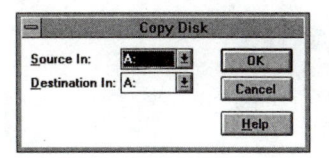

Fig. 5.30
The Copy Disk dialog box.

6. In the **D**estination In list in the Copy Disk dialog box, select the drive letter for the destination drive (even if it is the same as the source drive).
7. Choose OK, or press ⏎Enter in the Copy Disk dialog box.

To use the Copy Disk command, the disks must be identical. For example, you cannot copy from a 3 1/2-inch disk that holds 1.4M of data to a 5 1/4-inch disk that holds 1.2M of data. To duplicate a disk, you therefore use the same source and destination disk drive. File Manager prompts you to switch disk when necessary. Labeling your disks before you begin may help.

Warning: Note that copying disks always completely erases the destination disk. Before you use the Copy Disk command, make sure that you will not delete important files from the destination disk. The Copy Disk command formats the destination disk if it is not already formatted.

Chapter Summary

The File Manager may help you sleep better at night. Having backup copies of your important document files stored in a location separate from your computer has a very calming effect.

The File Manager is also an excellent tool for organizing your hard disk. Use the File Manager to keep directories and files organized, just as you organize a filing system. And don't let old and unused files overwhelm you. They waste space, slow performance, and are hard to get rid of when you don't remember what they contain.

In Chapter 6, you learn about linking different files together.

Testing Your Knowledge

True/False Questions

1. The directory tree occupies that right portion of the screen, showing files in the selected directory.
2. Electronic or primary memory is volatile and limited in size.
3. To activate different areas of the File Manager screen with the keyboard, you press [Tab⇄].
4. When you double-click the plus (+) sign in a directory icon, you collapse the directory.
5. To select nonadjacent files in the contents list, you click the files while holding down the [⇧Shift] key.

Multiple Choice Questions

1. Which of the following types of storage is where data and programs are kept magnetically for long periods while the computer is off?
    A. primary storage
    B. electronic memory
    C. secondary storage
    D. RAM (Random-Access Memory)
2. Which of the following file names would select all files that begin with *T* and have an extension that begins with *X*?
    A. *T.*X
    B. T*.X*
    C. T.X
    D. T?.X??
3. If you choose to display the files and directories in the File Manager by type, you expect to see
    A. files and directories sorted alphabetically by file extension and then by name.
    B. files and directories sorted by time of day.
    C. files and directories sorted by last date saved, from newest to oldest.
    D. files and directories sorted alphabetically by file name.

Testing Your Knowledge

4. What keystrokes copy a file(s) to the same disk?
    A. double-click
    B. drag
    C. Alt+drag
    D. Ctrl+drag
5. Which of the following is the reason to make copies of your disk?
    A. Bad sectors may suddenly appear on your disk.
    B. Someone may accidentally spill Coke on your disk.
    C. There may be a hurricane, and your disk may be blown to Timbuktu.
    D. All of the above.

Fill-in-the-Blank Questions

1. A volume label on the disk you are formatting can have _____ number of characters, both upper- and lowercase.
2. A directory within another directory is called a _____.
3. The File Manager follows the primary rule of all Windows programs: _____, then do.
4. The default condition in the Select Files dialog box (which selects all files) is _____.
5. If you are reasonably sure that your disk doesn't have bad areas, you may select _____ Format to save time.

Review: Short Projects

1. Organizing Your Data

    While in the File Manager, examine the way all the information is organized. Does it make sense to you? Can you identify which files are system files (those with EXE, COM, PIF, or BAT extensions) and what they are used for? Are your data files organized in the best possible manner? Think about the way you use data, and design a structure for the data. Create and remove directories as needed. Remember, you don't want too many files in one directory, making reading and retrieving files cumbersome; on the other hand, you don't want too many directories, making navigating the directories cumbersome. Think about your work, and design and implement your solution.

Managing Files

2. Exploring Your Own Disk

   How many drives do you see in the File Manager? Do you know the purpose of each drive? If you are on a Local Area Network (LAN), you will probably see drives that are unknown to you. Ask your instructor or someone at the Information Center to explain the purposes of these drives. Is there a central repository (file server) of data for your class? What is the letter of that drive, if it exists? Do you know how to copy data from that file server to your hard or floppy drive? If not, practice this.

3. Establishing a Backup Procedure

   Format two floppy disks. Label them A and B both electronically and on the paper label. You can use these backups on consecutive days. Create a paper log of the important backup information: date, time, and operator. Copy all the files and directories to disk A. Record that fact in the log. The next day copy all the files and directories to disk B. On the third day, copy to disk A. Continue alternating between the disks in this fashion, so that you always have two days of backups. This time period is a good comfort zone to establish. It is also excellent practice in good procedures to keep a log of all backups. This log not only gives you written documentation of your backups but also helps establish a routine.

Review: Long Projects

1. Creating a File Management System

   As CEO and president of Bella's Ice Cream Parlor, one of your critical responsibilities is the management of data—a key resource. Managing files is perhaps not the most glamorous part of the job but is nonetheless mission critical. Plan the directories that will be used by the applications you identified in Project 1 in "Long Projects" at the end of Chapter 4. Think about the most efficient way to organize these directories. Now make a backup log for the files, including the time of day, person responsible, and date. Create a daily and weekly backup schedule. Consider what would happen in the event of a unforeseen disaster to your facility. Should you store an extra copy of the weekly backups off site? If so, where would you store them? In your home? In a vault at the bank? Make plans for these possibilities. Keep clear records of your decisions.

Testing Your Knowledge

2. Using Wild Cards

   Learning to use wild-card characters in Windows is very useful. The File Manager is not the only place where they can be used. Explore all the functions and features that you have learned thus far in Windows. Can you find additional places to use wild-card characters? Now try using them. Consider the different groups of files you might want to retrieve at one time. Practice using both the single-place character, ?, and the *.

Using Object Linking and Embedding

6

Windows programs have the unique advantage of being capable of exchanging and linking information easily with other Windows programs. This capability is called *object linking and embedding*, or *OLE*. It enables you to create compound documents made up of objects created by different applications. If you are accustomed to working with a single program, the value of linking and embedding data is not always immediately apparent. After you begin to use this capability, however, you will see how it can help you communicate your ideas without being constrained by applications.

Here are some examples of uses for linking and embedding:

- You can link a mailing list in a Windows database to a mail-merge data document in a Windows word processing program.
- You can create sales projections, financial analyses, inventory reports, and investment analyses with Microsoft Excel or Lotus 1-2-3 for Windows, and link or embed them into Windows word processing documents.
- You can maintain target reminder letters and callbacks by linking PackRat, a personal information manager, to Word for Windows through the WordBASIC macros that come with PackRat.

Using Object Linking and Embedding

- You can embed drawings or schematics into Word for Windows or Ami Pro, and then update them from within the word processor using Microsoft Draw.
- You can link Microsoft Excel to a Windows database or SQL Source to monitor and analyze inventory.

Objectives

1. To Link Data between Programs
2. To Manage Links
3. To Embed Data in a Document

Key Terms in This Chapter	
Applets	Small programs that run within larger programs to enhance or add features to the large program.
Source	A document or program supplying linked or embedded data.
Target	A document or program receiving linked or embedded data.
Data	Text, worksheet, database, or graphics information.
Embed	To store data from the source document within a target document.
Link	A reference from within a target document to data in a source document. The link transfers data from the source document to a target document.
Object	Information created by one program and stored within another.
Object linking and embedding	The capability of certain Windows programs to transfer or store data from the source document to a target document.
Packages	An icon (pictorial) representation of data stored within a target document.

Objectives

You will see the terms *source* and *target* throughout this chapter. The *source* is the file or program supplying data. The *target* is the file or program receiving information. Some programs are both a source and a target; others are one but not the other. For example, Microsoft Write and Cardfile are targets—they only receive information. Windows Paintbrush, however, is a source; it only supplies information.

Copying and pasting is the simplest method of transferring small amounts of data or graphics from one program to another. You use the same method to move text or graphics within a document. If you are not familiar with copying and pasting between programs, you should review Chapter 4, "Editing, Copying, and Moving in Windows."

Copying, linking, or embedding data between Windows programs may require the same or similar commands, and the results may appear the same on-screen or in the document. Copying, linking, and embedding, however, fit different situations and have different advantages and disadvantages. Table 6.1 lists these methods of data transfer, the situations in which you should use each method, and each method's advantages and disadvantages.

Table 6.1 Methods of Transferring Data

Method	Usage
Copying	Use this method when you do not want to update data. To update this data, you must replace it.
	Advantages
	Data is not changed when you update other parts of the document.
	Less memory and storage is required to use or save the document.
	Disadvantages
	Pictures may print at a lower resolution if you copy them as bitmapped images.
	Updating data requires recopying the original data and repasting it into the target document.
Linking	Use this method when you want to update the source document and have the changes automatically transfer into multiple target documents.

continues

Using Object Linking and Embedding

	Table 6.1 Continued
Method	Usage
	Advantages
	Less memory is required than for an embedded object.
	Updates many target documents by changing one source document.
	Older Windows programs incapable of embedding objects can still link data.
	Disadvantages
	Links between the source and the target may be broken if you change or delete the source file name or path name.
	Automatically updated links may slow Windows operation.
	You must save source data and maintain its name and path name.
Embedding	Use this method when you have only a few target documents that need updating, and you want to include the source data (an embedded object) as part of the document.
	Advantages
	Target document and source data are stored as a single file so that you do not have to maintain links, path names, and source files.
	You do not have to keep the source data, because it is saved as part of the target document.
	You can stay within the source document and use the target program to update the embedded object.
	Disadvantages
	Documents containing embedded objects are larger than other documents because they contain both target and source data.
	Updating an embedded graphic may result in a file with lower printer resolution than the original.
	You must update each target document individually.

Objective 1: To Link Data between Programs

You can transfer data between Windows programs by *linking* documents. A link creates a reference to data in another program or to a different document in the same program. The data remains stored in the source document, and a copy is sent through the link to the target document.

Exercise 1.1: Creating a Link

Between Windows programs that are capable of linking, creating a link is as easy as copying and pasting. When you use one of the Paste commands to create a link, you have the option of making a link that updates automatically or a link that requires manual updates. The command to paste a link may vary between programs. If your source program does not have linking capabilities, it will not have an Edit Paste Link command, nor will it have an Edit Paste Special command with a subsequent Paste Link button.

To create a link, follow these steps:

1. Open both Windows programs: Microsoft Excel (or your own spreadsheet program) and your word processing program. The source document will be an Excel spreadsheet you create. The target document will be a word processing document you create.

2. Activate the blank target document (in your word processor). Type the text as seen in figure 6.1. After you have entered the text, press ⏎Enter three times to create blank spaces at the bottom of the page. Save the document as TARGET1.DOC.

3. Activate the blank source (Excel) document. Enter the data as seen in figure 6.2. Use the cursor-movement keys (arrow keys) to move around the spreadsheet. Save this source document as SOURCE1.XLS.

    Warning: You must use the correct file name when creating a link.

4. Select all the cells with data in the source document (including the labels, month, lab, quizzes).

5. Open the Edit menu, and choose the Copy command.

6. Activate the target document, TARGET1.DOC. (You can use Alt+Tab⇥ to move between programs.) Move the insertion point to the end of the document.

Using Object Linking and Embedding

7. Open the **E**dit menu, and choose the Paste **S**pecial command. You see the Paste Special dialog box, which displays the source of the link and presents a list of different forms in which you can paste linked data (see fig. 6.3).

   The Paste Special dialog box

   Note: If you are using a package that has a Paste Link command in the Edit menu, you don't need to use the Paste Special command.

8. From the **D**ata Type list, choose Formatted Text (RTF). Other link types are described in table 6.2. Note that some data types may not be available as a pasted link.

9. Choose the Paste **L**ink button. You have just linked your two documents.

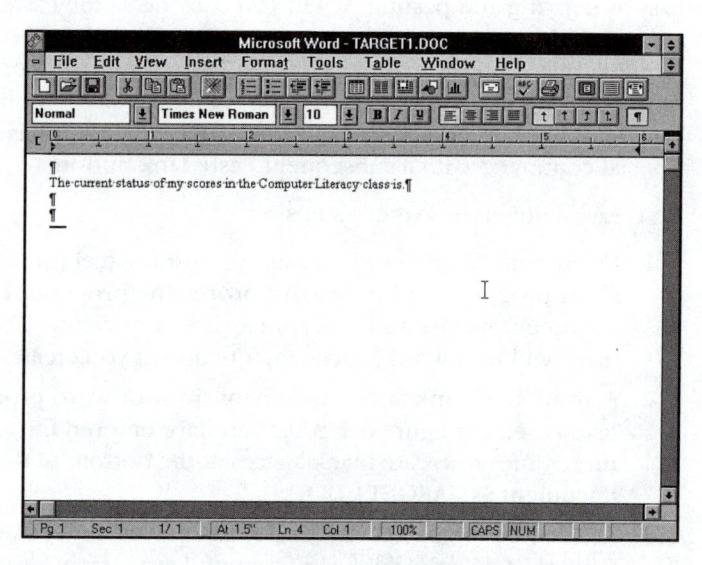

Fig. 6.1
A target document.

Pasted links automatically update to reflect a change in the source data. Later in this chapter, the sections under Objective 3 describe how to create a link that updates only when manually requested and how to change a link from automatic to manual.

When you create a link in the target document, you may be able to display the data from the source in different forms, depending on the source program. Table 6.2 describes some of the data types.

To Link Data between Programs

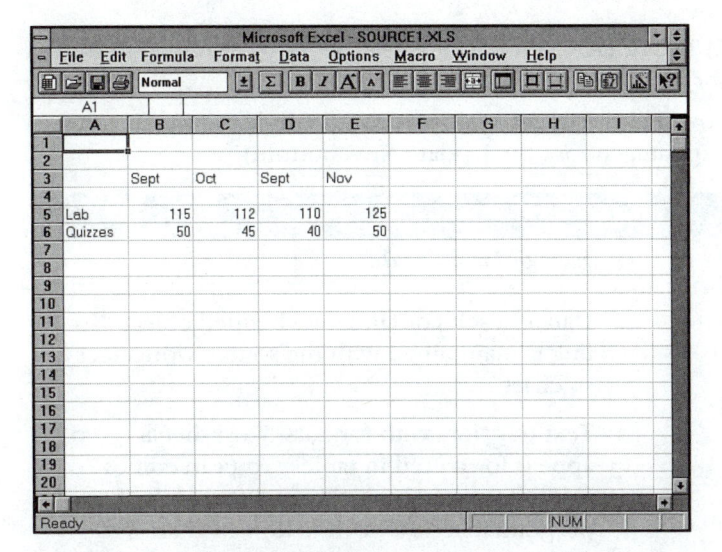

Fig. 6.2
Data entered in the source document.

Fig. 6.3
The Paste Special dialog box.

Exercise 1.2: Updating Linked Data

If your link is automatic, the linked data in the target document automatically updates when you make a change to the data in the source document. If your link is manual, however, you must tell the target program to update the link.

To update linked data, follow these steps:

1. Select the linked data from TARGET1.DOC.
2. Open the **E**dit menu, and choose the Microsoft Excel Worksheet **L**ink command. You are now back in the source document, SOURCE1.XLS.
3. Change the lab grade for September to 120.

Using Object Linking and Embedding

4. Activate the TARGET1.DOC. (You can use `Alt`+`Tab` to return to the word processor).
5. You can see now that the update was made in the linked data. (If you don't see the update, choose the **U**pdate Now button.)

Table 6.2 Data Types and Links

Data Type	Type of Link Created
Object	Data is a self-contained embedded object. No link is maintained with the source worksheet or chart.
Formatted Text (RTF)	Text transfers with formats. Worksheets appear formatted in tables. You can edit or reformat data. If you choose Paste **Link**, the program inserts a LINK field, which links to the source document. If you choose **Paste**, the data appears as unlinked text.
Unformatted Text	Text is unformatted. Worksheets appear as unformatted text with cells separated by tabs.
Picture	Pictures, text, database tables, or worksheet ranges appear as a picture. You can format items as pictures, but you cannot edit text. Unlinking changes items to Microsoft Draw objects.
Bitmap	Pictures, text, or worksheet ranges appear as bitmapped images at screen resolution. You can format them as pictures, but you cannot edit the text.

A link set to update manually does not update when you edit it. To see the update, you must use the **U**pdate Now button.

Some programs have a shortcut for updating manual links. In Word for Windows, for example, you select the linked data and press `F9` to update the link.

Exercise 1.3: Passing Linked Documents to Other Computer Users (or Breaking the Link)

If you break a link, you change the linked word processing and worksheet information into text, as though the text were typed in the target document. Graphics become pictures or bitmapped images. If you break the link, you do not have to include a copy of the source file with the target document; however, breaking the link also means that the person receiving the data cannot update it.

To break a link, follow these steps:

1. Select the linked data in TARGET1.DOC.
2. Open the **E**dit menu, and choose the **L**inks command.

   The Links dialog box enables you to freeze linked data by breaking the link.
3. Choose the **C**ancel Link button. If a dialog box prompts you to confirm that you want to cancel the link, choose **Y**es.

If you want to remove linked data rather than break the link, select the linked data and press Del.

Objective 2: To Manage Links

Keeping track of the many links included in a complex document can be difficult, but the **E**dit **L**inks command makes the job considerably easier. When you open the **E**dit menu and choose **L**inks, the Links dialog box displays a list including each link in the document and its type and indicates whether the link updates manually or automatically (see fig. 6.4). You can use the buttons and check boxes to update linked data, lock links to prevent changes, cancel links, and change the file names or directories in which the linked data is stored.

Before you can edit a link, you must select it. To select a link, click the link, or select the **L**inks list and press the up- or down-arrow key to select a link. To select multiple adjacent links in the Links dialog box, click the first link, and then Shift+click the last link. To select or deselect multiple nonadjacent links, hold down Ctrl as you click the links.

Using Object Linking and Embedding

Fig. 6.4
The Links dialog box.

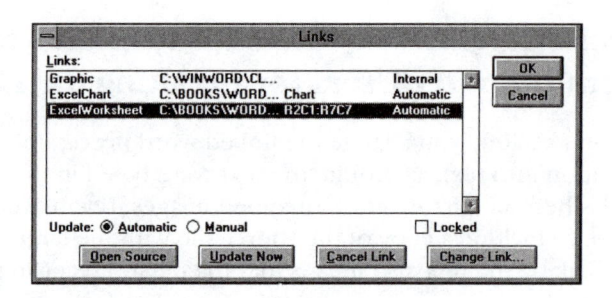

Updating Links

To update individual links in a document so that the destination file is refreshed with new information, select the linked data, and choose the Edit Links command. After the Links dialog box appears, select the links you want to update, and choose the Update Now button.

When you want to update all the links in an entire document, select the entire document or select all the links in the Link dialog box, and choose the Update Now button.

Exercise 2.1: Controlling Manual and Automatic Updates

In some programs you can specify whether a link should automatically update or whether it should be updated only under manual control. If you paste a link, the link updates automatically; however, you may want your linked data to update only when you request an update. Manually controlled updates improve Windows performance and enable you to control how frequently an update occurs.

To change an automatically updated link to a manual link, follow these steps:

1. Relink the Excel SOURCE1.XLS to the word processor TARGET1.DOC as you did in Exercise 1.1.
2. Select the linked data.
3. Open the **E**dit menu, and choose the **L**inks command. The Links dialog box appears.
4. Choose **A**utomatic if you want to update the link every time the source data changes.
5. Choose OK, or press ↵Enter.

6. Activate Excel to change the November quiz score to **100**.
7. Activate the word processor to see that the November quiz score was automatically changed to 100.

To update a manual link, use the procedure described in the preceding section, "Updating Links."

Unlinking Inserted Files or Pictures

When you want to unlink the source document and change the linked data to normal text or a graphic, select the linked data. Then open the **Edit** menu, and choose the Links command. Choose the **Cancel** Links button. A dialog box appears, prompting you to confirm that you want to cancel the link. Choose **Yes** to cancel the link.

Exercise 2.2: Editing Links When Source File Names or Locations Change

If a source document's location, file name, or the linked range within the document changes, you need to change the link so that the source data can be found. You use the Change Link dialog box when a linked file's name or directory changes.

To update a link that does not work, follow these steps:

1. Close SOURCE1.XLS.
2. Open the File Manager. Rename SOURCE1.XLS to SOURCE2.XLS.
3. Activate the word processor.
4. Open the **E**dit menu, and choose the **L**inks command.
5. Select the link to edit, and then choose the C**h**ange Link button to display the Change Link dialog box (see fig. 6.5).
6. Edit the **F**ile Name box to reflect the new name of the source document: change SOURCE1.XLS to SOURCE2.XLS.
7. Choose OK to change file name and then OK to change link.
8. Check that the link has been correctly renamed by updated SOURCE2.XLS and that TARGET1.DOC reflects the update.

Ensure that the program, path and file name, and range name are correct for the new source document. The **I**tem is the range name or bookmark that describes the linked data within the document. (For a discussion of the use of bookmarks, see Chapter 3.)

135

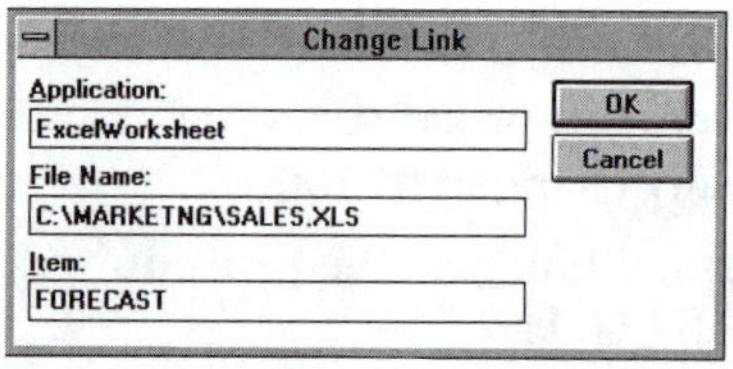

Using Object Linking and Embedding

Fig. 6.5
The Change Link dialog box.

Locking a Link To Prevent Accidental Changes

You may want to prevent accidental updating of a link but still be able to update it at your discretion. You can prevent accidental changes by locking the link; you can unlock it when you are ready to update the link. To lock or unlock a link, select the linked data, and choose the **Edit Links** command. Select the link you want to lock or unlock, and then check or clear the Loc**k**ed check box.

Objective 3: To Embed Data in a Document

Embedding is another method of inserting data from one program into another. Embedding enables a source document to store its data directly within a target program's document. For example, you can store a picture from Windows Paintbrush within a Windows Write letter or store a budget and chart from Microsoft Excel within a Word for Windows document. Not only can you see the budget table and chart, but the actual worksheet and chart data are stored in the target document so that you can make changes or review the originals.

Embedding data eliminates the need to include source data files when you send someone a document that contains links. Embedded data is stored within the target document, not as a separate file. This method, however, creates large files.

There are two basic types of object linking and embedding (OLE) source programs. Windows Paintbrush is one type: a stand-alone program you can use as an OLE source program or as you use any other program. You can embed a Paintbrush object in a target document by copying and pasting it or by inserting it.

The other type of OLE source program is called an *applet*: a miniature program you operate only from within a target program. The word processing program Word for Windows, for example, comes with several free applets, including Microsoft Draw, a drawing applet, and MS WordArt, an applet you can use to create logos.

To Embed Data in a Document

Exercise 3.1: Creating an Embedded Object

You can create embedded objects in two ways. You can copy data from the source program and embed that data in a target document as an object. Use this technique when you want to embed an object you created using a stand-alone OLE source program such as Paintbrush.

The other way to create an embedded object is to start the source program from within a target document, create the object, and then insert it into the target document. Use this technique whenever you are using an OLE applet.

To insert an embedded object by using any OLE source or applet, follow these steps:

1. Activate the word processing program, and open TARGET1.DOC. Move the insertion point to the end of the document.

2. Open the **I**nsert menu, and choose the **O**bject command. (Depending on your program, you may need to open the **E**dit menu and choose the **I**nsert Object command.) The Object dialog box appears, showing the types of objects you can embed (see fig. 6.6).

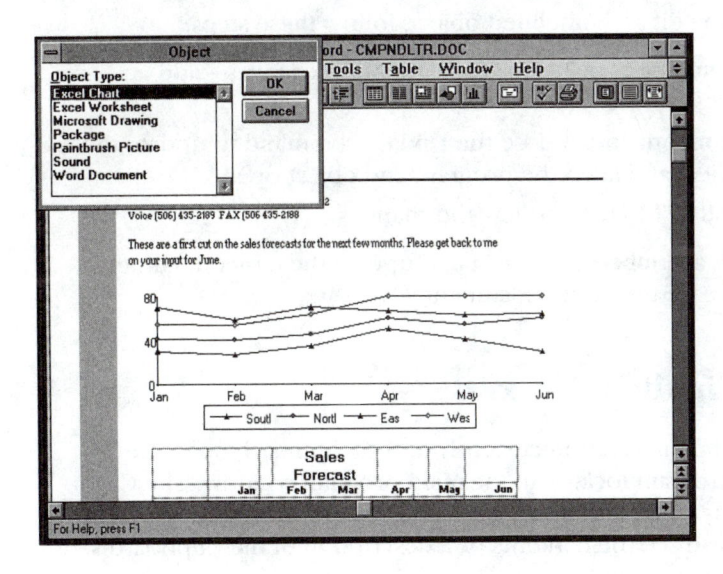

Fig. 6.6
The Object dialog box.

3. From the **O**bject Type list, select Microsoft Excel Worksheet Object, and then choose OK or press ↵Enter.

4. In the source program (you are now in Excel), create the data you want.

137

Using Object Linking and Embedding

Type 100, 90, 80 in the first three cells, respectively. (You could also copy an existing file into the source document.)

5. Open the File menu, and choose the Update command.
6. Return to TARGET1.DOC, and see the embedded data.

Some programs, such as Windows Paintbrush and Windows Write, enable you to embed an object by copying and pasting it. To embed a picture from Paintbrush into a letter in Write, for example, select and copy the picture in Paintbrush, switch to Write, and paste in the picture. The picture is automatically embedded.

Exercise 3.2: Editing Embedded Objects

You edit an embedded object by starting the source program from within the target document. When the source program starts, it also opens the file that contains the embedded object, enabling you to make changes. Make your changes; then update the target document. If you do not update the target document, you lose your changes.

To use the mouse to edit an embedded object, follow these steps:

1. Double-click the object in TARGET1.DOC. Make changes—add another row of test scores: 95, 80, 90.
2. Open the File menu, and choose the Update command to update the embedded object and keep the program and object open.
3. Go back to TARGET1.DOC to view the changes.

Note: After you edit an embedded object and update the target document, make sure that you save the target document.

Viewing Data in the Clipboard

If you need to see the information currently in the Clipboard, open the Clipboard Viewer program located in the Main program window. The Clipboard Viewer displays the contents of the Clipboard. From within the Clipboard Viewer, you can see the contents or a description of the Clipboard's contents.

Chapter Summary

This chapter discusses the techniques you need to create compound documents—documents created and collected from many different programs. Word for Windows and the Windows programs with which it can exchange data create the most powerful document-building system available.

Remember that to use Windows' object linking and embedding (OLE) technology, your programs must support OLE. For more information on using programs together, refer to Chapter 4.

Testing Your Knowledge

True/False Questions

1. The *source* is the file or program supplying the data.
2. An advantage of embedding is that less memory is needed compared to linking.
3. Links create a reference to data in another program or to a different document in the same program.
4. *OLE* stands for Object Look and Efficiency.
5. You can embed an object in a client document without ever leaving the client document.

Multiple Choice Questions

1. Which of the following is an advantage of linking?
    A. You must save source data and maintain its name and path name.
    B. You do not have to keep the source data, because it is saved as part of the target document.
    C. Updating data requires recopying the original data and repasting it into the target document.
    D. Linking updates many target documents by changing one source document.

Using Object Linking and Embedding

2. If you break a link to pass a document to another computer user,
   A. the source data is changed to text as if it were typed in the target document.
   B. the source data remains the same.
   C. you have to include a copy of the source file with the target file.
   D. none of the above

3. How can you edit an embedded object with the mouse?
   A. Select the object, open the **E**dit menu, and then choose the **O**bject command of the source program.
   B. Click and drag the object.
   C. Double-click the object.
   D. Select the object and do a cartwheel.

4. To choose manually or automatically updated links, you open the **E**dit menu, and choose the **L**inks command; then choose
   A. Cancel.
   B. the **U**pdate option.
   C. **O**pen Source.
   D. **L**ocked.

5. The easiest way to transfer small amounts of data or graphics from one program to another is by
   A. copying and pasting.
   B. embedding.
   C. linking.
   D. keeping your fingers crossed.

Fill-in-the-Blank Questions

1. _____ data is stored within the target document, not as a separate file.
2. A document or program supplying linked or embedded data is called the _____.
3. A document or program receiving linked or embedded data is called the _____.
4. A miniature program you operate only from within a target program is called a(n) _____.
5. The technology that enables Windows programs to exchange and link information easily is called _____ and _____.

140

Review: Short Projects

1. Embedding Spreadsheet Data in a Word Processing Document

    Using your spreadsheet program, create a list of all your grades for the current semester. Create subtotals for each subject, and leave room to add scores as you earn them. Now create a letter to the Dean of Financial Aid. Embed the spreadsheet data in the letter, and update the scores as the semester progresses. Update the letter to reflect the scores (for example, explain how you did so superbly in Computer Literacy 200, or why a Biology 202 lab score was lower than expected).

2. Linking Data

    Consider all the software packages available to you. Now think of the different ways you could link data between packages and between documents. Now create at least eight links. Manage these links by using the methods discussed in this chapter. What issues have you discovered? Make a printout of a list of the links and copies of the documents that use them.

3. Experimenting with Applets

    Explore your computing environment. Find out whether you have any applets available. Learn to use them. Try embedding them in different documents. What are they used for? When do you think you will use them?

Review: Long Projects

1. Using OLE

    In previous chapters, you identified the critical applications to be used in the operation of Bella's Ice Cream Parlor. Now think about which applications will be passing or sharing data. What method(s) will you use, linking or embedding, and why? Now that you know about OLE, have new uses come to your mind for the Ice Cream Parlor business? (Be sure to check the list of examples at the beginning of this chapter.) Make a list of all OLE uses for the Ice Cream Parlor.

2. Applications and OLE

    Using table 6.1 as a guide, develop a list of specific applications and uses for each of the methods of transferring data: copying, linking, and embedding. Give reasons based on the listed advantages and disadvantages for each choice. Can you develop a rule of thumb that will guide you?

Using Desktop Accessories

One of the greatest advantages of using Windows is that you can run several programs at the same time. Instead of using your major programs side-by-side, however, you may want to work with only one program and keep small accessory programs close at hand. That's where the Windows accessory programs shine. Suppose that you are working in Word for Windows and need to do a quick calculation. Open Calculator, add up your figures, and copy the total back into Word. At the end of the day, you may want to relax with a game—why not challenge yourself with Solitaire?

Calendar, Calculator, and Clock are small, so they don't use much of your computer's memory. And they're easy to use, so they don't use much of *your* memory! Located in the Accessories group window, these programs are useful companions to your primary programs.

Objectives

1. To Start the Windows Accessory Programs
2. To Track Appointments with Calendar
3. To Make Calculations with Calculator
4. To Watch the Clock
5. To Develop Skills with Solitaire and Minesweeper

Using Desktop Accessories

Key Terms in This Chapter	
Insertion point	The flashing vertical line where text appears (sometimes called a cursor).
Scroll	To move horizontally or vertically in a document. Most programs have scroll bars to make scrolling easy.
Select	To highlight text for editing.
Cut/copy and paste	To move or copy text within a document or between programs.
Clipboard	The temporary file in Windows that stores any text you cut or copy. You can paste the contents of the Clipboard at the insertion point.
Search or find	To look through a document for a specific word or phrase.
View	To look at a document in a different way; for example, you can look at Calendar in the Day view or Month view.

Objective 1: To Start the Windows Accessory Programs

Windows accessory programs are located inside the Accessories group window. When the Accessories group icon is open as a window, you can see the programs it contains (see fig. 7.1). Each accessory program appears as an icon with its name below it. To start any program, just double-click its icon. Alternatively, open the Accessories window, press an arrow key to select the program item icon, and press ⏎Enter.

After you start the accessory programs, you may want to minimize them as icons at the bottom of the screen until you need to use them.

144

To Track Appointments with Calendar

Fig. 7.1
The Accessories window.

Objective 2: To Track Appointments with Calendar

The Windows Calendar program is a computerized appointment book you can use to record appointments, mark special dates, and even set an alarm to remind you of an important event. Calendar operates in two views: Day and Month.

Opening Calendar

Open Calendar as you open any Windows program—by double-clicking the Calendar icon in the Accessories group window, or by pressing the arrow keys to select the icon and then pressing (←Enter). A new Calendar file appears, displayed in the Day view (see fig. 7.2). Calendar's Day view is marked in hourly intervals. You can scroll through the times and enter appointments for each hour.

Below the Calendar window's menu bar is a status bar showing the current time and date. Calendar's two views, Day and Month, both share the status bar.

Exercise 2.1: Typing Appointments in the Day View

When you open the Calendar window, you see the Day view for the current time and date. Times are listed on the left side of the Calendar window; you can type appointments next to each time. To type an appointment, move the insertion point to the correct time; then type the text. You can type 80 characters on each line.

145

Using Desktop Accessories

Fig. 7.2
Calendar's Day view.

Labels: Menu bar, Status bar, Times, Scratch pad, Title bar, Scroll bar, Appointment area

Although only part of the day is displayed in the Calendar window, all 24 hours are available. To enter an appointment for a time not displayed, use the scroll bar on the right side of the Calendar window to scroll up or down to the time you want. Alternatively, with the keyboard, use the up- and down-arrow keys or PgUp and PgDn to scroll up and down.

To type an appointment in a Calendar file, follow these steps:

1. Open the Calendar window by double-clicking the Calendar icon.
2. Scroll the Calendar window to display 7:00 a.m.
3. Move the insertion point to 9:00 a.m.
4. Type the appointment, as seen in figure 7.3. A 9:00 a.m. appointment is entered in the Calendar file.

Fig. 7.3
An appointment in the Calendar file.

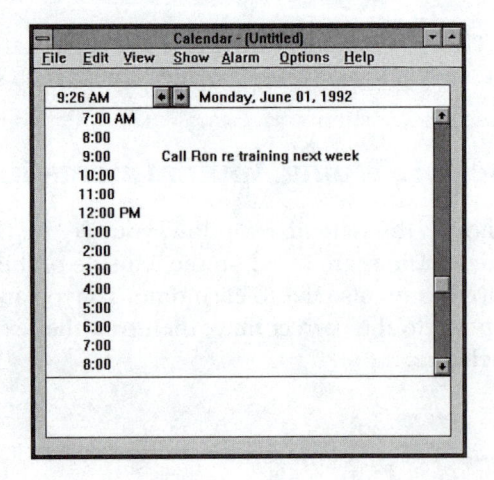

146

To Track Appointments with Calendar

5. Press `Enter` to move the insertion point to the next line.

At the bottom of each daily or monthly Calendar window is a three-line scratch pad in which you can type notes. A note stays attached to its date; whenever you turn to that date, the note appears in the scratch pad.

To type a note in the scratch pad, follow these steps:

1. Move to the scratch pad by clicking it or pressing `Tab`.
2. Type the text of your note as seen in figure 7.4.

   Calendar attaches your note to the date.

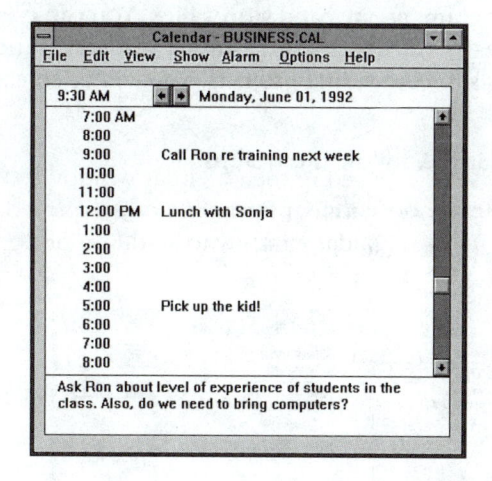

Fig. 7.4
A note in the scratch pad.

3. Move back to the appointment area by clicking it or pressing `Tab`.

Exercise 2.2: Saving a Calendar File

You can save as many different Calendar files as you want—for different projects, resources, clients, and so on. The first time you save a Calendar file, you must name it.

To save a new Calendar file, follow these steps:

1. Open the **F**ile menu, and choose the Save **A**s command.

   The Save As dialog box appears.

2. In the File **N**ame text box, type your first name (up to eight characters).

Using Desktop Accessories

3. From the D**ri**ves list box, choose the drive in which you want to save the file. From the **D**irectories list box, choose the directory in which you want to save the file.

4. Choose OK, or press [↵Enter].

To save an existing Calendar file without changing its name, open the **F**ile menu, and choose the **S**ave command.

Exercise 2.3: Opening an Existing Calendar File

Calendar, like any other program, creates and stores files. You can create as many different Calendar files as you want. For example, you may want to create separate Calendar files for individual projects. You can open each Calendar file as you need it.

To open an existing Calendar file, follow these steps:

1. Open the **F**ile menu, and choose the **O**pen command.

   The Open dialog box appears (see fig. 7.5).

Fig. 7.5
The Open dialog box.

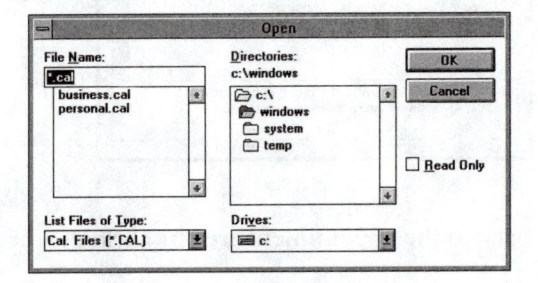

2. In the D**ri**ves list, choose the drive containing the calendar file you just saved under your first name in the preceding exercise. In the **D**irectories list, choose the directory containing that file.

3. In the File **N**ame list, choose the file saved as your first name.

4. Choose OK, or press [↵Enter].

Exercise 2.4: Editing and Moving Calendar Appointments

You can edit text in the appointment area and the scratch pad just as you edit text in any Windows program. For example, you can select text and then press

To Track Appointments with Calendar

⌊Backspace⌋ or ⌊Del⌋ to delete the text. To add text, position the insertion point where you want the new text, and then type. You can also copy or move appointments from one time or date to another time or date.

To copy or move appointments or notes, follow these steps:

1. Select Lunch with Sonja.
2. Open the Edit menu, and choose the Cut command to move the text.
3. Move the insertion point to 2:00 p.m.
4. Open the Edit menu, and choose the Paste command.

Exercise 2.5: Changing the Time Intervals and Starting Time and Setting an Alarm

The starting calendar displays the time in hours, but you can change the intervals on your calendar, and you can change the starting time. You can also add special times.

To change the time intervals and starting time, follow these steps:

1. Open the Options menu, and choose the Day Settings command. The Day Settings dialog box appears.
2. From the Interval group, select 30-minute intervals.
3. In the Starting Time box, type a different starting time; how about starting at 10:00 a.m.?
4. Choose OK, or press ⌊↵Enter⌋.

To add a special time, follow these steps:

1. Open the Options menu, and choose the Special Time command. The Special Time dialog box appears.
2. In the Special Time box, type the time about five minutes from the current time as it is shown on the calendar.
3. Choose Insert, or press ⌊↵Enter⌋.

To remind yourself of an important appointment, you can set an alarm that alerts you when the time for the appointment arrives. You can set alarms for as many appointments in a Calendar file as you want. When you set the alarm, a small bell appears to the left of the appointment time in the Calendar window (see fig. 7.6).

Using Desktop Accessories

Fig. 7.6
The bell shows that the alarm has been set.

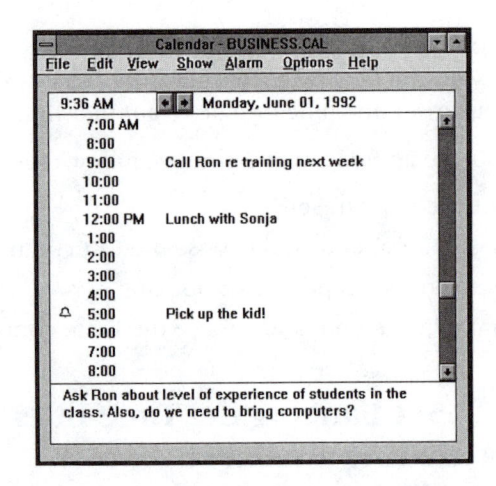

To turn on the alarm, follow these steps:

1. Move the insertion point to the special time you just inserted.
2. Open the **A**larm menu, and choose the **S**et command. Wait for the Alarm dialog box (see fig. 7.7).

Fig. 7.7
The Alarm dialog box.

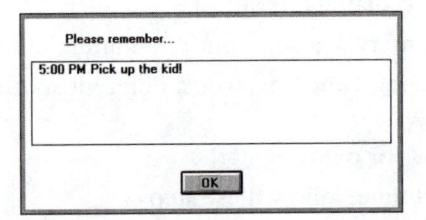

To turn off the alarm, follow the same procedure.

When the appointed time arrives, the alarm sounds a beep (unless you have turned off the sound), and the Alarm dialog box flashes to remind you of your appointment.

Using Calendar's Two Views

As stated previously, Calendar has two views: Day and Month. The Day view shows the details of each day's appointments. The Month view shows an overview of an entire month.

To Track Appointments with Calendar

Switching between the views is easy. To switch to the Month view, open the View menu, and choose the **M**onth command. To switch to the Day view, open the View menu, and choose the **D**ay command.

If you have a mouse, you can double-click the date in the status bar to switch between the Month and Day views. In the Month view, you can double-click any date (or select the date and press `↵Enter`) to switch to the Day view for that date.

Viewing Calendar by the Month

Like the Day view, Calendar's Month view shows the current time and date in the status bar below the menus. The day selected in Calendar's Month view is the same day displayed when you switched from the Day view.

In the Month view, today's date appears between angle brackets (> <) (see fig. 7.8).

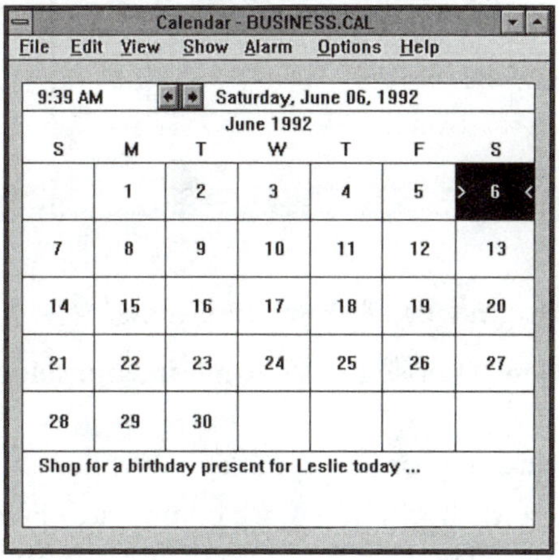

Fig. 7.8
The Month view.

Notice that the scratch pad for the selected day in the Month view is the same as the scratch pad for that day in the Day view. You can move into the scratch pad to type or edit text by either pressing `Tab⇆` or clicking in the scratch pad.

To select a different day in the Month view, move with the arrow keys, or click the day you want to select. You can move in the monthly calendar just as you move in the daily calendar; these movement techniques are listed in table 7.1.

151

Using Desktop Accessories

Exercise 2.6: Marking Important Days

In the Month view, you can mark a date to remind yourself of a special event, such as a report due date, a project completion date, or your sister's birthday. (As a reminder, you should make a note in the scratch pad area to specify *why* you marked the occasion.)

You can use one of five symbols to mark a date in Calendar's Month view (see fig. 7.9).

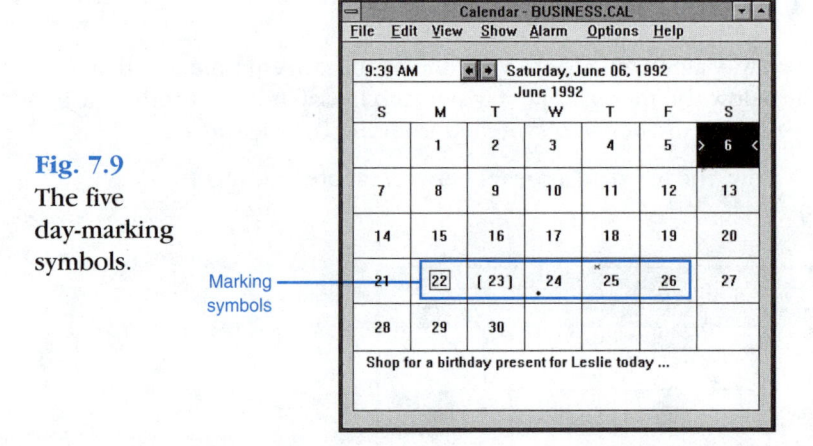

Fig. 7.9
The five day-marking symbols.

To mark a date in Calendar's Month view, follow these steps:

1. To switch to the Month view, choose the **V**iew menu, and select the **M**onth command.
2. Select your birthday by clicking it or pressing the arrow keys.
3. Open the **O**ptions menu, and choose the **M**ark command. (Figure 7.9 shows the possible symbols.) The Day Markings dialog box appears (see fig. 7.10).

Fig. 7.10
The Day Markings dialog box.

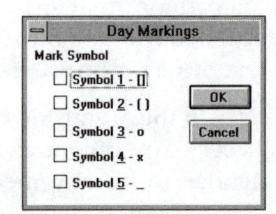

152

To Track Appointments with Calendar

4. Select symbol 4.
5. Choose OK, or press ⏎Enter.
6. Now click in the scratch pad area, and write **Today is my day. Happy Birthday!**

Displaying Different Dates and Times

When you open a new or existing Calendar file, you always see the current date in the Day view or the current month in the Month view. You can move between different dates and times by using the techniques listed in table 7.1. Many of the techniques include commands in the **Show** menu.

Exercise 2.7: Removing Appointments from a Calendar File

Old appointments take up disk space, and you probably don't want them cluttering your Calendar files. You can remove appointments for an individual day or for a range of days. (You can remove appointments only in the currently open Calendar file.)

To remove appointments from the currently open Calendar file, follow these steps:

1. Open the **E**dit menu, and choose the **R**emove command.

   The Remove dialog box appears, enabling you to specify a range of dates to remove (see fig. 7.11).

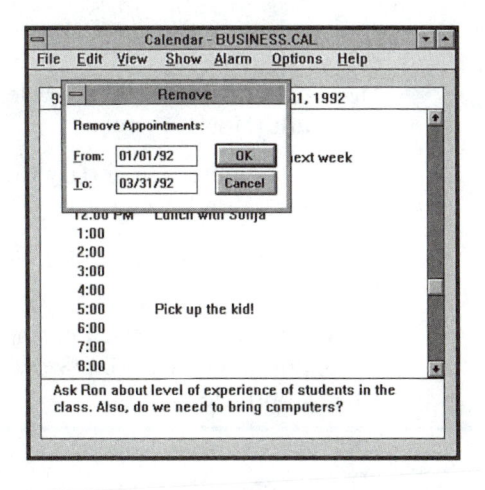

Fig. 7.11
The Remove dialog box.

153

Using Desktop Accessories

2. In the **F**rom text box, type the first date you want to remove, using the format suggested in the box (for example, type **01/01/92**).
3. In the **T**o text box, type the last date you want to remove, using the suggested format.
4. Choose OK, or press ⏎Enter.

Table 7.1   Moving in a Calendar File

Action	To
Open the **S**how menu, and choose the **P**revious command	Move to preceding day or month
Click the left arrow in the status bar	Move to preceding day or month
Open the **S**how menu, and choose the **N**ext command	Move to the next day or month
Click the right arrow in the status bar	Move to the next day or month
Open the **S**how menu, and choose the **T**oday command	Move to the current date
Open the **S**how menu, choose the **D**ate command, type the date (such as **9/1/92**), and press ⏎Enter	Move to a specific date
Press ↑ or ↓	Move to a different time (Day view) or month (Month view)
Press PgUp or PgDn	Move to a different time (Day view) or month (Month view)
Click the scroll bar arrows	Move to a different time (only Day view)
Press Tab⇥	Move between the scratch pad and the appointment area (Day view) or date (Month view)

If you want to remove appointments from just one date, type the date in the **From** text box, and leave the **To** text box empty.

Closing a Calendar File and Exiting the Program

You can close a Calendar file in two ways: open another file or close the Calendar program. To open a new or existing file, open the **File** menu, and choose the **New** or **Open** command. To close the Calendar program, open the **File** menu, and choose the **Exit** command.

Objective 3: To Make Calculations with Calculator

Like the calculator you may keep in your desk drawer, the Windows Calculator is small, but it can save you much time (and help prevent mistakes, too). The Calculator performs all the math of a standard calculator—addition, subtraction, multiplication, and division—but has some added advantages. For example, you can keep the Calculator on-screen alongside other programs, and you can copy numbers between the Calculator and other programs.

The standard Windows Calculator works so much like a pocket calculator that you need little help getting started. See figure 7.12 for a look at the Calculator.

Fig. 7.12
The Windows Calculator.

The Calculator's "keypad" contains familiar number keys, along with memory and math keys. A display window just above the keypad shows the numbers you enter and the results of calculations. The Scientific view of the Calculator (described in a following section) performs more advanced calculations.

Using Desktop Accessories

Although you cannot change the size of the Calculator as you can change other Windows programs, you can minimize the Calculator to an icon so that it's available as you work in another program.

Opening and Closing the Calculator

Open the Calculator program just as you open any Windows program—by double-clicking the Calculator icon in the Accessories group window, or by pressing the arrow keys to select the icon and then pressing [↵Enter]. The Calculator opens in the view (Standard or Scientific) in which it was last displayed.

To close the Calculator program, open the Control menu: with the mouse, click the square to the left of the title bar; with the keyboard, press [Alt] and then the space bar, and choose the **Close** command. If you plan to use the Calculator frequently, minimize it to an icon instead of closing it; that way, you can access it quickly when you need it.

Exercise 3.1: Using the Calculator

Operating the Windows Calculator is nearly the same as operating a desk calculator—you "press" the appropriate buttons (by selecting them), and the result displays at the top of the Calculator.

To use the mouse to select numbers and math functions on the Calculator, click the keys just as you press buttons on any calculator. Numbers appear in the display window as you click them, and results appear after you perform calculations.

Operating the Calculator with the keyboard is just as easy. Enter numbers with either the numeric keypad or the numbers across the top of your keyboard. To calculate, press the keys on the keyboard that match the Calculator's keys. For example, if the Calculator button reads +, press [+] on your keyboard.

The basic math functions are easy to perform. For instance, to add 2 plus 2, choose **2**, choose **+**, choose **2**, choose **=**. These selections produce the formula 2+2=.

To use the Calculator to add (+), subtract (–), multiply (*), or divide (/), follow these steps:

To Make Calculations with Calculator

1. Enter **8883**. The number appears in the display area at the top of the Calculator.
2. Choose the mathematical function *.
3. Enter the second number, **939**. This number now appears in the display area.
4. Choose the = button on the Calculator, or press =| on the keyboard. The result, 8341137, appears in the display.

   The other three math functions—finding a square root, calculating a percentage, and inverting a number (the 1/x button on the Calculator)—operate differently.

To find a square root, follow these steps:

1. Choose the **sqrt** button, or press @.
2. The result, 2888.10266438, appears in the display.

To calculate a percentage, follow these steps:

1. Enter the number **40**.
2. Choose the * button (for multiply), or press *.
3. Enter **50**.
4. Choose the % button, or press %| to display the result: 20, or half of 40.

For example, to find 15 percent of 80, enter **80*15%**. The result, 12, is displayed in the Calculator's display area.

Note: Be sure to press the C button to clear all numbers and functions after calculating a percentage.

The Calculator can work with positive or negative numbers. A negative number is indicated by a minus (–) sign to its left. To change any number's sign, select the number to display it; then choose the +/- button, or press F9.

Editing Numbers in the Calculator Display

Three buttons on the Calculator—C, CE, and Back—are used for editing a number or function. These buttons (and their keystroke alternatives) carry out the operations listed in table 7.2.

157

Using Desktop Accessories

Table 7.2 Editing in Calculator

Calculator Button	Keystroke Alternative	Function
C	[Esc]	Clears (erases) the Calculator of all numbers and functions
CE	[Del]	Deletes the displayed value
Back	[←Backspace]	Deletes the last number in the displayed value

Working with the Calculator's Memory

You can use the Calculator's memory to store numbers. The memory holds a single number, which starts as zero. You can add to, display, or clear that number; or you can store a different number in memory. You can display the number in memory at any time and perform calculations on the number, just as you can on any other number. Any time a number is stored in memory, the letter M appears in the box above the sqrt button on the Calculator. The Calculator's memory functions are listed in table 7.3.

Table 7.3 Calculator's Memory Functions

Calculator Button	Keystroke Alternative	Function
MC	[Ctrl]+[L]	Clears (erases) the memory
MR	[Ctrl]+[R]	Reveals (displays) the value in memory
MS	[Ctrl]+[M]	Stores the displayed value in memory
M+	[Ctrl]+[M]	Adds the displayed value to memory

To Make Calculations with Calculator

One use for the Calculator's memory is to sum a series of subtotals. For example, you can sum the first series of numbers and then add that sum to the memory by clicking the M+ button or pressing `Ctrl`+`P`. Then clear the display, and calculate the second subtotal. Add the subtotal to memory. Continue until you have added all the subtotals to memory; then display the value in memory by clicking the MR button or pressing `Ctrl`+`R`.

Exercise 3.2: Copying a Number from the Calculator into Another Program and Back Again

When working with many numbers or complex numbers, you are less likely to make mistakes if you copy the Calculator results into another program instead of retyping the results. The Calculator is easy to use with other Windows programs and DOS programs.

To copy a number from the Calculator into another program, follow these steps:

1. Perform the math calculations required to divide 22 by 7 so that 3.142857142857 appears in the Calculator's display area. (That's pi to some of you.)
2. Open the **E**dit menu, and choose the **C**opy command to copy the displayed value (or press `Ctrl`+`C`).
3. Activate your word processing program, into which you want to copy the number.
4. Position the insertion point where you want to copy the number.
5. Open the **E**dit menu, and choose the **P**aste command (or its equivalent in the new program).

You can copy a number from another program and paste it into the Calculator. When the number is in the Calculator, you can perform calculations with the number and then copy the result back into the other program.

To copy a number from another program into the Calculator, follow these steps:

1. Change the number by deleting all the decimal places.
2. Select the number.
3. Open the **E**dit menu, and choose the **C**opy command (or its equivalent for that program).
4. Activate the Calculator, open the **E**dit menu, and choose the **P**aste command.

159

Using Desktop Accessories

Exercise 3.3: Using the Scientific Calculator

If you have ever written an equation wider than a sheet of paper, you're a good candidate for using the Scientific Calculator. This special version of the Calculator offers many scientific functions (see fig. 7.13).

Fig. 7.13
The Scientific Calculator.

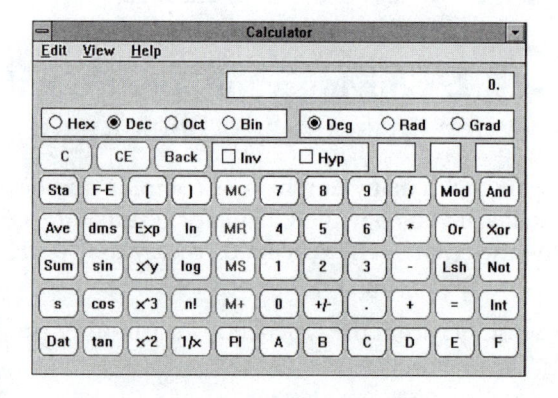

To display the Scientific Calculator, follow these steps:

1. Activate the Calculator.
2. Open the **V**iew menu, and choose the **S**cientific command.

The Scientific Calculator works the same as the Standard Calculator, but contains many advanced functions.

The advanced functions of the Scientific Calculator aren't described here, but they're well documented in the Calculator's **Help** command. To learn more about using the Help feature, refer to "Getting Help" in Chapter 3.

Objective 4: To Watch the Clock

Windows comes equipped with a standard clock, which you can display on the computer screen in almost any size by simply resizing the clock's window. When you minimize the Clock program to an icon at the bottom of the screen, you can still read the hands or digital readout (see fig. 7.14).

To Watch the Clock

The Clock program has one menu—the Settings menu. From this menu you can choose whether to display the clock in Analog or Digital view. The Analog view shows a round clock face with ticking hands; the Digital view shows a numerical readout of the time. You can change the font used in the Digital view. In either view, you can remove the title bar and choose whether you want to display seconds and the date (in the title bar). Windows remembers the settings you choose and uses those settings the next time you start the Clock program.

Fig. 7.14
The Clock.

Exercise 4.1: Varying the Clock Settings

To change the settings for the Clock, follow these simple steps:

1. Open the Settings menu, and choose the Analog command to display a clock with hands. Choose the Digital command to display a clock with numbers.
2. Choose Set Font to change the font used in Digital view.
3. Choose No Title to remove the title bar from the clock display. Double-click anywhere on the screen to put the title bar back on the screen.
4. Choose Seconds to display seconds (or deselect Seconds to remove seconds from the display).
5. Choose Date to display the date (or deselect Date to remove the date from the display).

The time displayed by the clock is based on your computer's internal clock (if it has one) or the time you specified when you started your computer. If the time on the clock is inaccurate, use the Control Panel to reset the clock. The Control Panel is part of the Main group.

Using Desktop Accessories

Objective 5: To Develop Skills with Solitaire and Minesweeper

The discussion of the games Solitaire and Minesweeper is included at the *end* of the chapter for a good reason: many Windows users stay up until the wee hours of the morning trying to beat their computer at a challenging game! You have a good excuse for playing these games: you can claim that you're developing your strategic skills and learning how to use the mouse more adeptly.

Opening and Closing Solitaire and Minesweeper

Open either game by double-clicking its icon in the Program Manager. Both games are included in a group window called Games, rather than in the Accessories group window, which contains the other Windows accessory programs. Close either game by choosing Exit from the **Game** menu.

Playing Solitaire

When you start the Solitaire game, you see a screen with three active areas: the *deck* in the upper left corner of the playing area, four *suit stacks* in the upper right corner of the playing area (the stacks start out empty), and seven *row stacks* in the bottom half of the screen (see fig. 7.15).

The object of the game is to move all the cards out of the deck, on to the row stacks in the middle of the playing field, and from there to the suit stacks at the top right corner of the screen. You build the row stacks in descending order and in alternating colors; you build the suit stacks upward, in sequential order, from ace to king, one suit per stack, in the same color. Suit stacks must start with an ace.

To move a card between the stacks or from the deck to the stacks, drag the card you want to move. When you release a card over a valid position, the card stays in that position. In the lower stacks, you can move either a single card at a time or a group of cards.

To get new cards, click the deck to turn over the top card, or move cards off face-down cards in the lower stacks. Click face-down cards to turn them over.

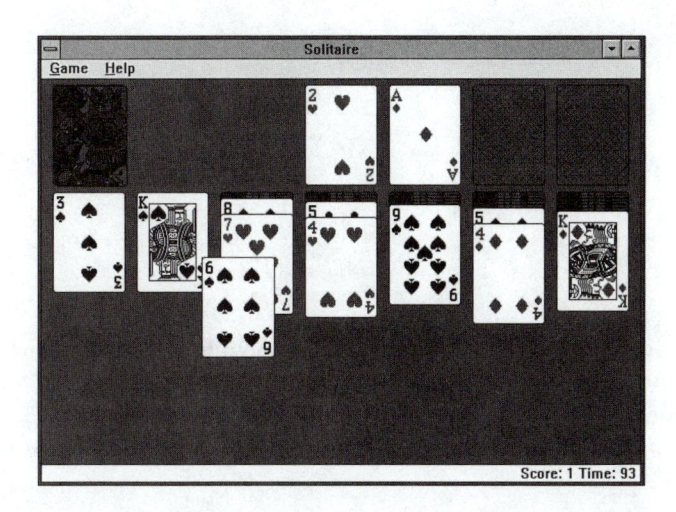

To Develop Skills with Solitaire and Minesweeper

Fig. 7.15
A Solitaire game in progress.

Solitaire offers several options. Open the **G**ame menu, and choose the **D**eck command to choose a different deck illustration. Open the **G**ame menu, and choose the **O**ptions command to select the **D**raw (one or three cards) and **S**coring options. Solitaire even has an Undo command in the **G**ame menu to undo your last action.

When you're finished playing and want to start a new game, open the **G**ame menu, and choose the **D**eal command. To learn the rules of Solitaire, browse through the information in the **H**elp command.

Playing Minesweeper

When you open Minesweeper, you are faced with a grid of squares that represents a mine field (see fig. 7.16). The goal of the game is to mark all the mines; if you step on a mine, the game is over.

When you step on a square, three outcomes are possible: the square contains a mine, and the game therefore ends; the square does not contain a mine, and your Minesweeper indicates that no mines are in the surrounding eight squares; or the square does not contain a mine, and your Minesweeper indicates that a certain number of mines are in the surrounding eight squares (displaying the number in the square).

Using Desktop Accessories

Fig. 7.16
What happens when you step on a mine.

As you successfully uncover squares without stepping on a mine, the information provided by Minesweeper helps you deduce which squares contain mines. When you know a square contains a mine, you can mark that square, effectively deactivating that mine. The idea is to mark all the mines before you step on any of them.

To uncover a square, click it. If the square does not contain a mine, either a number appears in the square, indicating the number of mines in the surrounding eight squares, or a blank space appears. If the square contains a number, you can then try to deduce which of the surrounding squares contain mines, and mark those squares. To mark a mine, click the square with the right mouse button.

You can clear the squares around an uncovered square if you have marked all the mines around that square. To clear the squares, point to the uncovered square, and click both mouse buttons. If you try to clear the squares and you have not marked enough mines, nothing happens. For example, if the number *3* appears in the square, but you have marked only two squares, you cannot clear the surrounding squares. If you have incorrectly marked the surrounding mines, the game ends when you attempt to clear the squares. For example, if you know that two mines are surrounding a square, but you mark the wrong ones, the game ends when you attempt to uncover the surrounding squares. For this reason, haphazardly marking squares does not pay.

From the **Game** menu, you can choose from three predefined skill levels of Minesweeper: **Beginner**, **Intermediate**, and **Expert**. The difference between the levels is the size of the mine field (and therefore the total number of mines). You can use the **Game Customize** command to define your own mine field. For additional information on the rules of Minesweeper, and some strategic hints on playing the game, choose the **Help** command.

7

164

Chapter Summary

The Windows desktop accessories are so convenient to use that they can quickly become part of your daily business tools. Calendar is useful every day. After checking appointments and your To Do list, you can minimize these accessories to icons, or close them if you need maximum memory. The Calculator is a handy tool for quick mathematical functions, and the Clock tells time even when minimized to an icon. Solitaire and Minesweeper challenge you to a little fun at the end of the day.

Chapter 8 introduces you to Windows Paintbrush.

Testing Your Knowledge

True/False Questions

1. While in Calendar, to move the insertion point to the next line, you press Ctrl + Alt + Del.
2. While in Calendar, you can edit text in the scratch pad and the appointment area just as you edit text in any Windows program.
3. In Calendar, you can remove appointments only one at a time to ensure that you don't lose any dates.
4. When the Alarm dialog box displays in Calendar to remind you of your appointment, you can choose Snooze to continue working.
5. You can view the Calendar in either Day or Month view.

Multiple Choice Questions

1. Using the Calculator, if you enter 50, *, 10, %, the result is
   A. 5.
   B. 500.
   C. .5.
   D. 40.

165

Using Desktop Accessories

2. When using the Clock, you may select **N**o Title to remove the title bar from the clock display. How do you restore the title bar?
    A. Press the right mouse button.
    B. Press `Ctrl`, `T`, `T`.
    C. Click anywhere on the screen.
    D. Double-click anywhere on the screen.
3. Which of the following applications is *not* part of the Windows accessory group?
    A. Paintbrush
    B. File Manager
    C. Calendar
    D. Character Map
4. When editing numbers in the Calculator display, which keystroke clears the calculator of all numbers and functions?
    A. `Home`
    B. `Esc`
    C. `Ctrl`
    D. `↓`
5. What is the extension that Calendar automatically assigns a new file?
    A. CLD
    B. XLS
    C. DOC
    D. CAL

Fill-in-the-Blank Questions

1. To display a clock with hands, select the _____ command.
2. At the bottom of each daily or monthly Calendar window is a three-line area called the _____ pad.
3. When you set the alarm in Calendar, a small _____ appears to the left of the appointed time in the Calendar window.
4. You can open the Calculator—as you open any Windows program—by _____ the icon.
5. The Calculator button _____ deletes the displayed value.

Testing Your Knowledge

Review: Short Projects

1. Using the Calendar

   Practice using the Calendar by creating a calendar for your work and life. Put in important assignment dates, personal dates, and events to remember. Use the scratch pad liberally. Use the daily appointment sheet by creating it (and printing it for use if you are not around a computer all day). During your sessions at the computer, use the alarm to remind yourself of deadlines and important times. What do you think of this accessory? Make a printout of your efforts, and evaluate its usefulness.

2. The Value of Games

   Practice playing the games Solitaire and Minesweeper. Can you see why people who enjoy playing computer games may be initially more comfortable using a Windows environment? Make a list of the skills you use while playing these games. What did you learn about not only the games, but the rules and conventions of the environment? Write a two-page paper on the value of learning computer games as an introduction to the use of computers. Are there any games you would like to see created? Can you make a case concerning skill transferability? You may be on your way to a new career!

3. Using the Calculator and Clock

   The Calculator and Clock are handy to have in your environment if you are comfortable keeping them on the desktop and flipping to them. Practice using both these tools. Try different formats and sizes. Try using them as minimized at the bottom of the screen and as an additional window. Which way is most comfortable? How do you like to retrieve them if they are minimized—by using Ctrl + Tab, minimizing your current work window, or another way? Experiment with different methods so that you can use these accessories in a natural way, the way you might look up at the clock or grab your calculator to do some calculations. Write down your decisions and reasoning.

Review: Long Projects

1. Using the Accessories

   As CEO and President of Bella's Ice Cream Parlor, you have many important dates to remember. Use the Windows Calendar program to track the delivery of ice cream, payroll and payroll tax, staff meetings,

Using Desktop Accessories

cleaning and maintenance of the facilities, booking of entertainment, and any other pertinent dates. Use Notepad to jot down important points to remember as you enter the Calendar dates. Can any other Desktop Accessories be helpful in your job? List all the uses and specific accessories you will use. Make a printout of the Calendar file, Notepad file, and any other tools you have used.

2. Sharing Accessories

Suppose that you are working on a project with five to seven other people. You each have your own calendar system on your personal computer. Can you think of the advantages of having your calendars connected so that you could plan a meeting or check on a deadline? Calendars are just one example of software used by a group of people—a very hot topic right now in the business world and in the computer industry. Some people, like Andrew Grove, President and CEO of Intel Corp., the largest maker of computer chips, think that shared software will be the next big wave of personal productivity growth. Mr. Grove calls this concept Computer Supported Collaboration, but it is also commonly known as Groupware. Do some research in the library of business periodicals, and find out what the fuss is all about. Write a short paper on Groupware and how you think it might be useful.

Using Windows Paintbrush

8

You may wonder why you would ever need a program like Windows Paintbrush. You may think that you're not the artistic type—what's more, you may think that you don't have time for Paintbrush because you have "real" work to do. What does drawing pictures have to do with work?

Plenty. Think about a long report filled with facts and numbers—but not one illustration. How many people want to read a report like that? But imagine the same report spiced up with a few well-placed charts and graphs. Those illustrations not only would make the report more inviting to readers but also would help clarify otherwise abstract points.

Windows Paintbrush is a simple program that you can use to create all kinds of illustrations—from free-form drawings to precise charts and graphs. You can copy the illustrations into many other Windows accessory programs, such as Write, Cardfile, or Notepad. Or you can use the illustrations in Windows programs, such as Word for Windows, a powerful word processing program; PageMaker, a desktop publishing program; or PowerPoint, a slide-show presentation program.

Objectives

1. To Use the Toolbox, Line-Width Box, and Palette
2. To Save a Drawing
3. To Use the Painting Tools
4. To Add Text
5. To Edit a Drawing
6. To Print a Drawing

Using Windows Paintbrush

Key Terms in This Chapter	
Draw	To draw a line, box, circle, or polygon in Paintbrush.
Paint	To paint a free-form line or shape in Paintbrush.
Toolbox	The box, on the left of the Paintbrush screen, that contains all the drawing and painting tools.
Line-width box	The box, at the bottom left of the Paintbrush screen, from which you can select the width for lines, for the borders of shapes, and for some tools.
Palette	The palette of colors (if you have a color monitor) or shades (if you have a monochrome monitor) you can use in your Paintbrush drawings.
Zoom in or out	To enlarge a drawing so that you can edit it dot by dot, or to reduce the drawing so that you can see the whole page.
Font	An alphabet of letters in a particular style.

8

Paintbrush is a simple program, but it's powerful enough to illustrate your reports, presentations, newsletters, instruction manuals, training guides—anything you create on your computer (see fig. 8.1).

Fig. 8.1
A Paintbrush illustration.

170

Starting Windows Paintbrush

To start Paintbrush, you must first start Windows (refer to Chapter 2, "Getting Started," if you need help starting Windows). When you first start Windows, a window called the Program Manager appears on-screen. The Program Manager contains at least four program groups: Main, Accessories, StartUp, and Games. A group called Applications is also among the program groups if you specified that it be created when you installed Windows. (Because you can create your own program groups, you may see more than four or five groups on-screen.) The program groups appear as *icons* (pictures) or as open windows.

You can expand the Accessories icon into a window by double-clicking the icon or pressing Ctrl+Tab until the Accessories icon is selected and then pressing Enter. When the Accessories program group is open as a window, you can see the programs it contains. Windows Paintbrush is a Windows accessory program located in the Accessories program group (see fig. 8.2).

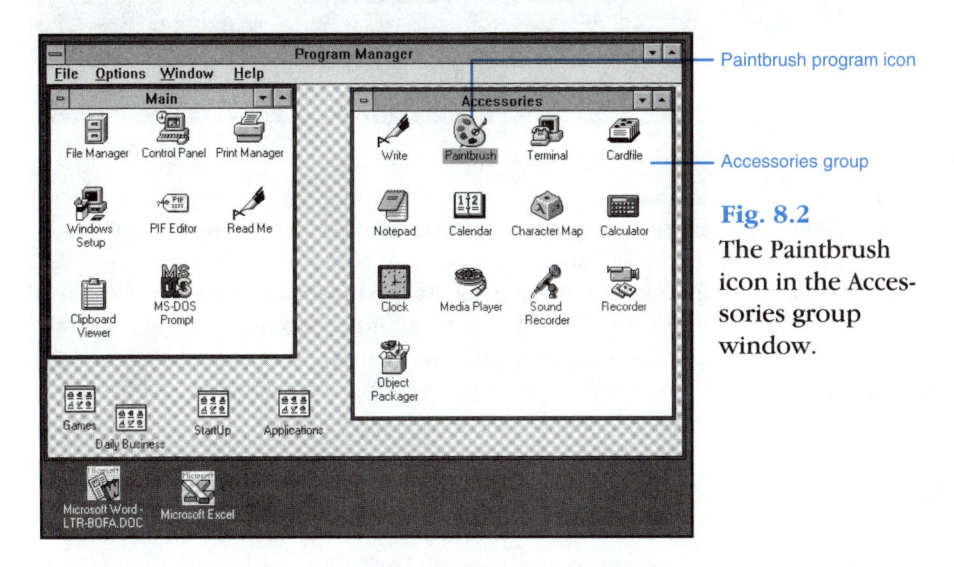

Fig. 8.2
The Paintbrush icon in the Accessories group window.

To start the Paintbrush program, double-click the Paintbrush icon; or with the Accessories window selected, press an arrow key until you select the Paintbrush icon and then press Enter. This procedure is the same one you use to start any Windows program.

When you first open Paintbrush, a new window appears, containing a blank Paintbrush document. Some parts of the window are like those in other

Using Windows Paintbrush

windows (see fig. 8.3). A title bar across the top tells you the name of the program and the name of the document (untitled until you name it). A menu bar is below the title bar, and scroll bars are located on the right and bottom sides of the window.

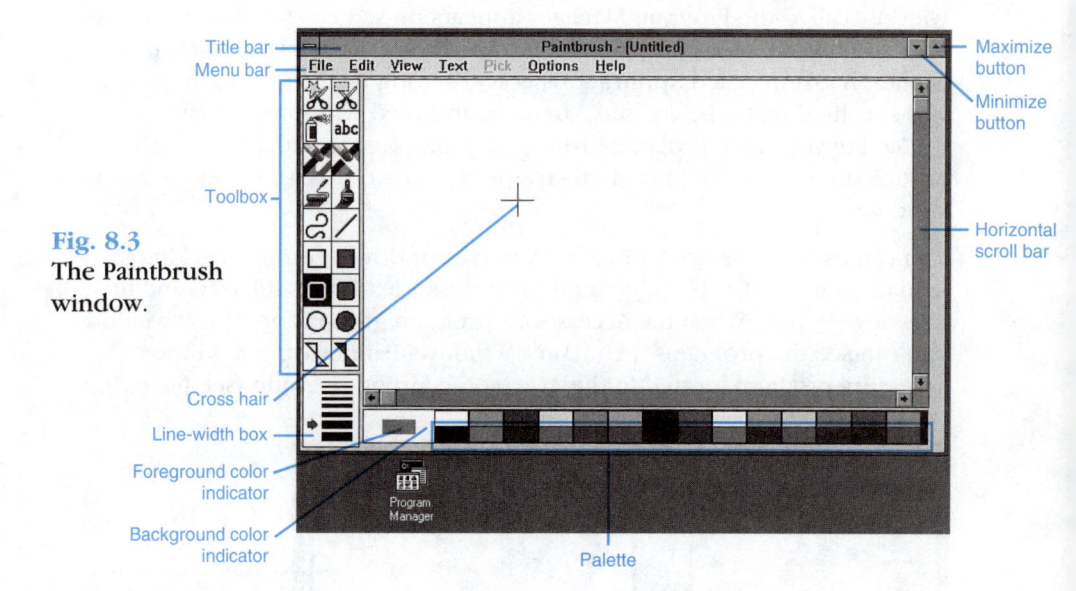

Fig. 8.3
The Paintbrush window.

Besides these familiar window parts, Paintbrush has several unique features. A *toolbox* appears along the left side of the screen, containing the tools you use to create a Paintbrush drawing or painting. At the lower left corner is the *line-width box*, which you use to select the width of lines. A *palette* at the bottom of the screen contains the colors or shades you use to fill shapes. *Foreground* and *background color indicators* show you which colors are selected from the palette.

Also on-screen is a pointer that moves as you move the mouse. The pointer may appear as a cross hair (when you select a drawing tool), as a special tool (when you select an eraser tool or a painting tool), as an arrow (when you move the pointer over a menu name or scroll bar), or as an I-beam (when you type text).

Understanding How Paintbrush Works

Before you plunge into using Paintbrush, you should understand how the program works.

To Use the Toolbox, Line-Width Box, and Palette

The blank area of the screen is the drawing area, where you create your Paintbrush masterpiece. To draw or paint, you must first select a tool by pointing to its icon in the toolbox and clicking the mouse button. For example, if you want to draw a straight line, you select the Line tool. After you select a tool, move the pointer into the drawing area, where the pointer becomes a cross hair or another drawing (or painting) icon.

Although the procedure varies from tool to tool, you generally draw or paint by holding down the mouse button, dragging the mouse, then releasing the mouse button. To draw a line, for instance, position the cross hair where you want the line to begin, hold down the mouse button, drag the cross hair to where you want the line to end, and release the mouse button.

The line-width box and the palette function as accessories to the tools. For instance, when you draw a line, it appears in a certain width. You determine that width by selecting a line from the line-width box. Similarly, when you draw a filled shape, its fill pattern is determined by the color or shading choices you make in the palette.

You can make additional refinements to a drawing by selecting commands from the Paintbrush menus. For example, you can select a type style or size for any text you add to the drawing. You can also tilt, flip, or shrink objects in the drawing.

Objective 1: To Use the Toolbox, Line-Width Box, and Palette

The toolbox is the heart of Paintbrush, containing all the tools you need to create the lines and shapes that make up a drawing (see fig. 8.4). The exercises in this chapter illustrate some of the tools, but you can probably figure out how to use them just by trying them. Don't be afraid to experiment.

You use the Scissors and Pick tools to select objects in a drawing or to select within the drawing areas that contain several objects.

The Airbrush, Paint Roller, and Brush tools are for painting. The Airbrush tool sprays a translucent mist of paint. The Paint Roller tool fills a shape with paint. And the Brush tool paints a line of color. Before using any of these tools, make sure that the color or shade with which you want to paint is selected in the palette.

With the Text tool, you can add text to a drawing. You use the Text menu to control the appearance of text.

Using Windows Paintbrush

Fig. 8.4
The toolbox.

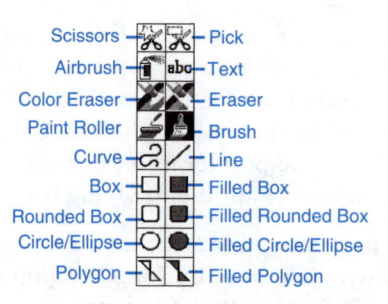

```
Scissors ─ ✂ ✂ ─ Pick
Airbrush ─ 🜸 abc ─ Text
Color Eraser ─ ✕ ✕ ─ Eraser
Paint Roller ─ 🖌 🖌 ─ Brush
Curve ─ ∽ / ─ Line
Box ─ □ ■ ─ Filled Box
Rounded Box ─ ▢ ▣ ─ Filled Rounded Box
Circle/Ellipse ─ ○ ● ─ Filled Circle/Ellipse
Polygon ─ ⌐ ◣ ─ Filled Polygon
```

The Color Eraser and Eraser tools enable you to change the colors in your painting or erase parts of the painting.

The Curve and Line tools are for drawing lines. The Curve tool draws curved lines, and the Line tool draws straight lines. Be sure to choose a line width from the line-width box before you draw a line.

The Box and Rounded Box tools draw boxes. The Box tools (filled and unfilled) draw boxes with right-angle corners; the Rounded Box tools (filled and unfilled) draw boxes with rounded corners. Before you draw any box, choose a line width to define the width of its borders. If you are drawing a filled box, select a fill color or shade from the palette.

Use the Circle/Ellipse tools (filled and unfilled) to draw circles and ovals. To draw a perfect circle, hold down ⇧Shift as you draw. Select a line width before you draw a circle or ellipse, and if you draw a filled shape, select a color or shade from the palette.

The Polygon tools (filled and unfilled) draw multisided objects with straight sides. Select a line width before you draw a polygon, and if you draw a filled polygon, select a color or shade from the palette.

Using the Line-Width Box

At the lower left corner on-screen is the line-width box, containing eight lines of different widths. An arrow points to the selected line width (see fig. 8.5).

The selected line width determines the width of the lines you draw and the width of the borders around boxes, circles, and polygons. If, for example, you select the thin line width at the top of the box, the next line you draw is thin. The selected line width also controls the width of some tools, such as the Airbrush, Brush, and Eraser tools. Selecting a line width doesn't change the width of lines already drawn.

To Use the Toolbox, Line-Width Box, and Palette

Fig. 8.5
The line-width box.

Using the Paintbrush Palette

At the bottom of the Paintbrush screen is a palette containing the colors or shades you use to draw, paint, and fill objects (see fig. 8.6). If you have a color monitor, the palette shows colors; if you use a monochrome monitor, the palette shows shades of gray. You must select the colors or shades you want to use.

Fig. 8.6
The color palette.

Note: Throughout this chapter, the term *color*, when referring to the palette, refers either to colors or to shades, depending on the monitor you have.

You actually get two choices in the palette: a *foreground* color and a *background* color. The foreground color is the color you draw with, using the line or shape tools, and it is the color you paint with when you use one of the painting tools (Airbrush, Paint Roller, or Brush). The foreground color also is the fill color that goes inside filled shapes. The *background* color is the color of the border around the edges of filled shapes and the background color of your screen when you start a new Paintbrush file.

If you look at the left end of the palette, you see a rectangle within a rectangle. These rectangles are foreground and background color indicators—they show you the colors currently selected. The inside rectangle shows the foreground color; the outside rectangle shows the background color. You choose foreground and background colors by clicking them with the mouse: click the *left* mouse button to select a foreground color and the *right* mouse button to select a background color.

Drawing Lines and Shapes

Paintbrush has two line tools, for straight and curved lines, and eight shape tools, for filled and unfilled boxes, circles and ellipses, and polygons. You use a similar process when you draw with any of these tools: select a tool, select a line width, select foreground and background colors, move the pointer into the drawing area (where the pointer becomes a cross hair), and draw the line or shape.

Using Windows Paintbrush

Lines and unfilled shapes are always drawn in the selected line width and selected foreground color. Filled shapes are filled with the selected foreground color and bordered with the selected background color. (If you want a filled shape with no border, select a background color that is the same color as the background of the drawing area—usually white.)

Note: Although you draw lines and shapes with the left mouse button, the right mouse button has a special purpose with the line tools. To undo the line you are drawing, click the right mouse button before you release the left mouse button.

Exercise 1.1: Drawing Straight Lines

The Line tool draws a straight line in the foreground color and in the selected line width. While you're drawing the line, it appears as a thin black line. When you release the mouse button to complete the line, it assumes the selected width and color.

To draw a straight line, follow these steps:

1. Select the Line tool from the toolbox.
2. Choose a line width by moving the pointer to the thinnest line width from the toolbox. Click the left mouse button.
3. Select a foreground color by moving the pointer to blue and clicking the *left* mouse button.
4. Select a background color by moving the pointer to red and clicking the *right* mouse button. You have now selected the line width and foreground and background colors.
5. Move the pointer into the drawing area, where the pointer becomes a cross hair.
6. To begin drawing the lines shown in figure 8.7, position the cross hair where you want the bottom of the left-most vertical line.
7. Press and hold the left mouse button.
8. While holding down the mouse button, drag the cross hair straight up to draw the line.
9. Release the mouse button to complete the line.

    Remember that you can press the right mouse button to cancel a line—as long as you do it *before* you release the left mouse button.
10. Now draw the seven remaining vertical lines in figure 8.7. Remember to choose a new line width for each line.

To Use the Toolbox, Line-Width Box, and Palette

To make the lines "snap to" an invisible vertical, horizontal, or 90-degree axis, whichever is closest to the line you draw, hold down ⇧Shift as you draw.

11. Draw the three heaviest diagonal lines in figure 8.7 by holding ⇧Shift as you draw.

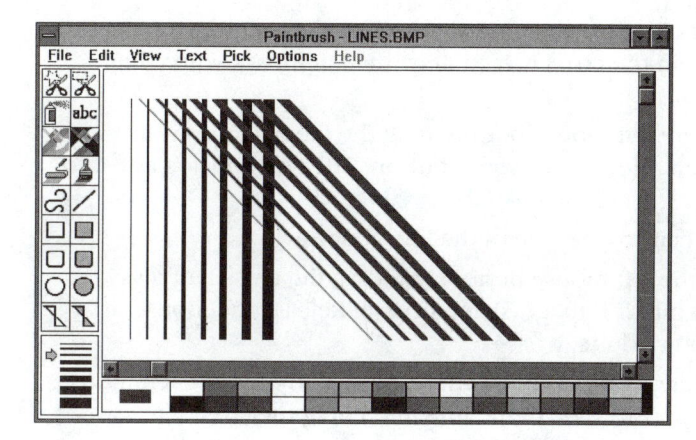

Fig. 8.7
The Line tool draws straight lines.

Exercise 1.2: Drawing Curved Lines

The Curve tool doesn't draw free-form curves; instead, it draws precise C-shaped or S-shaped curves (see fig. 8.8). Using the Curve tool requires a series of three drag movements with the mouse.

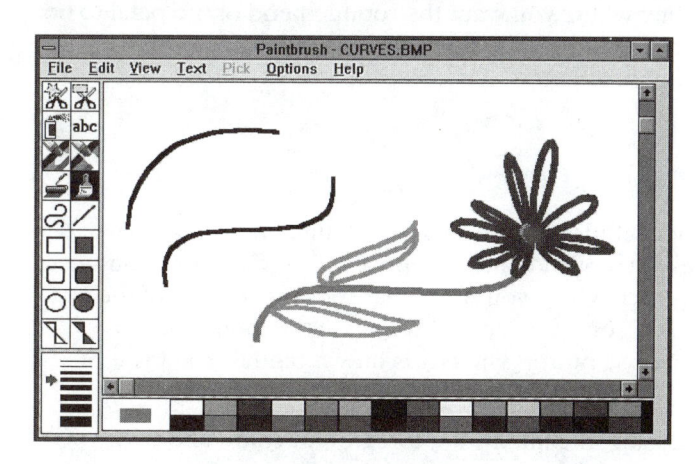

Fig. 8.8
S-curves and C-curves drawn with the Curve tool.

Using Windows Paintbrush

To use the Curve tool, follow these steps:

1. Open the File menu, and choose the New command to start with a new file. Answer No to saving current changes.
2. Select the Curve tool from the toolbox.
3. Select a line width and a foreground color.
4. Move the pointer into the drawing area, where the pointer becomes a cross hair. Position the cross hair to draw the left-most C-curve line seen in figure 8.8.
5. Press and hold the left mouse button, drag the mouse to draw a straight line; then release the mouse button. The line appears as a thin black line.
6. Move the cross hair to one side of the line you drew.
7. Press and hold the left mouse button, and drag the cross hair away from the line to pull it into a C-shaped curve. Release the mouse button when you're done.
8. To change the line to an S-shaped curve, press and hold the left mouse button on the opposite side of the line; then drag the cross hair away from the line to pull the line in the opposite direction. The line is complete when you release the mouse button.

You can cancel your line by clicking the right mouse button before you release the left mouse button.

A second method of using the Curve tool enables you to draw petal shapes. Select the Curve tool, and click once where you want the pointed end of the petal to be, a second time where you want the rounded end of the petal to be, then a third time to the side to indicate the width of the petal. Try drawing a flower like the one in figure 8.8.

Exercise 1.3: Drawing Boxes

The Box tools create four kinds of boxes: filled and unfilled square-corner boxes and filled and unfilled rounded-corner boxes. To draw a box, you select the Box tool you want, click where you want to anchor one corner of the box, drag diagonally to the size you want, and then release the mouse button. When you release the mouse button, the box is drawn (and filled, if you're drawing a filled box).

Note: Be sure that you select the line width, foreground color, and background color before you start.

178

To Use the Toolbox, Line-Width Box, and Palette

To draw a box, follow these steps:

1. Open the File menu, and choose the New command to start with a new file. Answer No to saving current changes.
2. From the toolbox, select the filled Box tool.
3. Move the pointer into the drawing area of the screen, where the pointer becomes a cross hair.
4. Position the cross hair where you want to anchor one corner of the box.
5. Press and hold the left mouse button.
6. Drag the cross hair in any direction to draw the box. Until you release the mouse button, the box appears as a thin black line.
7. Release the mouse button when the box is the size and shape you want. The box assumes the selected line width and color.

If you want to draw a perfectly square box, hold down ⇧Shift as you draw. Figure 8.9 shows various boxes created with the Box tools.

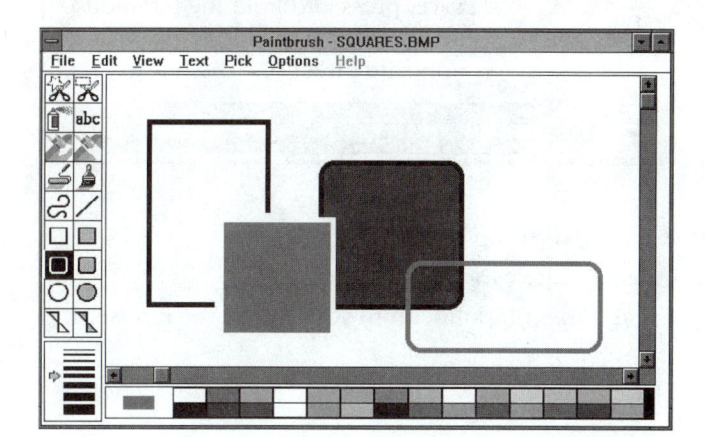

Fig. 8.9 Boxes drawn with the Box tool.

Exercise 1.4: Drawing Circles and Ovals

The Circle/Ellipse tools draw circles and ovals, either filled or unfilled. Both the Circle/Ellipse tools draw oval shapes by default; if you want a perfect circle, hold down ⇧Shift as you draw the shape.

To draw a circle or oval, follow these steps:

1. Open the File menu, and choose the New command to start with a new file. Answer No to saving current changes.

Using Windows Paintbrush

2. Select the unfilled Circle/Ellipse tool from the toolbox.
3. Move the pointer to the drawing area, where the pointer becomes a cross hair.
4. Position the cross hair where you want to start the left circle.
5. For a perfect circle, press and hold the left mouse button as you hold down ⇧Shift.
6. Drag the cross hair away from the starting point to the right until it is the approximate size of the unfilled circle in figure 8.10.

Fig. 8.10
Shapes drawn with the Circle/Ellipse tool.

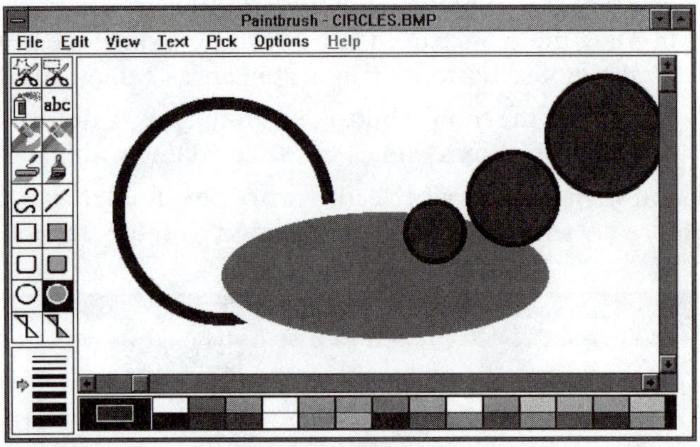

7. Release the mouse button to complete the circle.
8. Create the other ovals and circles seen in figure 8.10.

The circle or oval appears as a thin black line until you release the mouse button.

Exercise 1.5: Drawing Polygons

A polygon is a multisided shape with straight edges. The most familiar example of a polygon is a stop sign—an eight-sided polygon. A stop sign is symmetrical, but the polygons you create with Paintbrush can be any shape and have as many sides as you want.

Drawing a polygon is different from drawing a line or box. First, you draw one side of the polygon just as though you were drawing a line. As you continue drawing, you click to define each corner. Finally, you double-click to close the polygon by connecting the first point to the last point (see fig. 8.11).

To Save a Drawing

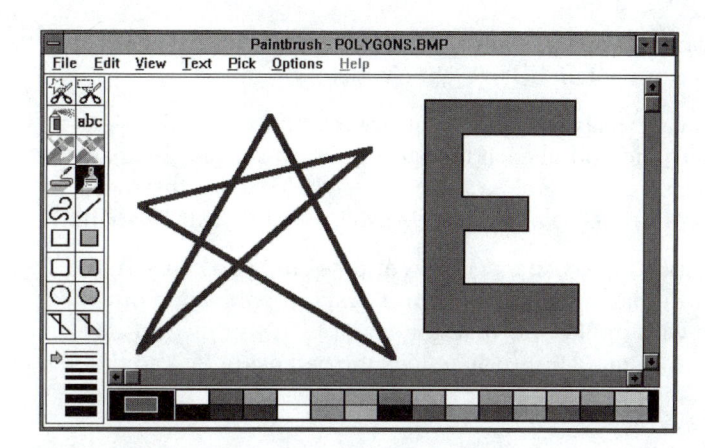

Fig. 8.11
The Polygon tool offers a variety of shapes.

To draw a filled "E" polygon similar to the filled polygon in figure 8.11, follow these steps:

1. Select the filled Polygon tool from the toolbox.
2. Move the pointer into the drawing area, where it becomes a cross hair.
3. Press and hold the left mouse button while pressing ⇧Shift to start the "E" polygon.
4. Drag the cross hair to draw one side of the polygon, and release the mouse button when the line is finished.
5. Position the cross hair where you want the polygon's next corner to appear; then click the mouse button.
6. Create the polygon's remaining corners by positioning the cross hair where you want them and clicking the mouse button. Each time you click, you add a side to the polygon.
7. To complete the polygon, double-click the mouse button to connect the first point to the last point.
8. By holding down ⇧Shift, you were able to create a straight-edged letter *E*. Now try drawing the same *E* without holding down ⇧Shift. Notice that you can still draw an *E*, but the sides are not straight. There may be times when you want this free-form look.

Objective 2: To Save a Drawing

To avoid losing any of your work, save your files frequently. Saving several versions of your evolving artwork is often a good idea. If you're creating a

Using Windows Paintbrush

chart, for example, you might name your successive files CHART01, CHART02, and so on. File names can contain up to eight characters.

Like most programs, Paintbrush saves files in its own file format and assigns a three-letter extension to the end of each file (an extension is like a last name). The extension that Paintbrush assigns to file names is *BMP*. If, for instance, you assign the name PAINTING to a file, Paintbrush saves it as PAINTING.BMP.

If you want to save a drawing to use in a different program, you can save the drawing in a different format. Many graphics and desktop publishing programs are compatible with the PCX format, for example. If you save a Paintbrush drawing in PCX format, Paintbrush assigns the extension PCX to the file name.

Exercise 2.1: Saving a Drawing

To save the Paintbrush file you just created, the "E" polygon, follow these steps:

1. Open the **F**ile menu, and choose the Save **A**s command.

    The Save As dialog box appears.

2. Type **EPOLYGON** in the File **N**ame text box.
3. From the Dri**v**es list, choose the drive on which you want to save the file.
4. From the **D**irectories list box, choose the directory in which you want to save the file.
5. If you want to save your picture in the PCX file format, select PCX file (*.PCX) from the Save File as **T**ype list.
6. Choose OK, or press ⏎Enter.

To resave your file later, without changing its name, open the **E**dit menu, and choose the **S**ave command.

Objective 3: To Use the Painting Tools

The Paintbrush drawing tools are rather constraining. You can draw straight lines, precise curves, and certain specific shapes, but you cannot draw freeform images. If you are more free-natured, you will appreciate Paintbrush's painting tools, which you can use to draw more imaginative shapes. All the painting tools "paint" in the selected foreground color. Before you start,

To Use the Painting Tools

remember to select the color you want by pointing to it and clicking the left mouse button.

Exercise 3.1: Using the Airbrush Tool

The Airbrush tool is much like a can of spray paint—it sprays a translucent mist of color instead of painting a solid color. If you select the Airbrush tool and click the left mouse button once, you get a round dot of misty color. If you click and drag the mouse, you get a misty line.

You control the diameter of an airbrush dot or line by selecting the line width you want from the line-width box: a thin line produces a small dot or thin line; a thicker line produces a larger dot or thicker line. You control the density of the mist by the speed with which you drag the mouse: a fast drag produces a light line; a slow drag produces a much denser airbrushed line.

To use the Airbrush tool, follow these steps:

1. Select the Airbrush tool.
2. Move the pointer into the drawing area, where the pointer becomes a cross hair.
3. Position the cross hair where you want to start the airbrush stroke, like the one seen in figure 8.12.

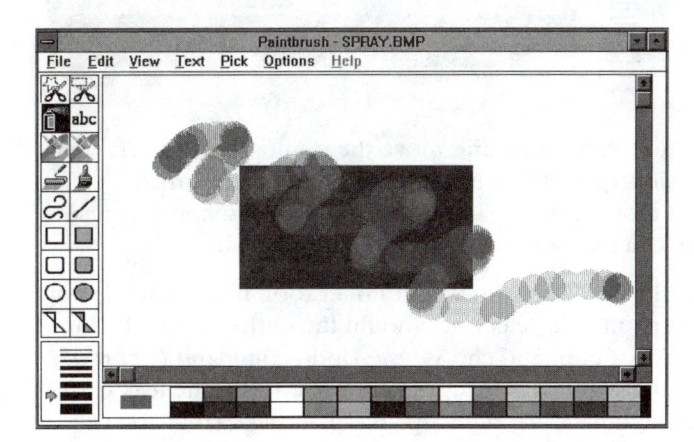

Fig. 8.12
The Airbrush tool works like a can of spray paint.

4. Press and hold the left mouse button.
5. Drag the cross hair to paint the airbrush stroke. Drag slowly for a dense line; drag quickly for a light line.

183

Using Windows Paintbrush

6. Release the mouse button.
7. Practice moving around the screen. Experiment with the way you move the mouse, and notice how the movement affects the density of the spray.

Exercise 3.2: Using the Paint Roller Tool

The Paint Roller tool fills a shape with a color. The shape you fill can be an open shape or one already filled with a solid color (but not with a pattern). In either case, the Paint Roller tool fills the shape with the selected foreground color (see fig. 8.13).

Fig. 8.13
The Paint Roller fills any shape with the selected foreground color.

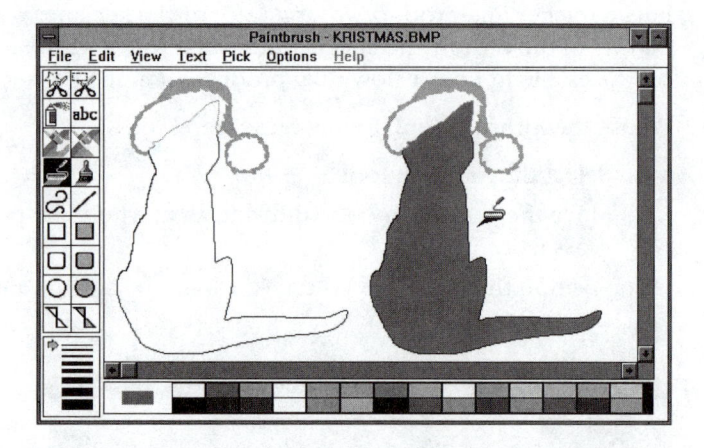

When you select the Paint Roller tool and move the pointer into the drawing area, the pointer turns into a tool that looks like a paint roller spreading paint. The pointed tip of this tool is where paint flows out to fill a shape. Because the tip is pointed, you can use this tool to fill a very small shape.

Be careful when you fill a shape with the Paint Roller tool. If the shape is not completely closed, the paint will "leak out" and fill the entire screen. If your paint leaks, open the Edit menu, and choose the Undo command (or press Ctrl+Z); then close the shape and try again. If you can't see the leak clearly, use the View Zoom In command to "blow up" the painting so that you can find and patch the leak. (The View Zoom In command is explained under Objective 5 in this chapter.)

To fill your "E" polygon with the Paint Roller tool, follow these steps:

1. Make sure that EPOLYGON is open.

To Use the Painting Tools

2. Select the Paint Roller tool from the toolbox.
3. Choose a foreground color from the palette by clicking the color you want with the left mouse button.
4. Position the pointed tip of the Paint Roller tool inside the shape you want to fill.
5. Click the left mouse button.

Use the Paint Roller tool to fill any shape with the selected foreground color. Have some fun with colors, and see how you can make the *E* jump off the screen!

You can also use the Paint Roller to fill a solid shape or line. Position the tip of the Paint Roller tool on the shape or line; then click. You cannot use the Paint Roller to fill a blended color made up of dots. You can fill a solid red box with blue, for example, but you cannot fill a blended green shape with blue.

Exercise 3.3: Using the Brush Tool

The Brush tool paints an opaque stroke of the selected foreground color. You can modify this versatile tool in two ways: by selecting a line width and by selecting a different brush shape. (Six brush shapes are available; if you don't choose one, you get the default square brush shape.) Like the other painting tools, the Brush tool enables you to paint free-form shapes.

To use the Brush tool, follow these steps:

1. Open a new file.
2. Select the Brush tool from the toolbox.
3. Select a foreground color from the palette.
4. Select a line width from the line-width box.
5. Move the pointer into the drawing area, where it assumes the shape of the brush you selected. The default brush shape is square.
6. Position the Brush tool to write the word *Calligraphy*, as seen in figure 8.14.
7. Press and hold the left mouse button, and drag the brush to paint a brush stroke.
8. Release the mouse button.

Using a line-shaped Brush tool, you can draw a line of variable width. You can change the Brush shapes, using the **Options** menu and selecting the **B**rush Shapes command. The Brush Shapes dialog box shows six different brush shapes (see fig. 8.15).

185

Using Windows Paintbrush

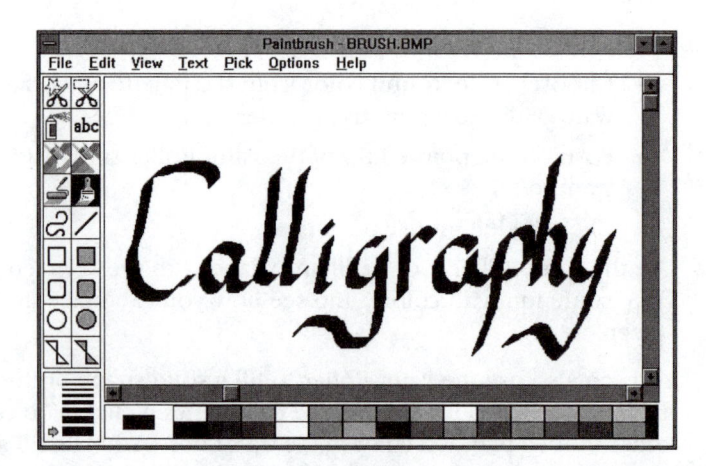

Fig. 8.14
The versatility of the Brush tool.

Fig. 8.15
The Brush Shapes dialog box.

To change the brush shape, double-click the Brush tool to display the Brush Shapes dialog box; then double-click the brush shape you want to select.

Objective 4: To Add Text

A picture may be worth a thousand words, but sometimes a few words can clarify your message. Using the Text tool, you can type text in your drawing by using any of several fonts, styles, sizes, and colors.

Typing with Paintbrush has some limitations. Unlike a word processing program, Paintbrush doesn't enable you to edit your text after you finish typing it. You can press `Backspace` to correct typing errors *while* you are typing, but after you click the mouse button, you can no longer use the Text tool to edit your text. Paintbrush also lacks a word-wrap feature; when you reach the edge of the screen, you must press `Enter` to move the insertion point to the next line.

When you type, text appears in the selected font, style, size, and foreground color. You can change any font and color selections *before* you start typing or

To Add Text

while you type—any time before you click the mouse button. The changes apply to all the text you have typed.

You can type text in black or in any color or shade—whatever you select as the foreground color.

Exercise 4.1: Entering and Enhancing Text

To type text, follow these steps:

1. Open a new file.
2. Select the Text tool from the toolbox.
3. Move the pointer into the drawing area, where the pointer becomes an I-beam.
4. Position the I-beam where you want to start typing; then click the left mouse button. The I-beam becomes a blinking cursor, or insertion point.
5. Type the first sentence of text as seen in figure 8.16 (press `↵Enter` when you want to start a new line). If you make a mistake, press `←Backspace` to erase it.

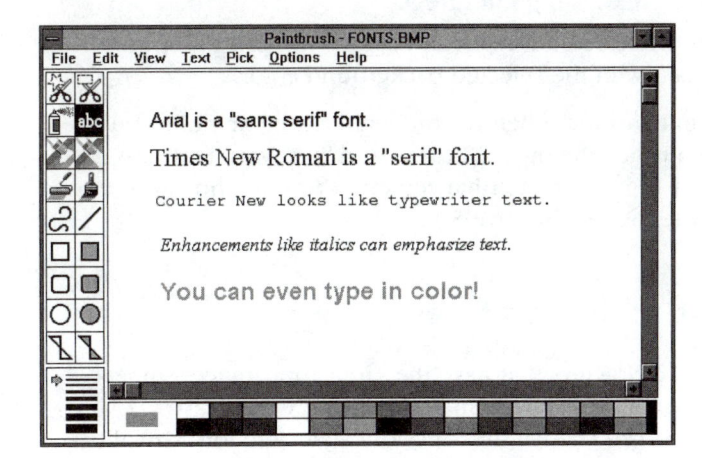

Fig. 8.16
Examples of text fonts.

6. Click the mouse button to "set" the text into your painting, but remember that after you set the text you cannot edit it.

A text enhancement is a variation of the selected font. Paintbrush offers several text enhancements: **R**egular, **B**old, **I**talic, **U**nderline, **O**utline, and **S**hadow (see fig. 8.17). You can use as many enhancements as you like, at the same

187

Using Windows Paintbrush

time. For example, you can type a title that is both bold and underlined. Select **R**egular to return to plain, unenhanced text.

Fig. 8.17
Shadowing is one way of enhancing text.

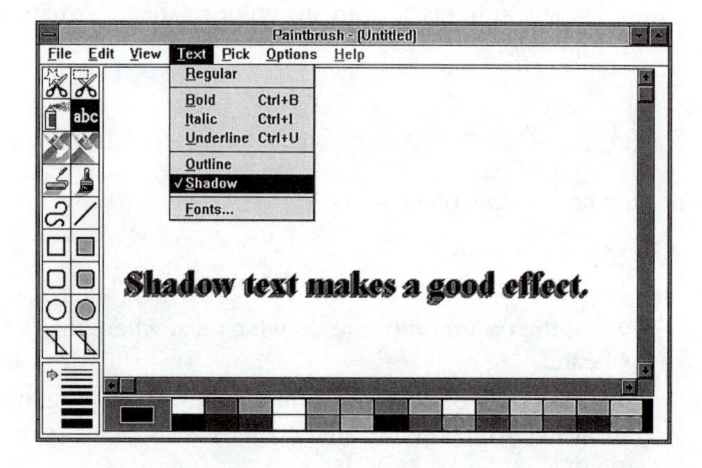

To enhance text, do the following:

1. Open the **T**ext menu, and choose **S**hadow
2. Type **Shadow text makes a good effect**.

Typed text appears in the selected foreground color, with one exception: shadow text adds a shadow in the selected background color.

You can select a text enhancement before you begin typing or while you are typing, but after you click the mouse button and "set" your text into the painting, you cannot change the text enhancement. (You can, however, erase the text and type new text; see Objective 5.)

Selecting a Font, Style, and Size

A font is an alphabet of characters that have the same appearance. Some commonly used fonts are Times New Roman, Arial, and Courier New. Using the **F**onts command, you can change the font, font style, and font size all at once. (Font styles are the same as the font enhancements listed in the Text menu.) You can also add one of two special effects—strikeout and underlining.

To select a font, style, size, and special effects, open the **T**ext menu, and select the commands you want.

188

When you select a font, that font applies to any new text you type and to the text you currently are typing, if you haven't clicked the mouse button.

Objective 5: To Edit a Drawing

You can modify a drawing in many ways. You can edit single objects, or you can change the whole picture. You can use the Undo command, which undoes your most recent action or series of actions. You can erase part of a drawing or change its colors. You can move or duplicate objects, and you can resize or tilt objects. For many editing procedures, you must first use either the Scissors or Pick tool to select the object or objects you want to modify.

Exercise 5.1: Using the Undo Command

Everyone makes mistakes. When you do, you will find a helpful ally in the Undo command. Undo erases everything you have done since the last time you changed tools, chose a menu command, used a scroll bar, opened another program, or resized the window. To avoid undoing something accidentally, reselect your tool each time you draw a line or shape you want to keep. That way, the next time you choose Undo, your work is undone only back to that point.

To undo your work, follow these steps:

1. Open EPOLYGON.
2. Select the Airbrush Tool, and "spray" all over the *E*.
3. Open the Edit menu, and choose the Undo command; or press Ctrl + Z.

You have now "un-vandalized" your *E*.

Erasing

Paintbrush has two tools you can use to erase—or recolor—parts of a drawing. Use the Color Eraser tool (on the left) to change the colors in the drawing. Use the Eraser tool (on the right) to change everything to the background color. Selecting either tool produces a square "eraser." To erase, just drag the square eraser across the drawing. The size of the eraser depends on the selected line width; you get a small eraser with a thin line width or a large eraser with a thick line width.

189

The Color Eraser Tool

The Color Eraser tool isn't really an eraser; it's a color switcher. It works two ways, and each way depends on the foreground and background colors you select from the palette. (This tool works only with colors, not shades.) The two ways to use the Color Eraser are

- Drag the Color Eraser tool across an area in your drawing. Every occurrence of the selected foreground color changes to the selected background color.
- Double-click the Color Eraser tool in the toolbox. Every occurrence of the selected foreground color in the visible area of your drawing changes to the selected background color. (The Color Eraser tool changes only the *selected* foreground color, whereas the Eraser tool, described next, changes *all* colors.)

Remember that the foreground color is the color in the center of the rectangle at the left end of the palette. You select the foreground color by using the left mouse button to click the color you want. The background color is the outer color in the rectangle in the palette box. You select the background color by clicking the right mouse button.

Exercise 5.2: Using the Eraser Tool

The Eraser tool "erases" by changing to the selected background color every part of your drawing that the Eraser tool touches. If the background color is white, passing the Eraser tool over an area turns it white (see fig. 8.18). If the background color is not white, the Eraser tool works more like a paintbrush than an eraser; everything you drag the tool over turns to the background color.

To use the Eraser tool, follow these steps (EPOLYGON should still be on your screen):

1. Select the Eraser tool from the toolbox (the tool on the right side of the toolbox).
2. Select a background color from the palette.
3. Move the pointer over the *E*, where it becomes a square eraser.
4. Press and hold the left mouse button.
5. Drag the Eraser tool across a part of the drawing to change to the background color.
6. Release the mouse button.

To Edit a Drawing

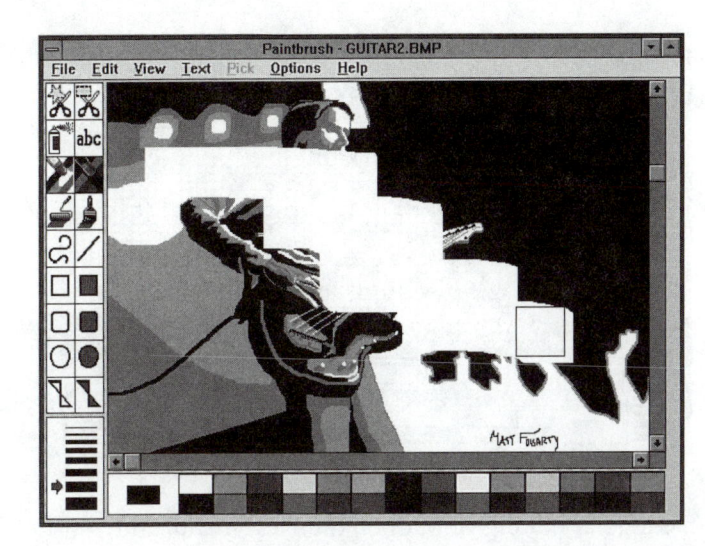

Fig. 8.18
The Eraser tool changes your drawing to the background color.

You can use the Eraser tool to erase your entire drawing by double-clicking the Eraser tool in the toolbox. When you do, Paintbrush closes the current file but first prompts you to save your changes. Choose **Yes** if you want to save them; otherwise, choose **No**. When a new document opens, its entire background is the color of the currently selected background color.

Exercise 5.3: Zooming In and Out

When you are doing detailed work, you can zoom in to get a close-up look at your drawing (see fig. 8.19). When you zoom in, you can edit a drawing dot by dot. (A dot is called a pixel in the lingo of computers.) To get an overview, you can zoom out to see the whole page.

Click the *left* mouse button to draw a dot in the selected foreground color; click the *right* mouse button to draw a dot in the selected background color. You can use the Paint Roller tool in Zoom In mode if you want to fill an area with the foreground color.

To zoom in for a close-up view of EPOLYGON, follow these steps:

1. Open the **V**iew menu, and choose the Zoom **I**n command. The Zoom box appears so that you can indicate where you want to zoom in.
2. Position the Zoom box over the spot where you want to zoom in.
3. Click the left mouse button to zoom in.

191

Using Windows Paintbrush

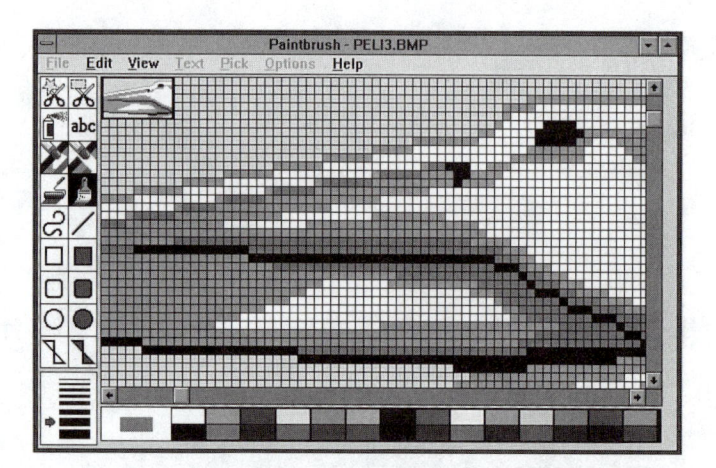

Fig. 8.19
A close-up view of a drawing.

To zoom back out to the regular editing view, open the View menu, and choose the Zoom **Out** command. If you're in the regular editing view, Zoom **Out** shows you a reduced picture of the entire page.

Viewing More of a Drawing

If your drawing is larger than your computer screen, you can see more of the drawing by hiding all toolboxes, menus, and scroll bars. You can only view in this mode; you cannot edit the drawing.

To view more of the drawing, you open the **View** menu and choose the **View Picture** command. To return to the regular editing view, click the mouse button, or press Esc.

Exercise 5.4: Moving Objects

You can move an object or group of objects to a different place in the drawing. First, you must select the object or objects with the Scissors or Pick tool.

To move an object, follow these steps:

1. Select the Scissors or Pick tool.
2. Draw an enclosure around the "E" polygon.
3. Move the pointer inside the selection enclosure, where the pointer becomes an arrow.

192

4. Press and hold the mouse button to "pick up" the selection.
5. Drag the selected object to the far-right corner.
6. Release the mouse button.

To move the selection as a transparent object, drag it with the left mouse button. To move the selection as an opaque object, drag it with the right mouse button.

Duplicating Objects

After you select an object, you can use the Scissors or Pick tool to duplicate that object. To duplicate an object, just copy and paste it. When you paste the object, it appears—selected—at the top left corner of the screen. You can then move the object, using the method described in steps 3 through 6 of Exercise 5.4.

Objective 6: To Print a Drawing

When you are ready to print your drawing, Paintbrush offers many options. For example, you can print a draft copy of the drawing to see a rough version of it, or you can print a final proof. You can print the whole drawing, or you can print only part of it. You can print one or more copies of the drawing, and you can print the copies at a reduced or enlarged scale.

Paintbrush prints on the printer currently selected in Windows. If you have been printing with another Windows program, you probably do not have to select a printer in Paintbrush; however, if you are printing for first time or if you need to change printers, be sure to use the Print Setup command to select a printer.

To select a printer, open the File menu, and choose the Print Setup command. When the Print Setup dialog box appears, select a printer from the Printer group. You can select the Default Printer, or you can select a printer from the Specific Printer list. From the Orientation group, you can choose to print either Portrait, vertically on the page, or Landscape, horizontally on the page. If necessary, choose options from the Paper group: to change the paper size, select an option from the Size list; to change the paper source on your printer, select an option from the Source list.

Using Windows Paintbrush

Exercise 6.1: Printing a Drawing

To print a Paintbrush drawing on the selected printer, follow these steps:

1. Open the **F**ile menu, and choose the **P**rint command.

    The Print dialog box appears.

2. In the Quality group, select **D**raft to print a rough draft, or **P**roof to print a final version of the drawing.
3. In the Window group, select **W**hole to print the entire drawing.
4. In the **N**umber of copies box, type the number of copies you want to print.
5. In the **S**caling box, type 66 to print at 66 percent of the total size.
6. Choose the **U**se Printer Resolution check box to print at printer resolution rather than screen resolution.

    If your drawing appears out of proportion the first time you print it, select the **U**se Printer Resolution option, and print the drawing again. This option may correct the problem.

7. Choose OK, or press ↵Enter.

If you select the option to print only part of the drawing and then choose OK to print, Paintbrush displays a reduced version of the drawing and gives you a cross hair. Use the cross hair to draw a box around the area of the drawing you want to print. As soon as you release the mouse button, printing begins.

If you print a *draft-quality* page, Paintbrush prints without printer enhancements but at a faster speed. If you print a *proof-quality* page, Paintbrush prints more slowly but uses all the printer's enhancements. On some printers, such as laser printers, no difference exists between draft- and proof-quality printing.

When you are finished working with Paintbrush, quit the program by opening the **F**ile menu and choosing the **E**xit command.

Chapter Summary

Paintbrush is a simple graphics program you can use to create illustrations for your work or to create computer drawings just for fun.

Paintbrush contains tools for drawing lines, boxes, circles, and polygons, as well as tools for drawing free-form lines and shapes. A line-width box offers a selection of line widths, and a palette displays an array of colors (if you have a color monitor) or a variety of gray shades (if you have a monochrome monitor).

You can type text in your drawing, selecting from a variety of fonts, sizes, and styles. To improve your drawing, you can erase or edit it.

Testing Your Knowledge

True/False Questions

1. To draw or paint, you must first select a tool by pointing to its icon in the toolbox and clicking the mouse.
2. You cannot use the drawings created in Windows Paintbrush in Word for Windows.
3. The polygon tools, both filled and unfilled, draw objects with no more than five sides.
4. To select the background color on the Paintbrush palette, move the pointer on top of the background color of choice, and click the right mouse button.
5. The lines you draw show the selected width and color only after you complete them.

Multiple Choice Questions

1. Which of the following tools are *not* for painting?
    A. Airbrush tool
    B. Curve tool
    C. Paint Roller tool
    D. Brush tool
2. When using the Line tool, what key do you hold down to make the lines "snap to" an invisible vertical, horizontal, or 90-degree axis?
    A. ⇧Shift
    B. Ctrl
    C. snap key
    D. Alt

Using Windows Paintbrush

3. What will happen if you press the right mouse button while you are drawing a line?

   A. The line will be doubled.
   B. The line will be perfectly horizontal.
   C. The line will be canceled.
   D. The line will be perfectly vertical.

4. If you want a perfect circle, which key should you hold down as you draw the shape?

   A. `Alt`
   B. `Shift`
   C. `Alt` + `Shift`
   D. `Ctrl`

5. When using the Paint Roller tool, if a shape is not completely closed, what happens?

   A. The paint leaks out, filling the entire screen.
   B. The paint stays within a defined distance from the closest object.
   C. The paint color changes as it leaks out of the object.
   D. None of the above

Fill-in-the-Blank Questions

1. An alphabet of letters in a particular style is called a _____.
2. When you select a drawing tool, the pointer appears as a _____.
3. A _____ at the bottom of the screen contains the colors or shades you use to fill shapes.
4. The _____ color is the color of the border around the edges of filled shapes.
5. The Curve tool doesn't draw free-form curves; instead, it draws precise ___-shaped or ___-shaped curves.

Review: Short Projects

1. Drawing a Pyramid

   Using Windows Paintbrush, create the pyramid figure that was introduced in Chapter 1 to illustrate the basic foundations of information

Testing Your Knowledge

systems. Use figure 1.1 as a guideline. Before you begin, think about what shapes you will use and in what order. Save the model as PYRAMID1.PCX, and print a copy of it.

2. Brushing Your Name

   Create a drawing of your name using the Brush tool. Experiment with different brush shapes, line widths, and foreground and background colors to create the image you want to project of yourself. You can use this drawing at the top of papers, as a sign on your door, or shrink it to be a "Hello, I'm...." badge. Be imaginative. Save the drawing under your name, and print a copy of it.

3. Mixing Text and Drawings

   Use Windows Paintbrush to create a document that shows each shape and then describes it. For example, draw an unfilled box and then next to it, type **Unfilled Box**. Document every shape you think that you might ever use in this way. This project will give you practice at integrating text and objects, in addition to practice at using the shapes. Save the file as TOOLS, and print a copy of it.

Review: Long Projects

1. Planning the Layout of the Ice Cream Parlor

   A drawing of the layout of Bella's Ice Cream Parlor would be a useful tool for thinking about how to arrange the facility. Make a drawing of the layout and include both the retail area and back offices, providing as much detail as you can. Areas to include are the counter, ice cream cases, tables and coffee bar, magazine racks, entertainment area, and so on. Save the file as LAYOUT, and print a copy of it.

2. Researching Other Drawing Software

   Windows Paintbrush is just one example of software for creating illustrations. In fact, Paintbrush is just the tip of the iceberg. There are many additional programs with far greater capabilities. Do a research project on the top five drawing programs for Windows. Find out what the best sellers are, what features and functions the top sellers offer, and what companies produce them. Write up your findings as a five-page paper, and print a copy.

Summary of Windows Shortcuts

General Windows Shortcuts

This appendix provides a list of the shortcuts you can use in Windows programs. This section lists the general shortcuts. Ensuing sections list the shortcuts you can use in the Program Manager, File Manager, and in Windows accessory programs.

Windows Shortcuts

You can use the following shortcuts in any Windows program:

Press	To
F1	Start Help (if the program has Help)
Ctrl+Esc	Display the Task List
Alt+Esc	Switch to the next program, if it is running in a window; select the next program, if it is running as an icon

continues

Windows 3.1 SmartStart

Press	To
Alt+Tab	Switch to the next or previous program, restoring programs running as icons. Hold Alt while repeatedly pressing Tab to scroll through each active program. Release Tab when the program or program name you want appears.
PrtSc	Copy an image of the screen to the Clipboard. On some PCs, you press Alt+PrtSc. (This shortcut works for DOS programs only if they are running in Text mode.)
Alt+PrtSc	Copy an image of the active window to the Clipboard
Alt+space bar	Open the Control menu for a program window
Alt+-	Open the Control menu for a document window
Alt+F4	Quit a program
Ctrl+F4	Close the active group window or document window
Alt+↵Enter	Switch a DOS program between a window and a full screen
← → ↑ or ↓	Move a window after you choose the **Move** command from the Control menu
	Or change the size of a window after you choose Size from the Control menu

Menu Shortcuts

Use the following shortcuts to select menus and choose commands in any program or in the Program Manager:

Press	To
Alt or F10	Select or deselect the first menu on the menu bar
letter	Choose the underlined letter or number in a menu or command

Appendix A

Press	To
← or →	Move among open menus
↑ or ↓	Move among commands in a menu
↵Enter	Choose the selected menu name or command
Esc	Cancel the selected menu name
	Or close the open menu

Dialog Box Shortcuts

Use the following shortcuts when you work in a dialog box:

Press	To
Tab	Move from option to option or group to group, left to right and top to bottom
⇧Shift+Tab	Move from option to option or group to group in reverse order
Alt+*letter*	Move to the option or group whose underlined letter or number you type
← → ↑ or ↓	Move the selection from option to option within a group of options
	Or move the cursor, respectively, left, right, up, or down within a list or text box
Home	Move to the first item or character in a list or text box
End	Move to the last item or character in a list or text box
PgUp or PgDn	Scroll up or down in a list, one screen at a time
Alt+↓	Open a selected list
space bar	Select an item or cancel a selection in a list
	Or select or clear a check box

continues

201

Windows 3.1 SmartStart

Press	To
Ctrl+/	Select all the items in a list box or window where multiple selections are allowed
Ctrl+\	Cancel all selections except the current selection
Shift+← → ↑ or ↓	Extend or cancel the selection in a text box, one character at a time, the direction of the arrow
Shift+Home	Extend or cancel the selection to the first character in a text box
Shift+End	Extend or cancel the selection to the last character in a text box
Enter	Implement a command
	Or choose the selected item in a list, and then implement the command
Esc or Alt+F4	Close a dialog box without completing the command

A Shortcuts To Move the Insertion Point

These shortcuts move the cursor or insertion point in text boxes and in programs where you can type text, such as in Notepad or Write:

Press	To move the insertion point
↑	Up one line
↓	Down one line
→	Right one character
←	Left one character
Ctrl+→	Right one word
Ctrl+←	Left one word
Home	To the beginning of the line
End	To the end of the line

Appendix A

Press	To move the insertion point
PgUp	Up one screen
PgDn	Down one screen
Ctrl + Home	To the beginning of the document
Ctrl + End	To the end of the document

Editing Shortcuts

Use these shortcuts to edit text in a dialog box or window:

Press	To
Backspace	Delete the character to the left of the insertion point
	Or delete selected text
Del	Delete the character to the right of the insertion point
	Or delete selected text
Shift + Del or Ctrl + X	Cut the selected text to the Clipboard
Shift + Ins or Ctrl + V	Paste text from the Clipboard to the active window
Ctrl + Ins or Ctrl + C	Copy the selected text to the Clipboard
Ctrl + Z or Alt + Backspace	Undo the last editing action

Windows 3.1 SmartStart

Text-Selection Shortcuts

When selecting text, you can use the following shortcuts in most Windows programs, but they may not work in all programs. All the following selections begin at the insertion point. If text is already selected, the shortcuts instead may deselect the text.

Press	To select
Shift + ← or →	One character at a time, left or right
Shift + ↑ or ↓	One line of text, up or down
Shift + PgUp	All text, one screen up
Shift + PgDn	All text, one screen down
Shift + Home	Text to the beginning of the line
Shift + End	Text to the end of the line
Ctrl + Shift + ←	The preceding word
Ctrl + Shift + →	The next word
Ctrl + Shift + Home	Text to the beginning of the document
Ctrl + Shift + End	Text to the end of the document

Program Manager Shortcuts

Use these shortcuts in the Program Manager:

Press	To
← → ↑ or ↓	Move between items within a group window
Ctrl + F6 or Ctrl + Tab	Move between group windows and icons
Enter	Start the selected program
Shift + F4	Arrange the open group windows side by side, or *tile* them

204

Appendix A

Press	To
⇧Shift + F5	Arrange the open group windows so that each title bar is displayed, or *cascade* them
Ctrl + F4	Close the active group window
Alt + F4	Quit Windows

File Manager Shortcuts

This section lists the shortcuts you can use in the File Manager to make your work in the directory tree, contents lists, and drive area more efficient.

Directory Tree Shortcuts

When working with the directory tree, use the following shortcuts:

Press	To
Tab ⇥	Move among the directory tree, the contents list, and the drive icons
←	Select the directory listed above the current subdirectory
→	Select the first subdirectory, if one exists, listed below the current directory
↵Enter	Display or hide any subdirectories
⇧Shift + ↵Enter	Open a new window displaying the contents of the selected directory
↑ or ↓	Select a directory listed above or below the current directory
Ctrl + ↑	Select the preceding directory at the same level, if one exists
Ctrl + ↓	Select the next directory at the same level, if one exists

continues

205

Windows 3.1 SmartStart

Press	To
PgUp	Select the directory one screen up from the current directory
PgDn	Select the directory one screen down from the current directory
Home	Select the root directory
End	Select the last directory in the list
letter	Select the next directory whose name begins with the letter or number you press
+	Expand the current directory
-	Collapse the current directory

Contents List Shortcuts

Use the following shortcuts when working with the list of files and subdirectories in the current directory:

Press	To
Tab	Move among the directory tree, the contents list, and the drive icons
PgUp	Select the file or directory one screen above the current selection
PgDn	Select the file or directory one screen below the current selection
Home	Select the first file or directory in the list
End	Select the last file or directory in the list
letter	Select the next file or directory whose name begins with the letter or number you press
Shift + ← → ↑ or ↓	Select or deselect multiple consecutive items
Ctrl + /	Select all items in the list

Appendix A

Press	To
Ctrl+\	Cancel all selections in the list, except the current selection
Ctrl+click	Select multiple nonconsecutive items
Shift+F8	Select or deselect nonconsecutive items. Press Shift+F8, and then press ← → ↑ or ↓ and space bar
← → ↑ or ↓	Move the cursor or scroll to other items in the window
Enter	Open a directory or start a program
Shift+Enter	Open a new window displaying the contents of the selected directory

Drive Area Shortcuts

Use these shortcuts in the drive area:

Press	To
Tab	Move among the directory tree, the contents list, and the drive icons
Click	Select a drive
Ctrl+*letter*	Change to the drive icon that matches the drive letter you type
← or →	Move between drive icons
space bar	Change drives
Enter	Open a new directory window
Double-click	Open a new window

A

207

Windows 3.1 SmartStart

Desktop Accessory Shortcuts

This section lists the shortcuts you can use in the Windows accessory programs, such as the Calculator, Calendar, Cardfile, Media Player, Notepad, Paintbrush, Write, and more.

Calculator Shortcuts

Use the following shortcuts for the Calculator:

Press	To
Esc	Clear (erase) the Calculator of all numbers and functions
Del	Delete the displayed value
Backspace	Delete the last number in the displayed value
Ctrl+M	Store the displayed value in memory
Ctrl+P	Add the displayed value to memory
Ctrl+R	Reveal (display) the value in memory
Ctrl+L	Clear (erase) the memory

Calendar Shortcuts

Use the following shortcuts in the Calendar's Day and Month views:

	Day View Shortcuts
Press	To
↑	Move to the preceding time
↓ or Enter	Move to the following time
PgUp	Move to the preceding screen
PgDn	Move to the next screen
Double-click status bar	Move to Month view

A

208

Appendix A

Press	To
Ctrl + Home	Move to the starting time
Ctrl + End	Move to 12 hours after the starting time
Tab	Move between the appointment area and the scratch pad
Shift + Del	Cut the selection to the Clipboard
Ctrl + Ins	Copy the selection to the Clipboard
Shift + Ins	Paste the Clipboard contents to the appointment area or scratch pad

Month View Shortcuts

Press	To
↑	Move to the preceding week
↓	Move to the next week
Double-click status bar	Move to Day view
PgUp	Move to the preceding month
PgDn	Move to the next month
Double-click date	Move to Day view (that day)
Tab	Move between a date and the scratch pad
Enter	Change to Day view

Cardfile Shortcuts

You can use these shortcuts in the Cardfile:

Press	To
PgDn	Scroll forward one card in Card view
	Or move forward one page of index lines in List view

continues

209

Windows 3.1 SmartStart

Press	To
PgUp	Scroll backward one card in Card view
	Or move back one page of index lines in List view
Ctrl+Home	Bring the first card in the file to the front
Ctrl+End	Bring the last card in the file to the front
Shift+Ctrl+*letter*	Bring a card to the front of the file. Cardfile displays the first card whose index line begins with the letter or number you type

Clipboard Viewer Shortcuts

Use the following shortcuts in the Clipboard:

Press	To
Del	Clear the Clipboard contents in the Clipboard Viewer
Shift+Del or Ctrl+X	In a document, cut a selection to the Clipboard
Ctrl+Ins or Ctrl+C	In a document, copy a selection to the Clipboard
Shift+Ins or Ctrl+V	In a document, paste the Clipboard contents to a document
PrtSc	In Windows, copy an image of the entire screen to the Clipboard. (This shortcut works for DOS programs only if they are running in Text mode.)
Alt+PrtSc	In Windows, copy an image of the active window to the Clipboard

A

210

Appendix A

Help Shortcuts

Use the following shortcuts to start Windows Help from a program:

Press	To
F1	Display the Help Contents for the program. If the Help window is already open, pressing F1 displays the Contents for How To Use Help
	In some programs (such as Program Manager and File Manager), pressing F1 displays a Help topic about the selected command, dialog box option, or system message
Shift+F1	Add a question mark to the pointer. You can then click the command, click the screen region, or press the key or key combination about which you want to know more. This feature is available only in some programs

Help Window Shortcuts

Use the following shortcuts after you start Help:

Press	To
Tab	Move clockwise among hot spots (where you can get further information) in the topic
Shift+Tab	Move counterclockwise among hot spots in the topic
Ctrl+Tab	Select all the hot spots in a topic
	Or deselect a hot spot
Ctrl+Ins	Copy the current Help topic to the Clipboard without displaying the Copy dialog box
	Or copy an entire annotation or a portion of it to the Clipboard
Shift+Ins	Paste the Clipboard contents into the Annotation dialog box
Alt+F4	Quit Help

211

Media Player Shortcuts

Use the following shortcuts in Media Player:

Press	To
`Tab`	Move among buttons and the scroll bar, left to right
`Shift`+`Tab`	Move among buttons and the scroll bar, right to left
space bar	Choose a button
←	Move back the playing position when the scroll bar is selected
→	Move forward the playing position when the scroll bar is selected
`PgUp`	Move back the playing position in large increments when the scroll bar is selected
`PgDn`	Move forward the playing position in large increments when the scroll bar is selected
`Home`	Move to the beginning of the sound when the scroll bar is selected
`End`	Move to the end of the sound when the scroll bar is selected

Notepad Shortcuts

See the cursor-movement, text selection, and Program Manager shortcuts in previous sections of this appendix.

Object Packager Shortcuts

Only one shortcut is available for the Object Packager:

Press	To
`Tab`	Move the selection cursor between the Content and Appearance windows

Appendix A

Paintbrush Shortcuts

Use the following shortcuts in Paintbrush.

Use these keys instead of using the mouse:

Mouse-Equivalent Shortcuts

Pressing	Is equivalent to
Ins	Clicking the left mouse button
Del	Clicking the right mouse button
F9 + Ins	Double-clicking the left mouse button
F9 + Del	Double-clicking the right mouse button

Use the following shortcuts to undo your last editing action:

Undo Shortcuts

Press	To
Backspace	Undo all or part of what you have drawn since selecting a tool. Press Backspace and then drag the eraser cursor over the part of the drawing you want to undo.
Alt + Backspace or Ctrl + Z	Undo everything you have drawn or typed since selecting a tool

Use these shortcuts for moving around the drawing area:

Movement Shortcuts

Press	To
Tab	Move the pointer among the toolbox, line-width box, palette, and drawing area in a counterclockwise direction
Shift + Tab	Move the pointer among the toolbox, line-width box, palette, and drawing area in a clockwise direction

continues

Windows 3.1 SmartStart

Press	To
← → ↑ or ↓	Move the drawing tool within a window
Shift + Home	Jump to the left side of a drawing
Shift + Del	Jump to the right side of a drawing
PgUp	Move up one screen
PgDn	Move down one screen
Home	Jump to the top of a drawing
End	Jump to the bottom of a drawing
Shift + ←	Move the cursor to the left one space
Shift + →	Move the cursor to the right one space
Shift + ↑	Move the cursor up one line
Shift + ↓	Move the cursor down one line

PIF Editor Shortcuts

Use the following shortcuts when you're working in PIF Editor:

Press	To
Tab	Move from option to option, left to right and top to bottom
Shift + Tab	Move from option to option in reverse order
Alt + *letter*	Move to the option or group whose underlined letter matches the one you type. If the option is a check box, this shortcut also sets or clears the option.
← → ↑ or ↓	Move the selection cursor from option to option within a group of options
space bar	Select or clear a check box

Appendix A

Sound Recorder Shortcuts

Use the following shortcuts in Sound Recorder:

Press	To
`Tab`	Move among the buttons and the scroll bar, left to right
`Shift`+`Tab`	Move among the buttons and the scroll bar, right to left
space bar	Choose a button
`←` or `→`	Move backward or forward when the scroll bar is selected
`PgUp`	Move back one second when the scroll bar is selected
`PgDn`	Move forward one second when the scroll bar is selected
`Home`	Move to the beginning of the sound when the scroll bar is selected
`End`	Move to the end of the sound when the scroll bar is selected

Write Shortcuts

The following shortcuts—movement and editing—help you work with Write. Note that when the key combination includes `5`, it refers to `5` on the numeric keypad with `Num Lock` turned off. (Refer also to the insertion point movement, text selection, and Program Manager shortcuts in previous sections of this appendix.)

Use the following shortcuts to move the insertion point within a document:

Movement Shortcuts

Press	To
`5`+`→`	Move to the next sentence
`5`+`←`	Move to the preceding sentence

continues

215

Windows 3.1 SmartStart

Movement Shortcuts

Press	To
[5]+[↓]	Move to the next paragraph
[5]+[↑]	Move to the preceding paragraph
[5]+[PgDn]	Move to the next page, according to the last repagination
[5]+[PgUp]	Move to the preceding page, according to the last repagination

Use these shortcuts to edit text:

Editing Shortcuts

Press	To
[Ctrl]+[↵Enter]	Insert a manual page break
[⇧Shift]+[Del] or [Ctrl]+[X]	Cut a selection to the Clipboard
[Ctrl]+[Ins] or [Ctrl]+[C]	Copy a selection to the Clipboard
[⇧Shift]+[Ins] or [Ctrl]+[V]	Paste the Clipboard contents to a document
[Ctrl]+[Z] or [Alt]+[⇐Backspace]	Undo the last typing or editing action
[↓]	Select a picture when the cursor is above the upper-left corner of the picture
[←] [→] [↑] or [↓]	Move the picture-sizing cursor after you choose the **Size Picture** command from the **Edit** menu
	Or move a selected picture after you choose the **Move Picture** command from the **Edit** menu
[Ctrl]+[⇧Shift]+[-]	Insert an optional hyphen
[Alt]+[F6]	Switch between the document and the Find or Replace dialog box
	Or switch between the document and the Page Header or Page Footer dialog box

216

Help, Support, and Resources

Windows is one of the most popular software programs ever written, which means that a great deal of support is available for it. The following resources will help you.

Telephone Support

Use the following telephone numbers to get technical support or product sales information about Windows or Windows programs. Telephone numbers and addresses in this appendix were accurate at the time of writing. Information is subject to change.

For questions specific to Windows installation, the Program Manager, File Manager, or Accessories, call

    Microsoft Corporation   206-637-7098

Windows 3.1 SmartStart

For technical or sales information regarding a major product, call

Manufacturer	Software	Telephone Support Line
Microsoft	Corporate	206-882-8080
	Technical (All software, Publisher, Money, and Project)	206-454-2030
	Windows	206-637-7098
	DOS (pay per call)	900-896-9000
	Microsoft Excel	206-635-7070
	Word for Windows	206-462-9673
Lotus	Corporate	617-577-8500
	Technical (recordings) (1-2-3 for Windows, Ami Pro, Freelance)	800-223-1662
	Technical (pay per call)	900-454-9009
WordPerfect	Corporate	801-225-5000
	Technical (WordPerfect 5.1 for Windows)	801-228-9907

Support Organizations

Most major cities in the United States have computer clubs. A Windows special interest group (SIG) usually exists within this club. Clubs usually have monthly meetings, demonstrate new software, maintain a list of consultants, and have free or low-cost training. To contact your local computer club, check newspaper listings under *computer*, or call local computer stores.

The Windows User Group Network (WUGNet) is a national organization devoted to supporting its members with information about Windows and Windows programs. It publishes a substantial bimonthly journal containing tips and articles written by members and consultants. Its staff is highly knowledgeable about Windows and Windows programs. Contact WUGNet for more information:

WUGNet Publications, Inc.
1295 N. Providence Rd.
Media, PA 19063
(215) 565-1861 Voice
(215) 565-7106 FAX

Computer Bulletin Board Forums

Computer bulletin boards are databases from which you can retrieve information over the telephone line by using Terminal—the communications program that comes with Windows. Some bulletin boards contain a wealth of information about Windows and Windows programs. One of the largest public bulletin boards is CompuServe.

CompuServe contains forums through which its members can discuss Windows and Windows programs. You can submit questions to Microsoft operators, who return answers within a day. CompuServe also contains libraries of sample files and new printer and device drivers. The Knowledgebase, available in Microsoft's region of CompuServe, has much of the same troubleshooting information used by Microsoft's telephone-support representatives. You can use keywords to search through the Knowledgebase. The Microsoft region of CompuServe is divided into many different areas, such as Windows users, advanced Windows users, Microsoft Excel, Microsoft languages, and sections for each of the major Microsoft and non-Microsoft programs that run under Windows.

After you become a CompuServe member, you can access the Microsoft user forums, library files, and Knowledgebase. To gain access to one these areas, type one of the following GO commands at the CompuServe prompt symbol (!), and then press ⏎Enter:

Type	To access
GO MSOFT	Overall Microsoft area
GO MSUSER	Overall applications and Windows areas
GO MSAPP	Microsoft applications areas
GO MSEXCEL	Microsoft Excel areas
GO WINNEW	New Windows user areas
GO WINADV	Advanced Windows user areas

continues

Windows 3.1 SmartStart

Type	To access
GO WINVEN	Overall non-Microsoft Windows applications areas
GO WINAPA	Non-Microsoft Windows applications area
GO WINAPB	Non-Microsoft Windows applications area
GO WINAPC	Non-Microsoft Windows applications area

Contact CompuServe for more information:

> CompuServe
> 5000 Arlington Centre Blvd.
> P.O. Box 20212
> Columbus, OH 43220
> (800) 848-8990

Consultants and Corporate Training

Microsoft Consulting Partners develop and support programs written using Microsoft products for the Windows environment. Microsoft Consulting Partners are independent consultants who have met strict qualifying requirements imposed by Microsoft.

Index

Symbols

* wild-card character, 109
<< help button, 65
>> help button, 65
? wild-card character, 109
386-Enhanced mode, copying in, 80-81

A

Accessories group, 29
accessory programs, starting, 144
Airbrush tool, 173, 183-184
alphanumeric keys, 37-39
applets (OLE), 126, 136
applications, *see* programs
arrow (mouse pointer), 35
automatic link update, 134-135

B

Back help button, 64
background color, 175
    indicators, 172
bookmarks (Help feature), 68-69
Box tool, 174, 178-179
Brush tool, 173, 185-186
bulletin boards for Windows, 219-220

C

Calculator, 155-157
    closing, 156
    copying to/from programs, 159
    editing numbers in display, 157
    memory functions, 158-159
    opening, 156
    Scientific, 160
    shortcuts, 208
Calendar, 145
    closing, 155
    editing appointments, 149
    intervals, changing, 149-150
    moving
        appointments, 149
        Calendar files, 154-155
    opening, 145, 148
    removing appointments from files, 153-155
    saving Calendar files, 147-148
    shortcuts, 208-209
    starting time, changing, 149-150
    typing appointments, 145-147
    views, 150-153
Cardfile, 209-210
check boxes, 51
choosing, 50
    commands, 52-54
    menus, 52-54

Windows 3.1 SmartStart

Circle/Ellipse tool, 174, 179-180
clearing Clipboard, 83
clicking, 24
Clipboard, 74, 78, 81-83, 144
    clearing, 83
    retrieving contents, 83
    saving contents, 83
    shortcuts, 210
    Viewer, 82, 138
    viewing contents, 82
Clock, 160-161
closing
    Calculator, 156
    Calendar, 155
    windows
        document, 40-42
        program, 43
collapsing directories, 96
Color Eraser tool, 174, 190
command buttons, 51
commands
    All File Details, 106
    Analog, 161
    Brush Shapes, 185
    Cascade, 102
    Character, 55
    choosing, 52-54
    Collapse Branch, 97
    Confirmation, 115
    Copy, 53, 78, 113
    Copy Disk, 118-119
    Create Directory, 113
    Cut, 149
    Day, 151
    Day Settings, 149
    Deck, 163
    Define, 68
    Delete, 114-115
    Edit Undo, 51
    Exit, 194
    Expand All, 97
    Expand Branch, 97
    Expand One Level, 97
    Fonts, 188
    Format Disk, 117
    Game Customize, 164
    Links, 133
    Mark, 81, 152
    Month, 151
    Move, 113
    New, 155
    New Window, 101
    Object, 137
    Open, 148, 155
    Options Confirmation, 114
    Partial Details, 106
    Paste, 53, 78
    Paste Link, 130
    Paste Special, 54, 130
    Print, 194
    Print Setup, 193
    Rename, 114
    Restore, 60
    Save As, 147
    Scientific, 160
    Search, 108
    selecting, 200-201
    Sort by Date, 106
    Sort by Name, 106
    Sort by Size, 106
    Sort by Type, 106
    Special Time, 149
    Tile, 102
    Undo, 51, 189
    View Name, 104
    View Picture, 192
    View Zoom In, 184
    Window Refresh, 105
    Zoom In, 191
    Zoom Out, 192
computer bulletin boards for Windows, 219-220
Contents help button, 64-66

Index

contents lists, 91
   shortcuts, 206-207
   specifying file information,
     104-105
control menu, 24
copying, 74, 127, 144
   directories, 110
   disks, 118-119
   files, 110-112
   from Calculator to/from
     programs, 159
   graphics between programs,
     12, 79
   positioning insertion point, 78
   text
     386-Enhanced mode, 80-81
     between programs, 12, 78-79
     in DOS programs, 79-81
crashes, 18-19
creating
   links, 129-130
   embedded objects, 137-138
cross hair (mouse pointer), 35
Ctrl+clicking, 24
cursor, 39
cursor-movement keys, 37-39
Curve tool, 174, 177-178
cutting, 74, 144

D

data, 88
Data Type list, 130
data types, links, 132
deleting
   character-by-character, 75
   directories, 114
   files, 114
   links, 133
   text, 76
deselecting, 50
   text, 77

desktop, 6, 10, 27, 30
destination (copying), 110
destination disks, 118
dialog boxes, 50
   selecting options, 54-55
   shortcuts, 201-202
directories, 88-90
   collapsing, 96
   copying, 110
   deleting, 114
   exanding, 96
   moving, 112
   names, 107-108
   new, creating, 113
   renaming, 113
   searching for, 108-109
   selecting, 97-98
     with File Manager, 93
   sorting display of, 106
directory
   tree, 89-91
     shortcuts, 205-206
   windows
     arranging, 102
     selecting, 101-102
disk drives, 89
   selecting, 94
disk operating system , *see* DOS
disks, 88
   copying, 118-119
   destination, 118
   floppy, 89
     formatting, 116-117
   hard, 89
   source, 118
document
   control menu, 32
   windows, 24, 28
     closing, 40-42
     parts of, 32

223

documents, 6
    linking, 133
    see also source document
    see also target document
DOS (disk operating system), 6
    disadvantages, 6
    programs
        copying/pasting in, 79-81
        running under Windows, 13
double-clicking, 24
draft-quality pages, 194
dragging, 24, 36
drawing, 170
    boxes, 179
    circles, 179-180
    lines, 175
        curved, 177-178
        straight, 176-177
    ovals, 179-180
    polygons, 180-182
    shapes, 175
drive area, 207-208
drive bar, 91
drop-down list boxes, 51, 55-56

E

editing
    Calendar appointments, 149
    drawings, 189
    embedded objects, 138
    links, 133-135
    numbers in Calculator display, 157
    shortcuts, 203
    text, 74-77
        keyboard shortcuts, 77
        multiple characters, 76-77
        single characters, 74-76
        with keyboard, 77
electronic storage, *see* primary storage
embedded objects
    creating, 137-138
    editing, 138
    inserting, 137-138
embedding, 126-128, 136-138
    between programs, 138
environment, 6, 15
Eraser tool, 174, 189-191
erasing drawings, 189-191
exiting Windows, 44
expanding directories, 96

F

file icons, 98-99
File Manager, 87
    active area, 93
    contents list, 91-92
    directory tree, 91-92
    local area networks (LAN), 94
    selecting
        disk drives, 94
        files/directories, 93
    selection cursor, 93
    shortcuts, 205
    starting, 90
    turning plus/minus signs on/off, 92
    warning messages, 115-116
files, 40, 88
    Calendar
        moving, 154-155
        opening, 148
        removing appointments from, 153-155
        saving, 147-148
    copying, 110-112
    deleting, 114
    moving, 112
    names, 88, 107-108
    renaming, 113
    searching for, 108-109
    selecting, 99-101
        with File Manager, 93
    sorting display of, 106

Index

specifying information appearing in contents lists, 104-105
finding, *see* searching
floppy disks, 89
    formatting, 116-117
fonts, 170
foreground color, 175
    indicators, 172
Formatted Text (RTF) format, 130
formatting floppy disks, 116-117
four-headed arrow (mouse pointer), 35
frozen keyboard, 18-19
function keys, 37-38

G

Games group, 29
Glossary help button, 64
Graphical User Interface (GUI), 6-7
graphics, copying between programs, 12, 79
Group window, 29
groups
    Accessories, 29
    Games, 29
    icons, 29
    StartUp, 30
GUI (Graphical User Interface), 6-7

H

hard
    boot, 19
    disks, 89
Help feature, 14, 62-69
    bookmarks, 68-69
    buttons, 63-67
    hypertext words, 63
    menus, 63
    shortcuts, 211
History help button, 64
horizontal scroll bar, 33
hourglass (mouse pointer), 35

hypertext, 14
    words, 63, 67-68

I

I-beam, 35, 74
IBM Enhanced keyboard, 37
IBM PC AT keyboard, 37
icons, 6, 9, 15, 171
    advantages, 16-18
    file, 98-99
    group, 29
    program, 32
    Program item, 25, 29
    restoring to windows, 60-61
inserting embedded objects, 137-138
insertion point, 39, 74, 144
    copy operations, 78
    moving, 202-203

K

key combinations, *see* keys
keyboard, 36-39
    choosing commands/menus, 53-54
    editing text, 77
    filling screen with window, 59-60
    frozen, 18-19
    IBM Enhanced, 37
    IBM PC AT, 37
keys
    alphanumeric, 37-39
    cursor-movement, 37-39
    function, 37-38
    numeric, 37
    shortcut, 36, 53
        editing text, 77

L

Line tool, 174-175
line-width box, 170-172

225

linking, 126-127
   between programs, 129-133
   creating links, 129-130
   Data Type list, 130
   data types, 132
   documents, pasting, 133
   editing links, 133-135
   Formatted Text (RTF) format, 130
   locking links, 136
   removing links, 133
   unlinking, 135
   updating links, 131-135
list boxes, 51
   drop-down, 51, 55-56
local area network (LAN), 94
locking links, 136

M

magnetic storage, *see* secondary storage
Main group window, 28
manual link update, 134-135
Maximize button, 32, 58
Media Player, 212
memory, 13
   Calculator memory functions, 158-159
   clearing Clipboard, 83
   primary storage, 88-89
   RAM, 88-89
   secondary storage, 40, 88-89
menu bar, 32
menus
   choosing, 52-54
   document control, 32
   program control, 32
   pull-down, 7
   selecting (shortcuts), 200-201
Microsoft Consulting Partners, 220
Minesweeper, 162-164
Minimize button, 32, 61

mouse, 35-36
   button, 24
   choosing commands/menus, 52-53
   copying files, 110-112
   deselecting text, 77
   dragging, 36
   filling screen with window, 58
   moving
      directories, 112
      files, 112
      windows, 57
   pointer, 24
      functions, 34-35
      I-beam, 74
      shapes, 34-35
   selecting disk drives, 94
   starting programs, 26
   switching between programs, 62
moving
   Calendar
      appointments, 149
      files, 154-155
   directories, 112
   files, 112
   insertion point, 202-203
   objects in drawings, 192-193
   text between programs, 78-79
   windows, 57
multiple programs, 10

N

Notepad, 212-216
numeric keys, 37

O

object linking and embedding, *see* OLE
Object Packager, 212
objects, 126
   embedded
      creating, 137-138

Index

    editing, 138
    inserting, 137-138
  packages, 126
OLE, 125
  applets, 136
opening
  Calculator, 156
  Calendar, 145
    files, 148
option buttons, 51

P

packages, 126
Paint Roller tool, 173, 184-185
Paintbrush, 172-173
  adding text to drawings, 186-189
  drawing
    boxes, 179
    circles, 179-180
    curved lines, 177-178
    lines, 175-176
    ovals, 179-180
    polygons, 180-182
    shapes, 175-176
    straight lines, 176-177
  editing drawings, 189
  erasing, 189-191
  line-width box, 174
  moving objects in drawings, 192-193
  painting
    with Airbrush tool, 183-184
    with Brush tool, 185-186
    with Paint Roller tool, 184-185
  palette, 175
  printing drawings, 193-194
  saving drawings, 182
  shortcuts, 213-214
  starting, 171-172
  toolbox, 173-174
  zooming in/out, 191-192

painting, 170
palette, 170
palettes (Paintbrush), 172, 175
pasting, 74, 144
  linked documents, 133
Pick tool, 192-193
PIF Editor, 214
pointers, 24
  I-beam, 74
  insertion point, 74
Polygon tool, 174, 181-182
positioning insertion point, 78
primary storage, 88-89
printing drawings, 193-194
program
  control menu, 32
  icon, 32
  restore button, 58
  windows, 24, 28
    closing, 43
    parts of, 32
Program item icon, 25, 29
Program Manager, 9, 15, 24, 28
  shortcuts, 204-205
  window 29
programs, 88
  copying
    between, 78-79
    graphics between, 12
    text between, 12
  embedding between, 138
  linking between, 129-133
  multiple, running, 10
  starting
    accessory, 144
    simultaneously with Windows, 27
    with mouse, 26
  switching between, 62
proof-quality pages, 194
pull-down menus, 7

Windows 3.1 SmartStart

R

RAM (random-access memory), 89
recovering from crashes, 18-19
renaming directories/files, 113
retrieving Clipboard contents, 83
Rounded Box tool, 174
RTF (Formatted Text) format, 130
running
    DOS programs under Windows, 13
    multiple programs, 10

S

saving
    Calendar files, 147-148
    Clipboard contents, 83
    drawings, 182
Scientific Calculator, 160
Scissors tool, 192-193
scroll
    bars, 33
    boxes, 33, 51
scrolling, 144
Search help button, 64-67
searching, 144
    for files/directories, 108-109
secondary
    memory, 40
    storage, 88-89
selecting, 50, 144
    commands, 200-201
    directories, 97-98
        with File Manager, 93
    directory windows, 101-102
    disk drives, 94
    files, 99-101
        with File Manager, 93
    links, 133
    menus, shortcuts, 200-201
    options from dialog boxes, 54-55
    text, 51-52, 76, 204-205
        deselecting, 77

selection cursor (File Manager), 93
shapes of mouse pointer, 34-35
Shift+clicking, 24
shortcuts
    Calculator, 208
    Calendar, 208-209
    Cardfile, 209-210
    Clipboard, 210
    contents lists, 206-207
    dialog boxes, 201-202
    directory tree, 205-206
    drive area, 207-208
    editing, 203
    File Manager, 205
    Help feature, 211
    keys, 36, 53
        editing text, 77
    Media Player, 212
    moving insertion point, 202-203
    Notepad, 212-216
    Object Packager, 212
    Paintbrush, 213-214
    PIF Editor, 214
    Program Manager, 204-205
    selecting
        commands, 200-201
        menus, 200-201
        text, 204-205
    Sound Recorder, 215
    undoing editing transactions, 213
    Windows, 199-200
    Write, 215-216
size box, 32
sizing windows, 57-58
soft boot, 19
Solitaire, 162-163
sorting display of files/directories, 106
Sound Recorder, 215
source, 110
    disks, 118
    document, 126
    program, 126

Index

starting
  File Manager, 90
  Paintbrush, 171-172
  programs
    accessory, 144
    simultaneously with Windows, 27
    with mouse, 26
  Windows, 25
StartUp group, 30
status bar, 32, 91
subdirectories, 89-90
suit stacks (Solitaire), 162
support organizations for Windows, 218-219
switching between programs, 62

T

target
  document, 126
  program, 126
telephone support for Windows, 217-218
text
  adding to drawings, 186-189
  boxes, 51
  copying
    386-Enhanced mode, 80-81
    between programs, 12, 78-79
    in DOS programs, 79-81
  deleting, 76
    character by character, 75
  editing, 74-77
    keyboard shortcuts, 77
    multiple characters, 76-77
    single characters, 74-76
    with keyboard, 77
  insertion point, 74
  moving between programs, 78-79
  selecting, 51-52, 76, 204-205
    deselecting, 77

Text tool, 173
title bar, 32, 91
toolbox (Paintbrush), 170-174
transferable skills, 50
transferring data (methods), 127-128
two-headed arrow (mouse pointer), 35

U

unlinking, 135
updating links, 131-135

V

vertical scroll bar, 33
viewing, 144
  Clipboard contents, 82, 138
virtual storage, 13

W-Z

warning messages (File Manager), 115-116
wild-card characters, 109
Windows
  advantages, 6-12
  computer bulletin boards for, 219-220
  exiting, 44
  running DOS programs under, 13
  shortcuts, 199-200
  starting, 25
    simultaneously with other programs, 27
  support organizations, 218-219
  telephone support, 217-218
  transferable skills, 50
windows, 6
  directory
    arranging, 102
    selecting, 101-102

229

    document, 24, 28
        closing, 40-42
        parts of, 32
    filling screen, 58-60
    Group, 29
    Main group, 28
    moving, 57
    program, 24, 28
        closing, 43
        parts of, 32
    Program Manager, 29
    reducing to icons, 60-61
    sizing, 57-58
Windows desktop, *see* desktop
workstations, 95
Write, 215-216
zoom in/out, 170, 191-192